Architect's Handbook of

Practice Management

Sixth edition 1998

RIBA Publications

Architect's Handbook of Practice Management
Sixth Edition 1998
Editors: Stanley Cox and Alaine Hamilton

ISBN 1 85946 035 6

© RIBA Publications 1998

1st edition published 1965*
2nd edition published 1967*
3rd revised edition published 1973*
4th revised edition published 1980*
* under the title RIBA Handbook of Architectural
Practice and Management
5th edition published 1991

Published by RIBA Publications,
a division of RIBA Companies Ltd,
Finsbury Mission, 39 Moreland Street,
London EC1V 8BB

Handbook design by RIBA Publications Design

Typography of Sixth Edition by James Shurmer
Typesetting by SPAN Graphics Ltd, Crawley, West Sussex

Printed and bound by Butler and Tanner Ltd,
Frome, Somerset

Architect's Handbook of
Practice Management

WITHDRAWN

Contents

Contents *continued*

Contents *continued*

Contents *continued*

Editors' Notes

This Sixth Edition of the Handbook revises and updates the information provided in the previous (1991) edition, and takes into account new legislation such as the CDM Regulations 1994 and the Party Wall etc Act 1996. Architects should be aware that Part II of the Housing Grants, Construction and Regeneration Act 1996 significantly affects all 'construction contracts' which, by definition, will include most forms of appointment for construction professionals. They should also monitor the gradual implementation of the Disability Discrimination Act 1995 over the next few years, which could bring new obligations for building designers.

A significant recent development has been the publication of the ARB Code of Professional Conduct and Practice, and some implications for architects are considered in Part A of the Sixth Edition, which is concerned with the professional context of practice. The coverage of Part B is extensive, dealing with the crucial elements of business practice and financial management. In this new edition, particular emphasis is placed on the importance of quality management and the disciplines it entails in terms of the regular auditing, control and correction of practice and project procedures.

Part C is about Communication, and is a departure from previous editions. Virtually every aspect of practice depends on effective communication, and the new section seeks to cover some of the basic tasks that face all architects and which many find difficult. These include dealing with practice correspondence, writing technical reports, minuting meetings, and the management of files and records, library material and archives. Some guidance is also given on developing an appropriate writing style.

Part D, Working with Staff, begins with a review of current employment legislation and its implications for practice, and then describes employers' general responsibilities including health and safety, insurance, and staff training and development. Guidance is offered on recruiting staff and conducting interviews. The section concludes with a general consideration of how to manage and motivate staff in the best interests of the practice as a whole.

Part E, Managing the Commission, is a valuable complement to the guidance offered in the *Architect's Job Book*. It considers roles and responsibilities, managing jobs in relation to practice resources, and the importance of teamwork and good lines of communication, all essential aspects of risk management while running a job. This theme is continued in Part F, Managing Risks, which deals more broadly with the subject in terms of the architect–client professional relationship, architects' liability and indemnity insurance, and the specific risks attaching to various one-off commissions such as house surveys and other inspections.

Architectural practice today is increasingly complex and diverse, and cannot be covered exhaustively in any manual or compendium. However, the guidance offered in this Sixth Edition is a compilation of RIBA and other authoritative guidance and is based on principles of sound practice and thoughtful management. Architects should nonetheless be sure to check matters of fact and currency for themselves as necessary.

Professional context

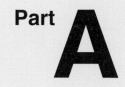

Part A

A1.1 Development

In the 18th century, architects could concern themselves primarily with visual matters of form, space and style. They were responsible for broad profiles and could confidently leave much of the detail in the capable hands of master craftsmen. Architects themselves often had a craft background. There was a directness of working which made conscious management almost unnecessary. Architects often enjoyed a personal working relationship with their patrons, many of whom were themselves knowledgeable about architecture.

In the 19th century, professionalism as applied to architecture was formalised and consolidated. Patronage was at an end. The number of architects increased as wealth and education spread, and the market for their services became predominantly commercial in character. No longer tied to patrons, they were free to offer their skills in return for a fee. Wider opportunities became available and a new way of commissioned working developed.

Then the construction industry itself underwent radical change. Master craftsmen were overtaken by firms of building contractors, headed by people whose aims were profit-orientated and sometimes speculative. Architects were criticised. Allegations of deficient or fraudulent practice were often vociferously expressed by the emerging new species of client industrialists, entrepreneurs, corporations and boards of guardians – some of them less than scrupulous.

Faced with such criticism, it was understandable that practitioners with a common professed interest should band together. In part this was for protection and so as to be able to present a unified approach when tackling injustices; in part it was for promotional reasons. Architects claimed to provide a uniquely impartial and independent service. They wished to have the status of professionals, offering a solid assurance of competence, honesty and integrity. They wished not to be confused with builders or surveyors. The image they sought to promote was that of professional people who were educated and responsible. They wished to be identified with, and to cultivate more explicitly a service of quality. They aspired to devise efficient methods and establish standards and, by learning from each other, to become more proficient.

Characteristics to be found in the newly emergent professions could be summarised as follows:

- *intellectual basis:* principles, theories and concepts capable of testing and implementation;
- *independence of practice:* integrity and impartiality in services, personal attention, reward by fee;
- *consultancy role:* advice, skills, resources, defined liabilities;
- *established practices*: conduct, conditions, procedures, performance standards;
- *representative institute:* protection of interests for members and clients, corporate voice and lobby, learned society role, advancement of knowledge and expertise.

These quickly became apparent in the practice of architecture, and are to a large extent still present in the profession today.

In the 1920s, Sydney and Beatrice Webb described the nature of professionalism as 'a vocation founded upon specialised educational training, the purpose of which is to supply disinterested counsel and service to others for a direct and definite compensation'. Practising any profession demands a level of commitment which makes vocation an apt description. In architecture today the educational pattern combines intellectual rigour and theory with practical training, and it is recognised that the need for structured learning and development continues after graduation and throughout professional life. The words 'disinterested counsel and service' are a reminder that architects are seen to be persons of professional integrity who supply advice without fear or favour and above self-interest. Working for a direct and definite compensation is still a straightforward and sensible way of doing business, particularly in a competitive world. The need for services to be adequately defined and the fee basis decided before work is started, is now an obligation as well as an efficient business practice. Providing a professional service has to be pursued with vigour and efficiency but also in line with business ethics.

A1.2 Change

Inevitably circumstances change, and this has had an effect on practice. The architect these days will not always be placed in a position of acting impartially between parties to a building contract. The reward for professional services may not always be a straightforward fee calculation. The architect will not necessarily be engaged to perform a lead role. Building procurement might not follow the traditional pattern; contractors might concentrate on the management of construction and be content to subcontract all the actual building operations. Clients might commission projects which they have no intention of occupying, and frequently the end users will have had no direct contact with the designers or any involvement with the design and construction process. Personal relationships, once such a strong feature of professionalism, often seem to be present only at operational levels.

Given such diversity, it is obviously difficult to devise professional codes and standard procedures to fit all possible permutations. Projects become more sophisticated in terms of design and construction technology and processes become more demanding in terms of information, organisation and programme. The tendency is for the construction professions to focus on functional requirements at the expense of traditional role perceptions, and for professional boundaries to become less clearly defined.

Nevertheless, even after taking into account the calls for deregulation, unfettered competition and free enterprise in today's consumer-orientated society, there is still a valid and significant role for the professions, the principles which they strive to uphold and the values which they aim to embrace. Trust and integrity are still the bedrock of fair business dealings and codes, standards and competence are still essential. In this context, professional practice today means having regard to the following:

- measures which are imposed through voluntary membership of a professional institution, and which regulate the conduct and performance of practitioners;
- consumer protection measures imposed by legislation, and which must be observed;
- declared standards of professional performance to be provided for all services undertaken, but particularly in order to avoid allegations of negligence in matters of design, specification, and contract administration;
- measures imposed by law, whether express or implied, concerning planning, design and construction of certain building types and classes, and relating to certain aspects of construction operations;
- generally held expectations relating to competent management and administration in business matters.

The knowledge and range of skills expected of the average practising architect has increased over recent years. For example, these might now include:

- an ability to prepare effective presentations to support funding operations;
- adequate knowledge of and a proper concern for health and safety in design and construction operations;
- balanced sensitivity towards matters of the environment, whether these relate to user requirements or to the wider context;
- reasonable understanding and operational skills concerning information technology and the use of computers.

In addition, today's architect might be expected to develop some area of specialisation (eg as adjudicator, planning supervisor, project manager, party wall surveyor etc). Given so much scope for diversification, it becomes very important to be accurate when supplying details as qualification for commissions, so that unwarranted assumptions are not made. Practice today is conducted against a background of ever increasing legislation and regulation in a society which has become less forgiving and more rights-conscious.

A1.3 Competence

Professional services are 'invisible', and initially at least have to be taken and given on the basis of trust. Traditionally, membership of a reputable professional body was regarded as providing a hallmark of a particular competence.

From 1932, evidence of professional competence has also been provided by entry in a Register of Architects set up under an Act of Parliament which restricted use of the title 'Registered Architect', and in 1938 this was followed by measures to give statutory protection to the business use of the title 'Architect'. Some of the intentions behind such legislation might have been questionable at the time, but undeniably it brought a measure of consumer protection, because the public were now able to distinguish between those properly qualified persons admitted to the Register of Architects and other persons who were no longer legally entitled to call themselves architects.

In 1997 the statutory Architects Registration Council of the United Kingdom was succeeded by the Architects Registration Board, which has greater powers to act in dealing with allegations of serious professional incompetence. Registered persons found guilty of unacceptable professional conduct or serious professional incompetence can be disciplined, and competence can relate to the way in which business is carried out as well as the service provided. Moreover the ultimate control in reaching such decisions may now rest with non-architects, as they have a voting majority of one on the Registration Board and the Professional Conduct Committee.

Over a long period the architectural profession has been rather reluctant to tackle the question of what should be done about incompetence, preferring to leave the remedy in the hands of the courts. The issue has now been faced, and competence is a matter included in code of professional conduct and standard of professional performance obligations on RIBA members. A real effort has been made to reinstate the traditional hallmark of competence. Evidence of competence may also be required to remain registered as an architect.

Clients sometimes seek additional reassurance in the form of professional indemnity insurance, warranties, certification of other competences, and quality management. Where such demands are reasonable and realistic, they may also be regarded as constituting further hallmarks of competence.

There are a number of bodies directly relevant to the practice of architecture, some of which can properly be described as representative professional institutes. These include the Incorporated Association of Architects and Surveyors (IAAS) and the Architects and Surveyors Institute (ASI). Note however that the only UK-wide professional body exclusively for architects is the Royal Institute of British Architects (RIBA) which is also by far the largest.

A2.1 RIBA – the background

The Royal Institute of British Architects was founded in 1834 under the style of the Institute of British Architects, and during its first fifty years it set up in embryo form many of the activities which characterise the work of the Institute today.

In the course of its first decade of existence, a register of architects seeking work was instituted, the first library catalogue was published, the first competitions committee was set up, and in 1837 the first Royal Charter was granted by William IV.

During the next 30 years there was the establishment of a professional practice committee, the granting of the Royal Gold Medal, and a great deal of activity directed at improving and rationalising architectural qualifications. The first board of examiners was set up in 1862 and the first voluntary architectural examinations were held in 1863. In the 1860s the first Scale of Charges and Conditions of Builders' Contracts were published, and in 1866 the first paid secretary was appointed. Also in 1866, the title 'Royal' was conferred upon the Institute by Queen Victoria.

The Supplemental Charter of 1887 made the examination in architecture compulsory for associate membership of the Institute, and made provisions for regulations to govern exclusion or suspension from membership. The first Code of Professional Conduct was published in 1900.

There were major initiatives in the early part of the 20th century directed towards unification of the profession and statutory registration, a policy adopted by the RIBA Council in 1905 following an intensive campaign by the Society of Architects. (This was a body formed in 1884 which consisted mainly of members of the RIBA who were dissatisfied with the Institute's inactivity on this matter.) The 1925 Supplemental Charter provided for the amalgamation with the RIBA of the Society of Architects, and the first draft architects' registration bill was published in 1926. Despite massive opposition and several amendments to the bill (including deletion of the provision for the RIBA to maintain the register), the Architects (Registration) Act 1931 came into force.

After World War II, the Institute became increasingly representative and democratic. It adapted to ensure that architects from specialist interest groups and those in the then burgeoning public service sector could feel that they were part of one professional body. A single corporate membership class was introduced following the Supplemental Charter of 1971, but under Byelaw 2.13, members who were elected before that time could continue to use the affix FRIBA or ARIBA as appropriate.

A watershed study, 'The Architect and his Office', was undertaken by the RIBA in 1962, and this brought to light the need for increased awareness of and skill in the business side of architectural practice. As a result, the RIBA published the first *Handbook of Practice and Management*, and the *Architect's Job Book*. Other studies were reflected in such significant reports as 'The Practical Training of Architects', 'Guide to Group Practice and Consortia', 'Competence', and 'Continuing Professional Development'. These were closely followed by other publications aimed at guiding and assisting practice, and in 1969 the RIBA Companies were formed to progress this work commercially. The most recent RIBA research initiative, to investigate clients' needs and perception of architects, has been the 'Strategic Study of the Profession', the results of which were published in phases commencing in 1992.

In recent years the RIBA has attempted to promote greater public understanding of architecture by means of Architecture Centres, and to provide better access to information for its Members via telephone help lines and the use of information technology. It has continued, with considerable success, to re-establish the case for fairer fees and conditions in relation to architectural services, and to engage government and funders in dialogue over environmental concerns, development priorities and best value in construction and architectural services.

A2.2 RIBA – the organisation

The headquarters of the RIBA is 66 Portland Place, London W1N 4AD. Here a Director General heads staff who are charged with administering Institute policy. The DG is supported by full time officials who in turn head Departments, each of which consists of a Directorate backed by specialist units as appropriate. These units are also responsible for servicing the various boards or advisory groups on which sit invited, nominated or elected members of the Institute who have particular expertise and interests.

At present the Departments have allocated responsibilities for Education and Professional Development; Practice; Finance and Administration; Library; Membership and International Affairs; Public Affairs. The DG's office deals with matters relating to arbitration, discipline, and professional conduct.

The RIBA Council, a body of some 60 members elected by ballot to ensure national and regional representation, is presided over by the President. This is an honorary office, and the Charter allows for 'such other Honorary Officers to be elected as the Byelaws prescribe'. At present these include Vice Presidents, an Honorary Secretary, and an Honorary Treasurer.

The RIBA is an Institute which functions internationally but with a UK focus. It is a considerable global force, particularly in those countries which are members of the Commonwealth Association of Architects (CAA). For RIBA members, contact with the Institute is likely to be through specific activities, Regional Offices and Branches. All RIBA members are allocated to membership of a Branch, of which there are about 80. Most members belong to the Branch in which they live or work, but the choice of Branch is the prerogative of the individual. Each Region has its own office with a Director and staff. This is the vital grass roots part of the network, responsible for organising seminars, courses, lectures and visits. This is where local practice contacts and support can flourish, and problems can be tackled at a personal level. The network also provides members with an opportunity to exercise considerable influence over RIBA affairs.

The traditional organisational framework of the Institute is both geographic and knowledge-based. The network of local offices is overlaid with a pattern of committees concerned with broad issues such as practice, education or marketing. The Strategic Study of the Profession took an in-depth client-centred look at architecture. It found a client group who sought to be able to distinguish one architectural practice from another on the basis of demonstrable specialist skills. New communication mechanisms have allowed the development of a locally accessible knowledge-based network superimposed on the old geographic structure. The new networks know no geographic or national boundary, and help the Institute both to meet clients' needs and to exploit its international potential. Recent activity, such as the establishment of client-led 'design quality forums', or professionally-led 'specialist interest groups', are evidence of this trend, as is the Institute's development of its own electronic network, Ribanet, and internet site, Ribasite.

A2.3 RIBA – the purpose

The RIBA Supplemental Charter 1971, in paragraph 2.1, states that 'the objects of the Royal Institute are the advancement of Architecture and the promotion of the advancement of the knowledge of the Arts and Sciences connected therewith'. Ever since the original Charter, primacy has been given to the advancement of architecture, not to the advancement of architects.

Currently RIBA efforts to advance the cause of architecture are expressed in many ways:

- by raising environmental and ecological concerns and seeking to influence government and public opinion;
- by facing the challenges to architectural quality in times of changing building procurement and technology;
- by providing support services for practitioners;
- by striving to improve the status and competence of architects through continuing professional education and research;
- by engaging in consultation on legal, technical and financial controls and constraints within which architecture is now practised;
- by maintaining the architect's professed concept of providing a unique design service.

From a list of support services now offered by the RIBA to members, the following are likely to be of particular interest to practitioners:

- Practice Register (details of all registered practices, published annually);
- Practice Database (computer-aided matching of suitable practices with client enquiries by the Clients Advisory Service);
- Appointments Bureau (for members looking for work or seeking to recruit staff);
- Members Information Line (professional library help service responding to most kinds of architectural queries);
- Specialist Advisors Panel (telephone advice on practice matters);
- Archives Collection (photographs, drawings, record documents);
- Office Library Service (helping practices to manage trade and technical information);
- National Building Specification (standard clauses and guidance kept up to date on a subscription basis);
- Register of Planning Supervisors (of accredited architects undertaking CDM work);
- Conciliation Service (for resolving disputes between architects and clients);
- Members Business Centre (rooms and facilities for hire at 66 Portland Place);
- Insurance Agency (RIBA approved policies for professional indemnity cover).

A2.4 RIBA representation

As befits a learned society, the RIBA also demonstrates through its Journal, sessional programmes, education policy, library and drawings collections, its right to be seen as a centre of knowledge upon which the practice of architecture is based. Through its code of professional conduct and standard of professional performance, its admission standards, appointing documents, and range of other publications, the Institute is able to assure the public of the standards of integrity and competence of its members.

The RIBA is affiliated to and represented on various associations of direct relevance to architects. Among these are the following:

Association of Consultant Architects (ACA)
Members with a particular involvement in private consultancy who also support the RIBA individually and collectively, especially concerning the business practices associated with architectural services.

Society of Chief Architects of Local Authorities (SCALA)
A select forum for members of local authorities.

Architects in Industry and Commerce
Open to all architects in industrial and commercial organisations.

Architects in Agriculture and the Countryside
A group to promote the involvement of architects in all aspects of agricultural and rural building.

Commonwealth Association of Architects (CAA)
An association of national architectural institutes covering nearly all Commonwealth countries.

Architects Council of Europe (ACE)
Architect representatives from the professional institutions of Member States in the European Union.

International Union of Architects (UIA)
Representing all the major architectural societies in the world, and providing a voice for architecture on bodies such as UNESCO, WHO, ILO etc.

Of particular concern to members in practice, the RIBA has direct representation on many bodies which, although outside the immediate profession, are prominent in the construction industry. These include the following:

Joint Contracts Tribunal (JCT)
The organisation which publishes and keeps under review the standard forms of building contract and subcontract generally used throughout the building industry. The RIBA is represented on the Tribunal itself, the drafting committee, implementation group, insurance group, research committee and various working groups.

Construction Industry Council (CIC)
The representative forum for most of the professional bodies, and some of the trade associations, in the construction industry. The RIBA is represented on committees and working parties concerned with appointments, adjudication, approved inspectors, energy and the environment, health and safety, and research.

Construction Industry Board (CIB)
Mainly concerned with the implementation of the recommendations in the Latham Report, for which the RIBA has representation on various working groups.

National House Building Council (NHBC)
A specialist but influential body, with RIBA representatives on its disciplinary and standards committees.

The RIBA is also actively represented on various bodies which are principally concerned with environmental matters, including urban and building conservation. These include the following:

Conference on Training in Architectural Conservation (COTAC);
Council of the National Trust;
Council for the Protection of Rural England (CPRE);
Countryside Commission;
Society for the Preservation of Ancient Buildings (SPAB).

A3.1 Control over entry to the RIBA

Most professional institutions lay down minimum standards for entry, and exert discipline on members through codes of professional conduct. The RIBA takes a keen interest in the way that architecture is handled in school curricula, and closely monitors the way that architecture is taught in higher education. It reviews courses and examinations in Schools of Architecture on a quinquennial basis jointly with Visiting Board representatives from the Architects Registration Board. Continued recognition depends on standards being maintained.

Many young aspirants glimpse their first possibility of a career in architecture through short periods of work experience in an architect's office. This is often initiated by the school careers teacher, who will be keen to establish and maintain a link with sympathetic practices. Such an arrangement can bring mutual benefits.

Practitioners may sometimes be asked about suitable courses and requirements for young people interested in pursuing a career in architecture. Information is available in the RIBA booklet, '*A Career in Architecture*', and through enquiries to the RIBA Education Department.

Entry requirements
The RIBA offers the recognised schools of architecture the following guidance on minimum entry requirements, but schools are at liberty to require higher standards, perhaps in specific subjects, and competition for places is keen.

The General Certificate of Education and the General Certificate of Secondary Education (England, Wales, Northern Ireland)
Candidates should have passes in two subjects at the Advanced level or one subject at A level with two AS levels of the GCE together with passes in three other subjects in the GCSE. Both the GCE A level subjects and at least two GCSE subjects should be drawn from the academic fields of study. The following are important:
(1) English
(2) Mathematics or a science subject. Botany, Zoology, Biology or Geology are acceptable GCSE subjects where accompanied by Maths at either level.

These subjects may be taken at either GCE A level or in the GCSE.

The traditional craft subjects are not sufficient in themselves for a career in architecture, but many schools will accept one of the newer courses which have a strong element of design and problem-solving rigorously taught and assessed within an academic framework.

The Scottish Certificate of Education
Requirements for the Scottish Certificate of Education are similar, except that at least three of the subjects should be passed on the Higher grade, but the other two subjects may be passed on the Ordinary grade. Passes in any two of the additional Maths subjects (Elementary Analysis, Geometry, and Dynamics) will count as one Higher grade for this purpose. All three Higher grade subjects and one Ordinary grade subject should be drawn from the field of study specified above.

BTEC Certificate
Under certain circumstances it is possible for students with a high standard of pass in the Business and Technician Education Council (BTEC) Certificate in Building Studies, supplemented by a pass in English in the GCSE syllabus, to be accepted by some schools, but others might also require three additional

subjects to include Maths. Candidates should apply to the school of architecture concerned for its specific views on entry requirements.

Schools of Architecture

There are currently 36 schools of architecture in the UK, with full-time courses and examinations recognised by the RIBA as giving exemption from its own examinations. The schools are inspected by the Joint RIBA ARB Validation Panel at least every five years.

A minimum period of seven years must elapse between embarking on a recognised course and being eligible to attempt the professional practice examination leading to RIBA Corporate Membership and UK Registration. Full-time courses traditionally require the equivalent of five academic years of full time academic study supplemented by at least two years' professional training. A few schools offer a four-year academic period with at least three years' monitored and assessed professional training. The RIBA publishes a booklet, *Schools of Architecture recognised by the RIBA*, which gives information about each school, the type and length of courses offered, and details of entry requirements.

As an employee in an architect's office it is also possible to study architecture as an external candidate with a view to qualifying by taking the RIBA's own examinations. Part-time courses are available at most schools of architecture, and at least for design submissions it is expected that some formal tutoring arrangement will exist. This external route is the only practical option for some students, but it is somewhat arduous. Anyone seeking to qualify in this way must be practice-based and have had the equivalent of at least six years' practical experience, and must satisfy the minimum entry requirements set by the RIBA.

The RIBA examinations currently comprise 'The Examination in Architecture for Office Based Candidates' (Parts 1 and 2), to be followed by 'The Examination in Professional Practice' (the so-called 'Part 3'). Information about the syllabus, regulations and submission requirements may be obtained from the Examinations Office, RIBA Education Department. The RIBA publishes a guide, *Examination in Architecture for Office Based Candidates*, and sets of previous examination papers are available.

Part-time courses, which may be modular, are offered at some colleges. In-company training programmes (which may recognise some work undertaken in the office) are another way of obtaining additional academic qualifications at the same time as professional development. Enquiries about such opportunities should be made directly to the academic institutions concerned.

Most schools of architecture also operate Higher Degree Schemes. These may entail a full-time commitment of between a few months (a taught course which might lead to a supplementary Master's degree at the end of Part 2) and three years (a research programme which might lead to a Master's degree or Doctorate). Many such courses are modular. A list of post-graduate courses is available from the RIBA Education Department, but the field is fast-moving and prospective candidates are advised to contact institutions directly.

Professional training

Professional training is an essential complement to academic learning. The fundamental objectives of the Professional Training Scheme are to ensure that through 'learning by doing' with responsibility in a busy office, those entering the profession in the UK should have:

- a practical understanding of the procedural, legal and contractual problems of architectural practice, which will be tested in an examination;
- practical experience of obligations of the kind entailed in architect–client and employer–employee relationships;
- direct experience, under supervision, of a range of the duties and responsibilities of professional practice;
- an understanding of the concept of professional judgement in architecture.

The first period of up to one year usually comes at the end of the first three years of the academic course (at a point equivalent to Part 1 of the RIBA Examination). The second period starts on completion of a further two years' academic study (at a point equivalent to Part 2 of the RIBA Examination). However, there are some variations to this pattern.

As far as practitioners are concerned, there are five undertakings which should be regarded as setting a minimum standard. Offices undertake:

- to give a student reasonable opportunities to gain an adequate breadth and depth of experience from the range described in the RIBA's *Professional Training Record;*
- to nominate an experienced architect who will be personally responsible for directing the student's work so that adequate experience is obtained;
- to allow visits from time to time by a school's Professional Training Adviser to discuss the student's progress;
- to allow up to ten paid working days per annum for professional activities which have the educational objective of broadening the student's professional training;
- to partner the student in assessing the learning outcomes.

Each school of architecture which offers a Part 3 programme is responsible for appointing a Professional Training Adviser who can cooperate with employers in a joint effort to secure the best training possible for students. Advisers welcome details of any likely vacancies for students and as much information as possible about the office and its work.

The status of a professional trainee is that of an employee first and a student second, and an Adviser is normally well qualified to comment on such matters as salary levels and student capabilities. Most Advisers have other responsibilities in their schools, but they will try to visit the office at least once during the year. The Adviser normally talks first with the student and then discusses progress separately with the employer or Office Supervisor. Advice given to students by an Adviser is impartial.

The usual pattern is for professional trainees to attend seminars of practice and management back at the school. The employer may expect confirmation by the school's Adviser that any proposed activity requiring formal leave of absence is of educational importance. The office should also arrange a programme of complementary activities such as visiting sites, attending client and contractor meetings, listening to planning enquiries, observing specialists' operations, and accompanying clerks of works, planning supervisors or quantity surveyors on their inspections.

Office Supervisor

The student should ensure that one person is nominated as the Supervisor, who will be responsible for supervising and guiding the student's training so that the range, quality and depth of the activities undertaken satisfy the objectives of the Scheme. The Office Supervisor should undertake to:

- direct and advise the student;
- inform the student of opportunities in various parts of the office to gain particular kinds of training;
- ensure that the student uses the *Professional Training Record* properly, regularly discussing its completion with the student;
- encourage the student to make the most of any opportunity to broaden his or her experience;
- keep in touch with the school's Adviser and report frankly and constructively on the student's progress.

The Rules of the Professional Training Scheme are set out in the *Professional Training Record* published by RIBA Publications.

Professional Practice Examination

Both the RIBA Examination and equivalent recognised courses at schools of architecture contain a strong professional studies element. The examination in professional practice is the final mechanism for controlling standards of entry to the profession and has the following components:

A documentary submission, which will contain some or all of the following:

- a professional cv;
- a professional training record;
- a professional training experience evaluation prepared by the candidate;
- a folio of professional case work.

A written examination, which will cover both job management and practice management.

A professional interview, at which the candidate's knowledge and experience generally will be probed.

This qualifying examination is intended to establish a high baseline of competence for entry to membership of the RIBA and registration, and with potential for continuing professional development. The range and quality of experience that candidates will be expected to demonstrate is unlikely to be acquired in less than three years and many candidates have four or five years' experience.

A3.2 Control over the professional conduct of Members

Issue 11 of the RIBA Code of Professional Conduct was published in 1997 and included the Standard of Professional Performance for the first time. The booklet is available from RIBA Publications.

The object of the Code is to promote the standard of professional conduct, or self-discipline, required of Members of the RIBA in the interests of the public. All Members, including Student Members, are required to uphold this standard, and their conduct is governed by the Code.

The Code comprises three Principles which are of universal application, dealing with competence, integrity, the interests of Members generally and the public who commission the services of an architect. This means keeping in mind the interests of all who use or might be affected by the work of an architect, and also having regard for environmental matters, such as use of natural resources, the cultural heritage etc.

The three Principles are supported by Undertakings which are essentially advisory and intended to illustrate the application of the Principles. The wording used in the Principles is pre-eminent, but it should be noted that Members must at all times be guided by the spirit of the Code and not just the words. This could prove to be a very wide obligation to satisfy.

Members are governed by the RIBA Charter, Byelaws and Regulations in addition to the Code. Disciplinary measures are provided for under the Byelaws. The RIBA can hold a Member personally accountable when acting through a corporate or unincorporated body, and Members will not be able to evade this by pleading a higher obligation.

Revisions to the Code, and relevant practice notes, may appear in the *RIBA Journal* from time to time. Members will be expected to be familiar with any new provisions right from the date of their introduction, and to comply with them. Ignorance will be no defence.

Principle One
A Member shall faithfully carry out his duties applying his knowledge and experience with efficiency and loyalty towards his client or employer, and being mindful of the interests of those who may be expected to use or enjoy the product of his work.

Principle One applies to all professional relationships, whether between an employer Member and a salaried staff Member, or between a Member and a client.

To uphold this Principle a Member **undertakes:**

1.1 When acting between parties or giving advice, to exercise his independent professional judgement impartially to the best of his ability and understanding.

1.2 When making any engagement, whether by an agreement for professional services, by a contract of employment or by a contract for the supply of services and goods, to state whether or not professional indemnity insurance is held, and to have defined beyond reasonable doubt and recorded the terms of the engagement and the scope of the service, responsibilities and any limitation of liability, the method of calculation of remuneration and the provision for termination and adjudication.

1.3 Before accepting or continuing with any work to establish that his competence and resources are adequate to provide a service which meets the **RIBA Standard of Professional Performance** and, if engaged as a full-time employee, give prior notice to both parties before accepting the engagement elsewhere.

1.4 To arrange that the work of his office and any branch office, insofar as it relates to architecture, is under the control of an architect.

1.5 Not to transfer his responsibilities, or reduce the scope of his services by sub-contracting, without the prior consent of his client or without defining the changes in the responsibilities of those concerned.

1.6 Not to evade his obligations by abandoning a commission.

---

* Note that these Undertakings require that the scope and precise terms of agreements between architect and client must be defined and recorded beyond reasonable doubt.
* Members are required to disclose whether or not professional indemnity insurance is held. As yet holding such insurance is not an RIBA requirement, but it is required under the ARB Code.
* It is essential to establish that both competence and resources are adequate for the commission to be undertaken.
* There is a requirement that work cannot be subcontracted without the consent of the client, and that Members cannot simply walk away from an undertaking once entered into.

Principle Two

A Member shall, at all times, avoid any action or situation which is inconsistent with his professional obligations or which is likely to raise doubts about his integrity.

Principle Two is relevant to all other business or personal interests which a Member might have which impinge in any way on a commission. The Member must then disclose this fact to the client. Preferably this will be before accepting the commission, but if a potential conflict of interests arises only after accepting the commission, then the Member must either withdraw or see to it that any cause of conflict is removed, or continue only with the express agreement of all parties concerned.

To uphold this Principle a Member **undertakes:**

2.1   To declare in writing to any prospective client or employer any business interest the existence of which, if not so declared, would or might be likely to raise a conflict of interests and doubts about his integrity by reason of an actual or apparent connection with or effect upon his engagement. If the prospective client or employer does not in writing accept these circumstances, the Member must withdraw from the situation.

2.2   When finding that in circumstances not specifically covered elsewhere in this Code his personal or professional interests conflict so as to risk a breach of this Principle, either to withdraw from the situation, or remove the source of conflict, or declare it and obtain the agreement of the parties concerned to the continuance of the engagement.

2.3   Not to make, support or acquiesce in any statement, written or otherwise, which is contrary to his own knowledge or bona fide professional opinion, or which he knows to be misleading, or unfair to others or otherwise discreditable to the profession.

2.4   Not to practise as or purport to be an independent consulting architect and simultaneously be a principal, partner, director or co-director in a firm which engages in the business of:
• trading in land or buildings; or as
• property developers, auctioneers, or house agents; or as
• contractors, subcontractors, manufacturers or suppliers in or to the building industry
unless that firm is distinct from the architectural practice and clearly identified as such.

2.5   Not to carry out or purport to carry out the independent functions of an architect or any similar independent functions in relation to a contract in which he or his employer is the contractor, or where the architectural practice and the contractor's firm are under substantially the same management or control.

(*continued*)

2.6   Not to disclose, or use to the benefit of himself or others, confidential information acquired in the course of his work without the prior written consent of the parties concerned.

2.7   Not to give or accept any commissions or gifts or other inducement to show favour to any person or body, or allow his name to be used in advertising any service or product associated with the construction industry.

2.8   Not to have or take as a partner or co-director in his firm any person who is disqualified for registration by reason of the fact that his name has been removed from the Register under Section 7 of the Architects (Registration) Act 1931, as amended by the Housing Grants, Construction and Regeneration Act 1996; any person disqualified for membership of the Royal Institute by reason of expulsion under Byelaw 5.1; any person disqualified for membership of another professional institution by reason of expulsion under the relevant disciplinary regulations, unless the Royal Institute otherwise allows.

2.9   Irrespective of the form of this practice, and notwithstanding the provisions of the Companies Acts, to conduct his business in a manner consistent with this Principle.

2.10   On becoming personally or professionally insolvent or being disqualified under the Company Directors Disqualification Act 1986, to notify the Royal Institute's principal executive officer of the facts.

2.11   To conform with the **Members' Rules for Clients' Accounts**.

* Note that Members must not make supportive statements, written or otherwise, including advertising material, which could bring discredit to the profession.
* Members must not act as independent consultants whilst also being part of a firm of estate agents, developers or contractors, unless the architectural practice is clearly separate.
* Members must not purport to act as independent contract administrators for a building contract where the architectural practice and the contracting organisation are under substantially the same management or control.
* Members must not disclose confidential information which has been acquired during a commission, without written consent from the parties concerned.
* Members must conform to the Rules for Clients' Accounts. These are printed in full in the current edition (Issue 11) of the Code.
* Reference to registration legislation in Undertaking 2.8 should be read in conjunction with the Architects Act 1997, which has repealed the legislation cited.

Principle Three

A Member shall in every circumstance conduct himself in a manner which respects the legitimate rights and interests of others.

Principle Three applies to all professional dealings, not just between Members but also with persons outside the profession in respect of legitimate (ie legal and moral) interests.

To uphold this Principle a Member **undertakes**:

3.1 Not to offer discounts, commissions, gifts or other inducements for the introduction of clients.

3.2 When offering services as an independent consultant, not to quote a fee without receiving an invitation to do so and sufficient information on the nature and scope of the project to enable a quotation to be prepared which clearly indicates the service covered by the fee.

3.3 When offering services as an independent consulting architect, not to revise a fee quotation to take account of the fee quoted by another architect for the same service.

3.4 Not to attempt to oust another architect from an engagement.

3.5 Not to enter any architectural competition which the Royal Institute has declared to be unacceptable.

3.6 Not when appointed as a competition assessor subsequently to act in any other capacity for the work.

3.7 Not maliciously or unfairly to criticise or attempt to discredit another Member or his work.

3.8 On being approached to undertake work upon which he knows or can ascertain by reasonable enquiry that another architect has an engagement with the same client, to notify the fact to such architect.

3.9 When engaged to give an opinion on the work of another architect, to notify the fact to that architect unless it can be shown to be prejudicial to prospective or actual litigation to do so.

3.10 Appropriately to acknowledge the contribution made to his work by others.

* Note that Members must acknowledge appropriately the contribution made to their work by others – and this presumably includes contributions from team colleagues who are not Members and may be from other professions.
* Members must, when employing other architects, make sure that their authority, responsibility and liability are clearly established.
* Members must ensure that full time staff have the benefit of subrogation waivers from the practice's indemnity insurers.
* Members must report to the RIBA any known alleged breaches of this Code, unless the law or the courts have imposed a restriction.
* Members must report to the RIBA any conviction for a criminal offence, including any disqualification from being a company director.

A3.3 Control over the performance of Members

The object of the Standard of Professional Performance, included with Issue 11 of the Code of Professional Conduct, is to establish a level of competence which the Royal Institute, in the interests of clients and the protection of the reputation of the profession, requires of Members and their practices.

The Standard applies to the service offered by the practising unit, whether it be a sole practitioner, sole principal, partnership or company.

An alleged failure to comply with the Standard may be investigated by the Royal Institute and, if it is concluded that the allegation is well founded, the Institute may instruct the practice to take action to ensure that the lapse in performance is not repeated.

While the primary objective is to offer advice to those Members who find themselves in difficulty, the Royal Institute may take disciplinary action where there is an extreme and irresponsible failure to meet the Standard, or where there is a repeated failure to comply with the Standard. It is only in exceptional circumstances that an isolated failure to meet the Standard would give rise to disciplinary proceedings.

A Member is required to follow the Undertakings which amplify the Standard, and honour them in his work according to his circumstances. It will be a material consideration in the assessment of a case if an investigation into an alleged failure to meet the Standard reveals that the Member has failed to do so.

THE STANDARD OF PROFESSIONAL PERFORMANCE

Members are required to maintain in their work and that of their practices a standard of performance which is consistent with membership of the Royal Institute of British Architects and with a proper regard for the interests both of those who commission and those who may be expected to use or enjoy the product of their work.

Members and their practices will meet the requirements of their engagements with commensurate knowledge and attention so that the quality of the professional services provided does not fall below that which could reasonably be expected of Members of the Royal Institute in good standing in the normal conduct of their business.

To uphold this Standard, the Member, and where appropriate the practice, **undertakes**:

1   To comply with all reasonable instructions, to carry out and complete the work entrusted to him honestly, competently, diligently and expeditiously in accordance with the timescale and any cost limits previously agreed so far as reasonably possible.

2   To fulfil CPD obligations and when employing other Members on a full-time basis to allow them reasonable time to do likewise.

3   To operate where appropriate an internal complaints procedure which should ensure that clients are informed whom to approach in the event of any problems with the professional service provided, and establish procedures which will ensure that complaints are properly and promptly attended to.

4   To make arrangements with an appropriately qualified person for the running of their offices and administration of contracts during a period of absence and inform clients of those arrangements.

5   To seek appropriate advice when faced with a situation which they recognise as being outside their own experience or knowledge.

6   When in practice as a sole practitioner or sole principal to make reasonable attempts to establish professional contact with other Members which could provide opportunities for the mutual exchange of experience and knowledge.

(*continued*)

7   As a partner or co-director of an architectural practice to have proper regard to the experience and capability of staff when delegating responsibility.

8   Not to lay claim to expertise which they do not have, or accept commissions which they know are beyond their skill and experience, without arranging for appropriate assistance and advice which will enable them to satisfy the **Standard of Professional Performance** in the discharge of their professional duties.

In upholding the Standard, the undertakings are both personal upon Members and upon practices. All Members undertake to engage in CPD activities, and to see that employees who are Members are also allowed reasonable time for this.

The term continuing professional development (CPD) is used by the profession to describe those activities which constitute part of the learning process which should continue throughout an architect's professional career. CPD is a matter both for individuals and collectively for offices and departments. It implies the need to formulate a positive plan of action rather than perfunctory attendance at a given number of random events. The RIBA has a national CPD Service, with convenors or managers at regional level.

What kind of activity constitutes CPD can be widely interpreted. For example, it could include:

- serving the profession in the branch or regional structure through work on various committees or ad hoc groups, and learning at the same time;
- a programme of self-directed learning activities;
- pursuing a formal educational course, which might result in an additional qualification or accreditation;
- attendance at external events such as seminars, lectures and workshops;
- participation in events arranged by the practice for its staff, such as discussions, workshops, design crits. Smaller practices might consider joining with others to establish a programme of regular activities.

A4.1 Registration of title

Registration for architects first occurred with the Architects (Registration) Act of 1931. Registration was a voluntary matter, but by the Architects Registration Act 1938 use of the word 'Architect' in any business style or title was restricted to those persons who were registered (with some exceptions, eg landscape architect or golf course architect). Much of the 1931 and 1938 legislation was repealed by the provisions of Part III of the Housing Grants, Construction and Regeneration Act 1996, and this was overtaken in turn by the consolidating Architects Act 1997.

In 1993, long-running arguments about the restriction of title and the protective undesirability of registration were revived in parliamentary circles. Consequently John Warne was appointed to enquire into whether statutory registration and protection of the title 'architect' should be retained. Warne concluded that he saw 'no merit in incurring the cost of retaining the Architects Registration Council United Kingdom (ARCUK) established under the 1931 Act, simply to fulfil a minimal role of keeping a register.' He said, 'If registration is to continue, I consider that instead it should be undertaken by the RIBA. My main recommendation is that the protection of the title "architect" should be abolished and ARCUK disbanded.'

The climate of opinion had changed somewhat by the time the Warne Report was published, and Parliament chose not to repeal immediately legislation for the registration of architects. However, reform was inevitable, and the Housing Grants etc Act included a Part III which related to the registration of architects. Under it the former ARCUK was replaced by a new Architects Registration Board (ARB), with powers to maintain a Register and discipline architects for breaches of its Code. The 1996 legislation was in a sense a measure of expediency, and all the provisions concerning architects' registration are now to be found in a logically structured Architects Act 1997. Generally the changes to the Act clarify the different roles of the professional institute, which is to promote professional knowledge, and the registration body, which regulates the use of the title 'architect' in the public interest.

A4.2 Architects Act 1997

ARB consists of seven elected members (elected by ballot from among registered persons but not necessarily RIBA Members) and eight appointed members (appointed by the Privy Council but not registered persons). The members elect their own chairman. Duties of the Board include the following:

- to appoint the Registrar of Architects;
- to establish a Professional Conduct Committee and other committees as may be necessary;
- to issue a Code of Practice;
- to publish a Register of Architects annually;
- to rule on various matters concerning registration.

The Registrar of Architects is appointed by the Board, and its duties include:

- to maintain the Register of Architects;
- to carry out various prescribed functions concerned with registration;
- to maintain a list of visiting EEA architects (ie from European Economic Area States).

The Professional Conduct Committee consists of four elected members of the Board (ie all architects, including at least one Scottish representative), three appointed members of the Board, and in addition two persons nominated by the Law Society.

A voting majority on both the Board and the Professional Conduct Committee lies with non-registered persons (ie outside the architectural profession). This is in line with the opinions expressed by Warne, that 'the views of professional men and women and their assessment of their own authority are no longer accepted automatically by governments and by the public which they serve'.

To become registered, a person must apply to the Registrar on the relevant form, and be able to provide evidence of:

- such qualifications and such practical experience as may be prescribed; *or*
- such standard of competence which, in the opinion of the Board, will be equivalent to the above.

An admission fee is payable on submission of the application, and if accepted a retention fee will become due annually.

Only persons who are registered may practise or carry on business using the name, style or title containing the word 'architect'. Any contravention will be an offence leading to a fine on summary conviction.

To remain registered, a person must:

- pay the annual retention fee at the appropriate time;
- notify the Board of any change of business address;
- not be found guilty of unacceptable professional conduct (ie conduct that falls short of the standard required) or serious professional incompetence;
- not be subject to a 'disciplinary order' which amounts to suspension or erasure.

The Professional Conduct Committee is empowered to make a disciplinary order which can be:

- a reprimand;
- a penalty order (this means paying a specified sum based on the standard scale of fines for summary offences). In the event of nonpayment, a name can be removed from the Register;
- a suspension order (this means removal of a person's name from the Register, with re-entry when the suspension period, not exceeding two years, is over);
- an erasure order (this means removal of a person's name from the Register). It will not be re-entered unless the Board so directs.

A4.3 ARB Code of Professional Conduct and Practice

The Code consists of an Introduction and Standards which are intended to be read together. It should be noted that the full title includes the words Conduct and Practice, understandable in view of the emphasis given in the Act to rejecting both unacceptable professional conduct and serious professional incompetence. As with the RIBA Code, it is stated that technical noncompliance will not necessarily result in proceedings, but that the spirit of the Code must be observed at all times. This could well turn out to be a demanding requirement in particular circumstances.

The Code applies to all architects whatever the form of practice or business they choose to adopt. Employer architects and employee architects are equally bound to respect and observe the Code obligations. UK registered architects are still subject to the ARB Code when they practise abroad, and only if it can be shown that compliance would be inconsistent with local law and customs will any relaxation be possible.

The Standards which are incorporated in the ARB Code of Professional Conduct and Practice are as follows.

Standard 1: An architect should only undertake professional work for which he is able to provide adequate professional, financial and technical competence and resources.

1.1 For the purpose of this Standard an architect does not undertake work when taking part in a competition or otherwise engaging in speculative work. The duty arises when a contract is entered into and continues throughout the term of contract.

1.2 Where work is carried out on behalf of an architect by an employee or by anyone else acting under an architect's direct control the architect is responsible for ensuring that that person is competent to perform the task and, if necessary, is adequately supervised.

Standard 2: An architect should only promote his professional services in a truthful and responsible manner.

2.1 In advertising his services or otherwise drawing them to the attention of a potential client an architect should not make untruthful or misleading statements. The making of a claim that is incapable of objective justification always carries a risk that it may be misleading.

2.2 Advertisements should conform, as appropriate, to the British Code of Advertising Practice and the ITC and Radio Code of Advertising Standards and Practice.

2.3 The business style of a practice should not be misleading, for example by being capable of being confused with that of another practice or service.

2.4 An architect offering consultancy services and other services should make it clear to a potential client that the other services are not independent of the consultancy services.

Standard 3: An architect should carry out his professional work faithfully and conscientiously and with due regard to any relevant technical and professional standards.

3.1 An architect should perform his work with due skill, care and diligence.

3.2 An architect should, so far as is reasonably practicable, carry out his work in accordance with a time scale and cost limits agreed with the client.

3.3 An architect should keep his client informed of the progress of work undertaken on his behalf and of any issue which may affect its quality or cost.

3.4 An architect should observe the confidentiality of his client's affairs and should not disclose confidential information without the prior consent of the client or other lawful authority, for example, when disclosure is required by order of a court.

Standard 4: An architect should manage his professional work responsibly.

4.1 An architect should not undertake work unless the parties have clearly agreed in writing the terms of the contract, notably as to:
- the scope of the work;
- the allocation of responsibilities;
- any limitation of responsibilities;
- the fee or method of calculating it; and
- any provisions for termination.

(*continued*)

4.2   An architect should not accept or continue work if he has a business, financial or personal interest that is or may be in conflict with an interest of the client. In a borderline case the architect should make full disclosure of an interest and leave it to the client to judge. However, some conflicts of interest are so extreme as to prevent an architect entering into or continuing work, even with the client's knowledge and consent. Particular care is needed with respect to the business and commercial interests of any partners or co-directors of the architect, which in this context are to be treated as his own.

4.3   Before agreeing to undertake work with two or more clients whose interests may be in conflict this fact should be made known to those concerned and, wherever possible, the work of the firm should be managed so as to avoid the interests of one client adversely affecting those of another. If it is not possible to disclose the existence of a conflict without a breach of confidence the architect should decline to work for or disengage from work with one of the clients. He should not however act or continue to act for a client while in possession of relevant confidential information concerning another client or potential client.

4.4   At the end of a contract or otherwise on demand an architect should promptly return to a client any papers, plans or other property to which he is legally entitled.

4.5   An architect should ensure that his firm has:
    • appropriate and effective internal procedures, including monitoring and review procedures, and
    • sufficient suitably qualified and supervised staff
    such as to enable it to function efficiently.

4.6   An architect should not take as a partner and should not act as a co-director with an unsuitable person. Examples of unsuitable persons are:
    • a person whose name has been removed from the Register of Architects otherwise than at his own request;
    • a person disqualified from membership of a recognised body of architects.

4.7   A sole practitioner should have adequate arrangements for the supervision of his work in the event of his death, incapacity or other absence from work.

4.8   An architect should observe the law concerning discrimination on grounds of race, sex, marital status and disability.

Standard 5: In carrying out or agreeing to carry out professional work an architect should pay due regard to the interests of anyone who may reasonably be expected to use or enjoy the products of his work.

5.1   In meeting his obligations under this Code an architect should have due regard to the need to conserve and enhance the quality of the environment and its natural resources.

Standard 6: An architect should preserve the security of monies entrusted to his care in the course of his practice or business.

6.1   When an architect has custody of monies belonging to a client or third party he he should arrange for its receipt to be carefully recorded and for it to be kept in an interest-bearing account in a bank or similar institution separate from any account of the firm or of himself.

6.2   Such an account should be designated a 'client account' and the bank should be given written instructions that all money held in it is held as client's money and that the bank is not entitled to combine the account with any other account or to exercise any right of set-off or counterclaim against it in respect of any sum owed to it by the firm.

6.3   Money may only be withdrawn from a client account to make a payment:
    (a) to or on behalf of a client; or
    (b) on the client's written instructions (for example, in order to defray the architects fees).

(*continued*)

6.4   Unless otherwise agreed by the client, any interest accruing to a client account should be paid to the client.

Standard 7: An architect should not undertake professional work without adequate and appropriate professional indemnity insurance cover.

7.1   The need for cover extends to professional work undertaken outside an architect's main professional practice or employment.

7.2   In the case of an employed architect the professional indemnity insurance cover may be provided by his employer.

Standard 8: An architect should ensure that his personal and professional finances are managed prudently.

8.1   The following are examples of acts which may be examined in order to ascertain whether they disclose a wilful disregard by an architect of his responsibilities or a lack of integrity, namely:
   • an order of bankruptcy;
   • the placing into liquidation of a company of which he was a director;
   • an accommodation with creditors; and
   • failure to pay a judgment debt.

8.2   Personal insolvency is an exception to the rule that an architect's private life cannot give rise to disciplinary proceedings, since it may affect his professional solvency.

Standard 9: An architect should maintain his professional competence in areas relevant to his professional work.

9.1   The fact that an architect has not maintained his professional competence may count against him in the event of that competence having to be investigated.

Standard 10: Complaints concerning the professional work of an architect or his practice or business should be dealt with promptly and appropriately.

10.1 (a) In the case of a firm or company comprising four or more partners or directors a partner of the firm or director of the company should be designated as being responsible for dealing initially with complaints.
       (b) Where the designated person is unable to resolve a complaint to the satisfaction of the complainant he should refer it promptly to the senior partner or managing director.
       (c) If, after reviewing the complaint, the senior partner or managing director is unable to resolve the complaint to the satisfaction of the complainant he should inform the complainant that architects are subject to the disciplinary supervision of the Board and that, if the complainant can demonstrate that an architect has been guilty of unacceptable professional conduct or serious professional incompetence, disciplinary proceedings may follow.

10.2 In the case of a sole practitioner or a firm of three or fewer partners or directors complaints should be referred to the sole practitioner, senior partner or managing director, who should deal with them as in sub paragraph (c) of the previous paragraph.

10.3 If a complainant wants more than an explanation and an expression of regret for whatever difficulties he has experienced, some formal means of dispute resolution, such as arbitration, should be considered.

10.4 Complaints should at every stage be handled courteously, sympathetically and in accordance with the following time scale:
       (a) not later than 15 working days from the receipt of a complaint an acknowledgement should be sent;
       (b) not later than 30 working days from the receipt of a complaint a response addressing the issues raised in the initial letter should be sent.

(*continued*)

All correspondence from the Architects Registration Board concerning complaints and/or compliance with the Code shall be handled within the same time limits as shown above unless otherwise instructed by the Board.

Standard 11: An architect is expected to promote the Standards set out in this Code.

11.1   It is not enough that an architect orders his own professional life according to the Standards in this Code; he should also do whatever can reasonably be done to ensure their observance generally by architects. For this reason an architect should report to the Registrar any serious falling short of these Standards on the part of any architect of which he is aware. (It is not necessary to report facts that have been widely reported in the media.)

11.2   An architect should report to the Registrar without delay if he:
   • is convicted of an indictable offence or sentenced to imprisonment in respect to any offence; *or*
   • is made the subject of an order of a court disqualifying him from acting as a company director; *or*
   • is made the subject of a bankruptcy order; *or*
   • if a company of which he is a director is wound up otherwise than for the purposes of amalgamation or reconstruction.

11.3   The fact that an architect has failed to make prompt report may count against him in the event of disciplinary proceedings.

11.4   An architect should not enter into a contract the terms of which would prevent any party from reporting to the Board the conduct of an architect.

11.5   An architect is expected to co-operate with an Investigator appointed under the Architects Act 1997 in his conduct of investigations into the professional conduct or competence of architects, including himself.

11.6   A failure by an architect to co-operate promptly and fully with inquiries by such an Investigator may result in adverse inferences being drawn against him in the event of disciplinary proceedings and in any consequential costs to the Board being reflected in the orders of the Professional Conduct Committee should he be found guilty. It may also itself constitute grounds for disciplinary proceedings.

There is reference in the Standards (by numbers 3–13 inclusive) to footnotes which relate to paragraphs in the Introduction to the Code, thereby also emphasising the integrated nature of the total document. There are also two Appendices. Appendix A refers back to the 1997 Act, and in particular sections 13 and 14; Appendix B cites the kind of criminal conviction which could be regarded as materially relevant to an architect's fitness to practise and which might lead to removal from the Register.

Some essential points of a practical nature should be noted. All registered persons are required to:

• bring adequate professional, financial and technical competence or resources to all work undertaken, and maintain that level of competence; [*cf Standards 1 and 9 with RIBA Code Undertaking 1.3*]
• promote their work only in a truthful and responsible manner, without the risk of misleading or confusing clients; [*cf Standard 2 with RIBA Code Undertaking 2.3*]
• perform to the standard of skill and care expected of a professional – and with diligence, particularly concerning timescales and cost limits agreed with clients; [*cf Standard 3.2 with RIBA Standard Undertaking 1*]

- see that the terms of an appointment are clearly defined and agreed in writing; *[cf Standard 4.1 with RIBA Code Undertaking 1.2. NB This will probably be classed as a 'construction contract']*
- be alert for any conflict of interests when accepting work, or which might arise during a commission, and take appropriate action; *[cf Standard 4.2 with RIBA Code Undertaking 2.1]*
- pay due regard to the interests of anyone who may reasonably be expected to use or enjoy his work *[cf Standard 5 with RIBA Code Principle One]*. This could have far-reaching implications, including giving proper consideration to environmental matters;
- treat client monies responsibly, and place them in a separate identifiable account. Architects must also manage their own personal and professional finances prudently; *[cf Standards 6 and 8 with RIBA Code Undertaking 2.11 and 'Members' Rules for Client Accounts']*
- have adequate professional indemnity insurance cover for all professional work undertaken; *[cf Standard 7 with the less demanding RIBA Code Undertaking 1.2]*

Standard 4 of the Code includes some sensible obligations relating to the management of professional work. For example, architects are required to:

- ensure that sufficient suitably qualified staff are available, and that they are properly supervised; *[Standard 4.5]*
- ensure that employment legislation, in particular that concerning discrimination, is observed; *[Standard 4.8]*
- ensure that there are appropriate procedures, including for monitoring and review, which will comprise a quality management system; *[Standard 4.5]*
- ensure, in the case of sole practitioners undertaking a project, that there are contingency plans in the event of enforced absence. *[Standard 4.7]*

Architects are under a duty to report to the Registrar information concerning convictions or disqualification orders imposed on them by the courts. However, personal observance of the Code with the Standards might not always be sufficient. Architects also have a duty to promote the Standards, to the extent that if they are aware of serious shortcomings on the part of other architects, then these must be reported to the Registrar. *[Standard 11]*

For all RIBA Members, who are also registered persons, the current Codes will need to be taken in conjunction. They have moved far beyond earlier notions of ethical behaviour. Matters of competence, performance and sound business practice have now been established as obligations. The Codes are as much concerned with the interests of those who commission the services of architects as with the protection of the profession and its members.

Practice management

Whatever their mode of practice, and regardless of their status within an organisation, all architects as professional people have some legal obligations for which they may be held personally or jointly accountable. These are most likely to arise in connection with:

- occupying premises for business purposes;
- running the business;
- employing staff;
- providing professional services under architect–client agreements
- carrying out projects.

Some of these obligations will be subject to common law, where actions which result in injury to others could result in claims for damages. Other obligations will arise from legislation where noncompliance could be a breach of statutory duty giving grounds for prosecution.

Architecture can be a high risk business and all persons involved in formulating briefs, writing specifications, reporting on the state or potential of land or buildings, designing, inspecting work and administering building contracts etc could at some time or other be faced with a reference to adjudication, arbitration, or litigation. Sometimes the architect may be forced into the position of claimant, or become caught up as a witness of fact, or be joined as co-defendant in proceedings, or have to face allegations of breach of contract or negligence.

Obviously legal considerations loom large in practice. The late Judge John Newey once remarked: 'No architect can be expected to have the knowledge and expertise of a professional lawyer, but, if an architect is to perform his own work properly, he must have sufficient knowledge of the sections of the law which bear upon it . . .'

B1.1 Claims in contract

Claims against professionals may arise in contract or in tort, sometimes under both heads. There are important differences.

A contract is an agreement enforceable at law, or for a breach of which the law will provide a remedy – usually monetary compensation or damages. Contractual obligations can arise from express or implied terms, the latter usually because of trade custom, or because they are necessary to make the contract workable, or most likely because they are implied by statute and cannot readily be excluded. Only the parties to a contract are bound by its terms, and the obligations which it gives rise to are therefore relatively controllable. By and large, the parties are free to agree whatever bargain they wish, and the courts will not be concerned about its fairness, only that it is workable and not contrary to public morality and the law.

Where a contract obligation is not met, an action for breach of contract may be brought and damages claimed in respect of all the losses suffered. An architect liable for breach of contract will often be in breach of an express or implied term to exercise that degree of skill and care expected of an ordinary competent architect. However, if the contractual duty is a strict liability one, ie to achieve a particular result, as for example with a 'fitness for purpose' warranty, then it will not be necessary to rely on a lack of skill and care. The fact of failure will, of itself, be sufficient to establish breach of contract. Contract law puts no restrictions on the kind of losses that are recoverable in damages, and economic losses are freely recoverable so long as they arise directly from the breach and it may be supposed that they could reasonably have been within the contemplation of the parties at the time they entered into the contract.

It is therefore important to consider carefully the terms of any contractual arrangement. It is essential that contracts for professional services are put into writing, and that the obligations of the parties are set down in clear and precise terms. Such contracts will usually be 'construction contracts', and subject to the terms of the Housing Grants, Construction and Regeneration Act 1996.

Under the Limitation Act 1980, the time for bringing an action for breach of contract will be six years from the date of the breach in the case of simple contracts, or twelve years in the case of a contract entered into as a deed.

B1.2 Claims in tort

Tort is a civil wrong outside of contract, although a tortious duty may exist in parallel with a contractual one. Many kinds of tort are relevant to the practice of architecture (for example, trespass, libel, nuisance), but actions in tort against architects are usually for alleged negligence.

We are all personally liable for any torts which we commit, whether these are the result of actions or a failure to act in particular circumstances. In general, anyone can sue or be sued in respect of injury so caused, provided it is not too remote. Normally it is the actual wrongdoer who will be liable, but the law imposes a responsibility also on persons who are vicariously liable for the actions of others under their control, for example their employers.

There are three essentials for a claim in tort to be established:

1 There must be a duty of care owed to the plaintiff by the defendant. For a professional person this will usually be a duty to use reasonable care and skill to the standard of the ordinary skilled man or woman exercising and professing to have that special professional skill. The standard of care expected of a reasonably competent person is likely to be judged in the light of the technical knowledge and standards prevailing at the time, ie the 'state of the art'. This is why it is important that architects retain all technical information and manufacturers' trade literature relating to specific projects.
2 The duty of care must have been breached by carelessness, to an extent which in law amounts to negligence.
3 Damage must have resulted from that breach.

Often the plaintiff will have no contract with the defendant, and therefore of necessity any claim has to be founded in tort. However, even where there is a contract, the courts may nevertheless find that a duty in tort also exists. There can be advantages for a plaintiff in bringing a tort action because:

- the time limits before an action becomes statute barred due to the Limitation Act 1980, could be greater in tort than in contract. This could be particularly important in the case of design defects where time will start to run from the date that damage first occurred, and of course this could be much later than the date of the breach of contract;
- differences in the basis for calculating damages as between tort and contract could also be advantageous to a plaintiff, even though it is usually easier to establish breach of contract than to prove negligence in tort.

Against this it should be remembered that recovery of damages for pure economic loss, unrelated to physical damage or personal injury, seems much less likely to succeed in tort than in contract with the law as it is at present. As a result, it is generally considered better for actions to recover economic loss to be framed in contract. Third parties such as funders, lessees, subsequent purchasers etc, who were not involved with the original contract and who would otherwise have to rely mainly on tort, usually try to establish contractual relationships by seeking collateral agreements or warranties. These should never be entered into if the terms are more onerous than the original contracts, but even so the additional contractual relationships can only increase liability.

The limitation period applicable for an action in tort is six years after the damage was first sustained, regardless of whether or not it was discovered. This is often likely to be far more favourable for a plaintiff than the period for breach of contract, and even this longer period can be further increased by the provisions of the Latent Damage Act 1986. This amends the Limitation Act 1980 in certain respects concerning tort actions. It introduces a three-year discoverability period, but also imposes a fifteen-year absolute time bar except where there has been deliberate concealment.

B1.3 Legislation

Legislation imposes conditions on the practising architect's work, and is increasingly used to reformulate areas of law which have become unwieldy. It is also used to introduce new areas of law, some of which are the result of complying with European Directives.

Legislation is made in Parliament, and only Parliament can introduce, amend or repeal it. Its interpretation, however, is solely a matter for the courts. Acts which have application nationwide form the bulk of legislation passed in each parliamentary session. Nonetheless a considerable number of local Acts are in force, particularly concerning matters of building and the environment, which should not be overlooked.

When a Parliamentary Bill has reached its final reading, it receives the Royal Assent and becomes an Act with a Chapter number for that year, a long title with a date, and is headed by a short title. It may or may not come into force immediately even though it will be on the Statute Book. If there is nothing to the contrary in the Act, it comes into force on the morning of the day on which it receives Royal Assent. More commonly these days, a commencement date some time in the future is given, or it may be indicated that a Secretary of State has the power to designate 'an appointed day'. Sections of an Act may fall into any of these categories, and it may be necessary to establish whether all or only part of the Act is in force. All Acts not immediately enforceable may be brought into force by a Statutory Instrument, or more than one if different dates are needed for various sections. It is therefore not always easy to establish whether certain provisions in Acts are actually in force.

An Act remains in force until it is repealed by another Act. A part or sections of an Act may be repealed, leaving the remainder unchanged; there is often a Repeal section or schedule in an Act. An Act may be amended by subsequent legislation – the wording may be altered and the effect of the Statute may be altered. The law, once in force, must be observed; ignorance of it is no defence. It will also be no excuse that printed copies were not available, as happened in recent years when supplies were interrupted by industrial action.

As well as the Acts themselves, there is an enormous amount of delegated legislation which can come out of provisions contained in an Act enabling a Secretary of State to move rapidly on matters of detail. Much of this delegated legislation is likely to be of considerable interest to the architect in practice, and may be in the form of:

- *Orders in Council*, where rule-making powers are vested in the Privy Council (these are generally used in emergencies);

- *Statutory Instruments*, commonly used when a Secretary of State makes regulations by virtue of delegated powers;
- *Bye-laws*, usually enforced by local authorities or public bodies and made under powers granted by Parliament.

It should be remembered that delegated legislation has the full weight of law and can be implemented without much warning, although in practice there tends to be a reasonable period for consultation.

Circulars or guidance notes are often published to accompany pieces of legislation. They are written in plain English and are an invaluable aid to a better understanding of legislation, sometimes giving a clear indication of what Parliament intended. However, they are not part of the law, unlike Approved Documents or Approved Codes of Practice, which often have legal standing to the extent that they describe minimum acceptable standards.

European law is now becoming a major influence on English legislation. Both the Council of Ministers and the European Commission can make 'Regulations'. These are directly applicable in all Member States and are published in the *Official Journal*. In other cases they may issue 'Directives' or 'Decisions', which are usually also published in the *Official Journal*. Directives, usually the most relevant for architects, are binding in substance on Member States, but the UK Parliament must then implement them in whatever form it chooses. Decisions are binding in their entirety on those to whom they are directed, and are enforceable in national courts. Mere recommendations and opinions have no binding force.

B1.4 Increasing awareness

Architects need an awareness of the legislation that applies to particular situations and a working knowledge of the consequences of its application. In a High Court case in recent years, the judge commented that where the client pays for independent and skilled advice he is entitled to just that, and the architect should not simply have accepted without question the view or opinions of a planning officer of a local authority, operating a policy which was wrong in law. He said that architects are not expected to have an expert knowledge of the legislation, but they need to know what is required in terms of compliance, and what procedures need to be adopted.

Acts of Parliament likely to be most relevant in connection with the practice of architecture are shown in the table of statutes given as Fig B1.1. Note that only Acts are included, and not the many Statutory Instruments which flow as delegated legislation, and which usually carry the detail so often important for the practitioner. Local legislation is not included either. Although the legislation included in the table was correct at the time of writing, it is always liable to change, and readers should check its currency and effectiveness for themselves.

Relevant texts and sources of information

Architects should have acquired a basic understanding of those areas of law generally relevant to the practice of architecture in order to satisfy the requirements for registration. As a refresher to this knowledge, easy to read books such as *Learning the Law* by the late Professor Glanville Williams, or *The Legal Obligations of the Architect* by Andrea Burns might be found helpful.

For a more detailed knowledge of law relevant to specific areas or for situations which arise in practice, architects are advised as follows:

- Refer to texts (preferably those written by lawyers with architect readers in mind). *The RIBA List of Recommended Books* is published annually and includes selected titles on practice and legal matters, eg procurement, design liability, building contracts, contract administration, arbitration etc. A law dictionary such as *Osborn's Concise Law Dictionary* will also be useful.
- Subscribe to, or make arrangements to access, case law reports and other authoritative texts, eg *Building Law Reports*, *Construction Law Reports*, *Construction Law Digest*, *Construction Industry Law Letter* etc. These will often be available for reference at libraries in universities with architecture or law departments.
- Refer to authoritative and up to date annotated legislation such as will be found in *Halsbury's Statutes*, *Current Law Statutes*, or *Statutes in Force*. Such reference works will usually be available at university law libraries. Data bases such as *Lexis*, which holds all reported recent case law, may also be available, but a charge will normally be made for this kind of service.
- Use the RIBA Members Information Line for specific queries, or seek advice by telephone from the RIBA Specialist Advisors Panel through the members' subscription line.
- Keep up to date on developments in the law relevant to practice by reading the technical press and perhaps compiling a file of articles from, for example, the *RIBA Journal*, *Architects' Journal*, and the legal sections from *Building*. Attend CPD events and seminars which feature practice issues and often include legal topics.

Some architects may wish to develop their expertise further and perform associated roles such as:

- *Adjudicator* The RIBA is an appointing body for qualified persons to act under the adjudication provisions of Section 108 of the Housing Grants, Construction and Regeneration Act 1996.
- *Arbitrator* The RIBA President is an appointor in cases of disputes to be determined by an arbitrator.
- *Conciliator* The RIBA administers a Conciliation Scheme in collaboration with its Regional Directors, where disputes arise over architect–client agreements.
- *Expert* Where the architect acts as an expert to determine disputes (although not as an arbitrator), or acts as an expert witness, a quite different role.

Such persons might also wish to join likeminded architects in membership of one or more of the specialist professional groups. Among these are:

Architects Law Forum, a law society for architects involved with or interested in construction law, under the aegis of the RIBA. It holds regular meetings at Portland Place and facilitates the dissemination and sharing of knowledge. It seeks to promote the cause and appointment of architects in arbitration, alternative dispute resolution, as expert witnesses etc. Further information from the Hon Sec Architects Law Forum, c/o 66 Portland Place, London W1N 4AD.

Society of Construction Law, formed in 1983 to enable those interested in construction law to meet and discuss matters of common interest. It provides a forum for lawyers and non-lawyers alike, and meets on a regular basis, usually at King's College, London. Further information from Society of Construction Law, The Old Watch House, King's College, London WC2R 2LS.

Chartered Institute of Arbitrators, founded in 1915 and a multi-disciplinary organisation with worldwide membership. Its primary object is to promote and facilitate the determination of disputes by arbitration, but it is also active in promoting other means of dispute resolution. Publishes a quarterly journal, *Arbitration*, and organises a wide range of activities nationally, internationally, and locally through its branch network. Further information from The Secretary General, Chartered Institute of Arbitrators, International Arbitration Centre, 24 Angel Gate, London EC1V 2RS.

Architects with a sufficient grasp of legal considerations should be able to recognise possible hazards, legal or otherwise, and the likely consequences if the right kind of professional advice is not sought at the appropriate time. Architects should take care to avoid making unwarranted assumptions or sweeping generalisations when faced with reports of case law and interpretations of legislation. They should be able to recognise the nature of the legal problems entailed, and seek appropriate legal advice.

Many architects enjoy long and mutually beneficial association with solicitors; sound legal advice can save a great deal of money and worry in the long term. Information on suitable firms of solicitors currently in practice, together with particulars of their expertise, may be obtained from The Law Society, or by referring to a recent edition of *Waterlow's Solicitors and Barristers Directory*, or similar.

Fig B1.1 Relevant legislation

Business premises
Occupiers Liability Acts 1957–84
Offices Shops and Railway Premises
    Act 1963

Running the business
Business Names Act 1985
Civil Liability (Contribution) Act 1978
Companies Acts 1985–89
Copyright Designs and Patents Act 1988
Data Protection Act 1984
Employers Liability (Compulsory
    Insurance) Act 1969
Health and Safety at Work etc Act 1974
Insolvency Act 1986
Interpretation Act 1978
Limitation Act 1980
Limited Partnership Act 1907
Partnership Act 1890

Employing staff
Contracts of Employment Act 1972
Disability Discrimination Act 1995
Employment Acts 1980–89
Employment Protection Act 1975
Equal Pay Act 1970
Race Relations Act 1976
Sex Discrimination Acts 1975–86
Wages Act 1986

Professional services
Architects Act 1997
Arbitration Act 1996

Consumer Protection Act 1987
Housing Grants Construction and
    Regeneration Act 1996
Supply of Goods and Services Act 1982
Trade Descriptions Acts 1968–72
Unfair Contract Terms Act 1977

Projects
Ancient Monuments and Archaeological
    Areas Act 1979
Building Act 1984
Control of Pollution Act 1974
Defective Premises Act 1972
Environmental Protection Act 1990
Factories Act 1961
Fire Precautions Act 1971
Highways Act 1980
Historic Building and Ancient
    Monuments Act 1953
Housing Acts 1974–96
Latent Damage Act 1986
Law of Property Acts 1925–69
Licensing Acts 1964–88
Museums and Galleries Act 1992
Noise and Statutory Nuisance Act 1993
Party Wall etc Act 1996
Prescription Act 1832
Rights of Light Act 1959
Rights of Way Act 1990
Safety of Sports Grounds Act 1975
Sale and Supply of Goods Act 1994
Town and Country Planning Acts 1990–91
Wildlife and Countryside Act 1981

B1.5 Forms of practice

The title 'architect'

Anyone can set up in practice as an architect provided they do not attach to their business name the word 'architect'. The Architects Act restricts the use of the title 'architect'. Where a company is being registered whose title includes the word 'architect' or 'architectural', the application may be referred to the Architects Registration Board (ARB). The normal pattern is for a certificate of non-objection to be issued where the company's articles of association include a form of words indicating that the control of the architectural work will remain in the hands of a person or persons on the ARB Register of Architects so long as the title subsists.

There are no legal restrictions on the form of practice architects might decide to adopt for the operation of their businesses.

The sole practitioner

Many architects practise alone, attracted by the freedom of carrying on a business on their own account, in tune with their own talents, over which they have absolute control. However, sole practitioners can sometimes feel isolated from their fellow professionals and whilst they are entitled to all the profits from the business, they also have to manage it single-handed and face the risks alone. Sole practitioners are responsible for debts and any damages awarded against them for breach of contract or tort, and are liable to the full extent of their personal and business assets. They can be made bankrupt.

The partnership

The internal management of a partnership will generally be governed by the Partnership Act 1890, but this needs to be varied to meet the needs of a modern professional practice, and it is usual for a partnership to be established by a formal deed of partnership which set out the rights and responsibilities of the partners. These should be discussed and agreed before they are written into the deed, which should ultimately be drawn up by a solicitor. Compatibility of skills, personalities and objectives is of crucial importance in a partnership, and the executive responsibilities of each partner must be clearly identified. Matters such as the name of the practice, the apportioning of profits and losses, payment of interest on capital, and banking arrangements and authority should be agreed and recorded in the partnership deed. Other matters it should clarify are pension provision, retirement, and the admission of new partners. In some cases, the partnership agreement provides for a salary to be paid to one or more of the partners in addition to a share in the profits. Such partners are referred to as 'salaried partners'.

Each partner is liable jointly with the others for all debts and obligations incurred while a partner, and should he or she die, this liability falls upon the estate. The partnership is liable for all negligent acts committed by any one of its partners, even though the others might have taken no part in such negligent action. The same applies to people who were partners at the time, but who have subsequently retired from the practice. A partner's liability extends to all his or her business and personal assets. To dissolve a partnership it simply requires one partner to give notice of an intention to dissolve, but if there is a deed, formal dissolution will be necessary.

In a partnership the equity is owned by those who manage it; they share both the profits and the risks, and have the right to participate in the daily management of the business.

The limited liability company (Ltd)

The limited liability company has no practice principals; it is owned by the company and its 'directors' are employees of the company. Under English law, directors and other employees, as agents of the company they serve, generally enjoy immunity from personal liability for the company's debts and its obligations towards third parties. However, all employees of a company owe a duty of care to the company itself.

A company has a clearly identified management structure administered by a board of directors. The senior level of management might include equity and non-equity directors. Under this structure, young architects of calibre are not deterred from reaching the top of a firm by the prospect of having to buy themselves in, as they might have to with a partnership – a formidable prospect in the case of a large thriving practice. Non-architectural staff of calibre, such as finance, computer or office managers, are able to enhance their status and progress their careers as well-rewarded directors, particularly if share options are available.

The public limited liability company (Plc)

A company that intends to offer its shares for sale to the public must register as a public company, include the letters 'Plc' after its name, and have a subscribed share capital. It cannot obtain a certificate from the Registrar or Companies to allow it to start trading until the stipulated sum has been subscribed. The difference between the Ltd company and the Plc is the level of share capital and the fact that the Plc has to operate under stricter rules.

Cooperative and collaborative arrangements

The terms cooperative and collaborative are used to describe various forms of practice. There are a number of registered architects' cooperatives and these are in effect workers' cooperatives. Those who work in the enterprise both own and control it.

A cooperative may be owned collectively, in which case nobody has an individual shareholding beyond a nominal £1, and it is a common ownership cooperative. This is the type most frequently found in architecture, often for ideological reasons.

There is also a co-ownership cooperative in which dividend-earning shares are held by the members. In some schemes the shares remain at a fixed value, whilst in others they increase or decrease according to the value of the business. Control is dependent on votes (one per person) and is independent of shares. Where an established partnership is converting to a cooperative, this model might be more appropriate, as long-standing partners can hold personal shares commensurate with the value of the assets they have built up.

Both types of cooperative can be legally established either by registering as a cooperative with the Register of Friendly Societies under the Industrial and

Provident Societies Acts 1965 to 1987, or with the Registrar of Companies as a company limited by guarantee of £1 per member. Both kinds of organisation carry limited liability.

Various other formal and informal collaborative arrangements may be made for the sake of business or professional expediency.

Two or more firms may arrange to assist each other with varying degrees of commitment on individual projects, or a range of specialisations, or other market activities. This is likely to be short term co-operation on an informal basis. Other firms might wish to engage in a continuing association, either for mutual help or the sharing of facilities, but stopping short of carrying out projects jointly. On a more formal basis, firms may wish to join in partnership for a particular project, exercising a joint venture method of working. This would need to be a legally constituted arrangement with joint and several liability.

Firms of different disciplines may elect to collaborate by establishing a consortium arrangement which could offer the benefits of an integrated approach. Such an arrangement could simply be a continuing informal association, or one which carried out projects jointly. The identity of each firm in the consortium could still be retained for other concurrent projects handled separately.

Whenever formal collaborative arrangements are contemplated, appropriate legal advice should be sought, and professional indemnity insurance arranged to cover the particular situation.

The opportunities for practice in the European Union are likely to increase as British architects explore the potential of the wider market. The forging of links between British and overseas practices provides informal means of promoting joint architectural opportunities. More formal associations and collaborative working can be expected to develop as business relationships are actively encouraged by Chambers of Commerce in the respective countries. In some cases British-based firms have opened branches or subsidiaries abroad, whilst others have elected to collaborate with local practices in carrying out projects. Legal systems and insurance obligations in particular differ throughout Europe, and any arrangements for collaborative working should be subject to appropriate legal advice.

B1.6 Considering incorporation

Numerous architectural practices sought incorporation in the 1980s and early 1990s, and while a notable few have prospered, many have not. With the benefit of hindsight, general reasons for such failures would appear to be over-optimism about economic prospects for the construction industry, misplaced confidence that the public would readily invest in architectural firms, and a mistaken belief that trading as a company would provide total protection of personal assets for proprietors/directors. However, a more obvious cause of failure in many instances was that firms did not seek the best available legal and financial advice.

A partnership considering incorporation may at first glance identify many attractive operational advantages:

- It is easier for a company to raise outside finance than it is for a partnership, as security can more readily be created over the assets of a company.
- The taxation position is relatively simple and overall taxation is likely to be lower than for a partnership.

- All employees, including directors, are subject to PAYE, avoiding sudden large tax demands later.
- Overall taxation is likely to be lower than for a partnership.
- All salaries, including directors', are deductible before calculation of profit for corporation tax purposes.
- An interest in a company may be given more readily than in a partnership, by making architects and non-architects with useful expertise directors or shareholders.
- It is easier to remove an unsatisfactory director than an unsatisfactory partner.

Management

Another apparent advantage of incorporation is that the separation of ownership from the management should lead to improvements in operational efficiency and cost-effectiveness. However, in the company situation there is always a danger that ownership may pass outside the original architectural proprietor, whose professional control and influence may thereby be diminished.

Companies have to comply with the formalities laid down by the Companies Act, which relate to all aspects of the Company's formation and operation. Management is therefore less flexible than with a partnership and there is a considerable additional administrative and financial burden. Companies whose turnover exceeds a certain limit are required to have their audited accounts published, whereas a partnership is able to keep its financial affairs confidential. Companies also have a duty to provide their shareholders with appropriate information, and this can be a significant extra cost.

Liability

The personal assets of a director of a company are not as safe as many think them to be, especially if the directors conduct their business without regard to the detailed legislation governing the management of companies. Trading through an incorporated business does, in theory, limit the liability of shareholders to the extent of the funds that they contribute as share capital, but this advantage tends to be eroded because shareholders and directors are often required to give personal guarantees to the company's bankers. However, there remains some protection for shareholders and directors where trade creditors are concerned.

Pension provision

The pension benefits that can be provided for directors and employees of a limited company tend to be more beneficial than those that can be provided via retirement annuity and personal pension schemes entered into by an individual.

The benefits that a company pension scheme can provide are, in the main, flexible and generous, depending on the type of scheme adopted. The company's contributions into the pension scheme are generally deductible in calculating the company's taxable profits. This should be compared with the fairly rigid limits that apply to the tax relief available on contributions into retirement annuity and personal pension schemes.

Professional indemnity insurance

In terms of exposure to indemnity claims, a change from partnership to limited company does not materially change the risk from the insurer's point of view. However, the insured will now be the company, a separate legal identity from its directors. The policy must therefore be extended to indemnify the individual directors and employees as well as the company. It is vital that any change, whether to a new partnership or to a company, does not leave the practice unprotected vis-à-vis its continuing liability for claims. It may be best to incorporate this cover in the new policy, but legal advice should be taken.

Tax and National Insurance

The implications of incorporation for tax and National Insurance can be significant because, at the time of writing, there are different rules for employees/directors of a company and self-employed persons/partners. However, a potential tax advantage for companies is the ability to defer tax liabilities by retaining profits within the company, and not paying them out as remuneration or dividends.

Passing on the business

The proprietors of the business should always consider their future intentions as regards disposing of or passing on a family business. Trading through a limited company has the advantage that shares in the company can be gifted to other members of the family as potentially exempt transfers for inheritance tax purposes. Therefore such gifts can be made without there necessarily being any effect on the running of the business.

A fundamental disadvantage of trading via the medium of a company is the potential double tax charge that can arise on winding up the firm. The company pays corporation tax on retained profits and also on any gains that it makes, and individual shareholders will also pay capital gains tax on the disposal of their shares. This only becomes a problem where assets or the business of the company are sold. If the business is expected to run for many years and pass to future generations, this point may not be of concern to the proprietors.

Overview

The practicalities of incorporating a business do tend to be underestimated, and it is important to consider all taxes and their impact on the parties involved. It should also be borne in mind that it is difficult to disincorporate a business once it has been incorporated, so it is not a decision to be taken lightly.

Clients should be advised of any change in the composition or form of a practice, and the firm's advisers should be asked about the legal implications and how clients may best be notified.

The strength of a business lies in the quality of its human, financial and physical resources and the way in which they are managed. It is important that the form of practice adopted suits the workload and staff complement. This should be reviewed from time to time, as shifts in the practice's philosophy, objectives and circumstances suggest the need for change. The matter should be given careful consideration, and sound legal and financial advice obtained.

At any point in its life, a practice should be operating in the context of a described strategy: it should know where it is going and how it is going to get there. It is important to set goals and work to them, both as a means of quantifying achievement, and as an expression of purposeful leadership, which unites the efforts of all those who work for the practice, and focuses them on worthwhile objectives.

Every new practice should formulate a business strategy. Its existence allows the principals to evaluate their decision-making against a described position, and the plan itself will constitute the basis of the practice's Business Plan when it needs to seek funds or financial backing. It should cover a period of between three and five years – the fluctuating nature of architectural work makes it difficult to make more distant assumptions and predictions. Short term targets will be set in the firm's annual budget. Formulating the strategy will take much time and thought, and an honest and objective attitude will be needed.

An existing practice will need, first, to evaluate the current position of the business; second, to decide where the principals would like the business to be in, say, five years' time; and third, to devise an operational plan for moving the business from its current position towards achieving its defined objectives. An example schedule of goals is given as Fig B2.1.

Fig B2.1. Example schedule of goals and targets

Goals	Targets
1 To achieve steady and significant growth in the existing design practice.	1 Set a target % growth rate over the next five years.
2 To expand the geographic base of the practice by opening new offices.	2 Establish a London office and an EU link-up by a given date.
3 To set up a separate section or wholly owned subsidiaries to exploit related fields, eg: • energy surveys and audits; • interior design and total furnishing contracts; • facilities management.	3 At least two sections or subsidiaries set up and providing positive contributions within the next five years.
4 To establish improved management throughout the practice.	4 Evaluate the current management structure and the effectiveness of staff training and career development.
5 To achieve a high reputation for design and quality of service.	5 Draw up an appropriate CPD programme immediately. Institute a quality management system and auditing procedures.
6 To achieve financial security for the practice as a whole.	6 Reassess the financial gearing of the firm. Aim to reduce debt capital by a specified amount.

The practice's current position could be assessed under the following headings:

- a review of its development and achievements;
- an evaluation of its position in the market-place;
- an assessment of its design philosophy and standards;
- a review of its staffing levels and organisation;
- an analysis of its financial performance over the last three years;
- a summary of its Strengths and Weaknesses, what its Opportunities are, and where it faces Threats (SWOT).

SWOT analysis

Self-analysis can make a valuable contribution to the practice's assessment of where it is and where it wants to go. Various techniques have been developed and the SWOT method is well-tried.

A SWOT analysis will enable managers at all levels to describe their current positions and think about the way the practice should be going in the future. They are invited to schedule their perception of the strengths and weaknesses of the organisation (ie internal issues) and what they see as its opportunities and threats (ie external influences). The results are reviewed and analysed by various working groups to identify priorities; the findings are then summarised and presented. An example SWOT exercise is included as Fig B2.2. An alternative would be to hold structured discussions or a 'brainstorming' at senior management level, which could work to an agenda of set questions on the same lines as the SWOT method.

Evaluating the implications

Once objectives have been defined, their implications will need to be evaluated, described and quantified. For example, if a principal objective is to increase turnover by a stated percentage, the implications might include:

- an increase in marketing effort;
- the prediction of future levels of income, expenditure and profit to support the growth targeted;
- an increase in staff resources by recruitment or retraining;
- increased logistical support, such as new information technology;
- the cost implications overall.

Most of these issues will require investigation in their own right and could be made the responsibility of various members of senior management.

The business strategy must be flexible enough to be able to respond to market forces and not to collapse if circumstances change. If its predictions fail to materialise it may have to be revised, and it is important to consider how this might affect the practice's staff, workload and finances.

Staff consultation

Principals are often reluctant to discuss strategic and financial matters with staff, but when anything as fundamental as the rationale and direction of the practice is under review, it is in the interests of the practice as a whole to allow as wide a

Fig B2.2 Example of a SWOT exercise

1 EVALUATION

Strengths
- Confident leadership
- Staff with good mix of skills
- Good commercial awareness
- Strong client base
- High quality professional service
- Plenty of repeat work

Weaknesses
- Senior management personality-dominated, youngest is over fifty
- Over-confidence about job-getting; some clients are known to be high risk
- Management decisions often intuitive; rule of thumb job costing
- Long term viability of firm may be threatened when top management retires
- Staff loyalty taken for granted, some acknowledged salary anomalies
- Old-fashioned administrative set-up

Opportunities
- Regional work opportunities materialising; could open a branch office
- Upturn in conservation work; could import specialist staff to exploit situation
- Demonstrable track record in green buildings; could tap into current public awareness
- Invitation to write one of a series of practice articles in technical press; could get some useful publicity

Threats
- Two new design practices recently opened in head office area
- Economic climate uncertain
- General election within the next 24 months may reverse funding policies
- Certain key staff have been approached by competitors
- Two former and one existing client have gone out of business

2 ASSESSMENT

What kind of picture emerges so far?

Here is an apparently thriving practice, well liked in the local business community, with strong leadership, competent staff and a reputation for providing a good professional service. Admits it has some weaknesses and fully intends to get round to dealing with them – one day. Doubtful about moving further into uncertain territory such as new construction or information technology. Is well aware that it might be advantageous commercially to seek QA certification, but feels that the practice is not suited to a procedures-dominated style of operation and dislikes the necessary disturbance that such changes will bring. Considers marketing to be unnecessary and slightly undignified.

Its attitudes might be expressed like this:
- 'You have to admit we're doing pretty well.'
- 'The trouble with change is it brings hassle and problems with staff – and clients might not like new procedures.'
- 'Everyone has problems: of course we'll deal with them – if they become serious.'
- 'Competitors? Good luck to them: our clients will stay loyal.'
- 'It's too soon to upgrade our computer system – and all that retraining.'
- 'Marketing is a bit pushy for a practice like ours. We don't really need it.'
- 'We're thinking about quality management, but clients may think our fees will go up. And to go the whole hog and seek certification takes years and years ...'

It may be that as long as the status quo continues, all will be well. Unfortunately the status quo is vulnerable to a great many influences that are outside a practice's control, and as soon as there is some significant change the whole management rationale may be overturned. One alternative is to leave well alone and hope for the best; the other is to recognise the potential dangers and take immediate and positive action.

3 ACTION

- Revise the management structure so that younger staff are given more responsibility and influence
- Review technical, financial and administrative procedures. Then consider, with experts if necessary, whether the practice would benefit from instituting a quality management system and/or installing an up to date computer system
- Fend off competition by instituting a marketing initiative directed at new and existing clients
- Deal promptly with any salary anomalies; this is the sort of aggravation that tempts staff to move on – particularly if there is competition close at hand
- Take steps to consolidate the financial basis of the firm: reassess gearing, consider whether a different form of practice could bring benefits and greater security

consultation as possible, since the operational matters arising are of immediate interest and importance to staff. They will be more prepared to identify with new thinking or a change in pace or direction if they have been involved in the decision-making leading up to it.

B2.2 Business advisers

The support of good advisers is essential for successful business management: the accountant and the solicitor are the two key long term professional consultants that all practices need sooner or later. It is wise to look for firms who have other architect clients and will know the kind of special needs that architectural work generates. A fellow practitioner may be able to recommend someone suitable, but otherwise the practice must either make its own enquiries or approach the relevant professional institute. It is important to consider a firm's reputation and prosperity, whether the range of services offered will meet its current and future needs, and whether its offices are conveniently placed. It is also wise to consider whether the attitude and philosophy of the firm is in tune with that of the practice – whether, that is, the professional chemistry is right.

Other advice that will be needed on setting up a practice will be from the bank (often to arrange a start-up loan), and from insurance brokers to arrange professional indemnity and, if appropriate, premises insurance.

Accountants

An accountant is a professional keeper and inspector of accounts. J Smith ACA would be a chartered accountant, ie an associate member of the Institute of Chartered Accountants in England and Wales. Accountancy firms vary in size from the small office that offers mainly auditing and tax advice, to the large prestigious firm with an international network of offices offering a wide range of financial and management services.

The standard services that an architectural practice might engage an accountant to provide are:

- preparation of the firm's annual audit;
- advice on tax matters;
- advice on book-keeping procedures;
- advice about the practice's financial state of affairs.

Many accountancy firms also provide management consultancy services, and some offer services connected with corporate recovery and insolvency, and corporate finance and investigations.

Under the Companies Act every company above a certain size is required to submit audited accounts to Companies House where they can be inspected by interested parties. Accounts also have to be submitted to the Inland Revenue. The auditors' duty is to review the accounts and the systems from which they are derived and give a professional opinion as to whether they give 'a true and fair view' of the company's results.

The question of fees should be clarified at the outset of the consultancy and it is important, particularly when any extensive piece of work is commissioned, to set a budget for it and to stipulate that this is not to be exceeded without express permission. It is desirable to build up a good working relationship with the accountant; not only can he or she save the practice money in the short term, but may be able to warn it of troubles ahead.

Legal advisers

Legal services are provided by solicitors and barristers. Lawyers qualified in other jurisdictions are available if such special advice is needed, and lawyers employed by banks and accountants will often offer an advisory service to third parties. Since 1990 it has been possible for architects to instruct barristers directly without having to use a solicitor as intermediary.

The legal services that an architectural practice might require are various. Its first needs might relate to the form of practice to be adopted and the conveyancing of practice premises, followed by a continuing general consultancy as the practice finds its feet. It may need specialist legal advice about building contract conditions and claims, professional indemnity, construction litigation, planning legislation, copyright of drawings and so on.

Fees are likely to be on a retainer basis to cover routine and day-to-day advice, and time-charged for major consultancies. As with architects' work, there are various hourly rates, and the procedures for charging expenses and disbursements and for billing will need to be agreed. Solicitors have to be meticulous in their work, and it may come as a surprise to the architect client to be charged for amounts as small as the price of a first-class postage stamp. There are lessons to be learned from the way the legal profession renders its accounts.

Clearing banks

It is in the interests of banks to support local business initiatives, and they are usually ready to lend money if they consider that a firm's approach is businesslike and its prospects are good. Banks make money from the interest they charge on loans and are usually prepared to allow a running overdraft provided they are confident that the architect will be in a position to pay the interest. Similarly they will be pleased to see sensible intentions for business expansion – which may mean an increased need for borrowing.

Although banking has become an intensively competitive business, banks are aware that the best way to keep their customers is to give them support and advice, and this can be invaluable, particularly to a new architectural practice.

A wide range of banking services is available, some of which may help a practice to streamline its financial administration. For example, payment of creditors' accounts can be made through BACS (Bank Automated Clearing Service) as an alternative to making payments by cheque, although this is probably only worthwhile where more than 100 or so cheques a month are prepared. Arrangements can also be made whereby surplus funds in current accounts are automatically transferred into an interest-earning account as soon as they reach an agreed level. New electronic services are coming on stream all the time, and it is always worth seeking the bank's advice about ways of making the most of the practice's finances.

Insurance brokers

A broker is an intermediary between two parties – in the case of insurance, between an insurer and the person buying the insurance. Until the 1977 Insurance Brokers (Registration) Act, anyone could call themselves an insurance broker; now only registered brokers can do this, although anyone can operate as a broker under any other name or description.

The insurance broker's remuneration is the commission he or she receives from the insurer. It is important to remember that insurance brokers are therefore not obliged to place the interests of the client first: they are commission-driven, and the service they offer should not be compared with that provided by, say, the accounting or legal profession. Insurance claims are evaluated and met (or not, as the case may be) by the insurer, not the insurance broker.

Insurance brokers are well placed to give advice about the best deals going among the insurance companies, their promptness or otherwise in meeting claims, and which companies specialise in the particular insurance cover required. Firms of insurance brokers tend to specialise in certain types of insurance cover, and as soon as the first job comes in an architect will need to look for one who specialises in professional indemnity insurance. Risk management, including trade credit risks, is another specialism of interest, and so is claims handling.

B2.3 Managing practice finances

Accountants provide the essential financial accounting services that every business requires, but continuing financial information will also be needed to allow the firm's management to forecast, plan and make decisions. The provision of such information is the function of management accounting, and a primary decision to be made is who in the practice is to be responsible for producing it.

Large practices may have an in-house management accountant at the head of an accounts department. J Smith ACMA would be an Associate Chartered Management Accountant. In a medium size practice, one of the partners may be responsible for managing finance with the help of an administrative assistant with book-keeping expertise and appropriate computer software. The senior (or sole) partner of a small practice will manage its finances, with or without human or electronic help in-house.

The development of standard accounting software has enabled businesses of all shapes and sizes to handle day to day book-keeping efficiently and to analyse and extrapolate financial information for the purposes of management and decision-making. However, it is important that architects recognise their limitations in this area and ensure that the practice's book-keeping system and accounting procedures are soundly based and appropriate, and are approved by the practice's accountant. (See also B3 below.)

The capital requirement

Capital is the money invested in the firm by the owners themselves (equity capital), plus any long terms financing loans (debt capital).

In a partnership, each partner has a fixed capital account and a current capital account, and these accounts represent his or her share of the capital invested in the firm. The fixed capital account shows the amount of capital subscribed by each partner on entry to the partnership, and any additional capital contributions or withdrawals are recorded in it. The current capital account exists to record adjustments in respect of profit shares, partners' salaries, interest on subscribed capital and private drawings.

The amounts in the capital accounts can only be increased with the agreement of all the partners. Profits made by the firm are distributed into the partners' current accounts or are withdrawn as partners' drawings. If a partner wishes to realise his or her capital investment it will mean withdrawing cash from the partnership, which may be damaging.

A company's debt capital may include long term loans, and bonds and debentures at a fixed rate of interest. In the case of a partnership, it usually takes the form of a long term loan from the bank. Debt capital has to be repaid and attracts interest, whereas equity only has to be repaid if the firm ceases to exist – the return on investment is participation in the firm's profits through dividend receipts.

Gearing

A primary decision to be made is what the gearing ratio is to be, which is an expression of the relationship between long term debt and equity capital. If Business X has a gearing ratio of 3 to 1 it means that for every £1 of equity capital invested, there exists £3 of long term debt (such as a bank loan). In the eyes of an investor, the higher the ratio, the riskier the investment in the business.

In times of recession, businesses with high gearing, ie a large proportion of long term debt, are far more prone to failure. The reason is that the interest payments, which are normally paid out of the cash receipts generated from trading, remain fixed regardless of the prevailing economic climate. Therefore if cash receipts are failing – as they are likely to do during a recession – a business with a large amount of debt may find that it is not generating enough cash to meet the interest bill. However, the reverse can be true when substantial trading growth is experienced.

A company with a high proportion of equity capital can always defer or reduce the payment of its annual dividend. This would certainly not be good news for shareholders, but if times are hard it should be possible to convince them of the need for such temporary restraint.

How much capital?

Deciding how much capital is needed is never easy. For an architect considering setting up in practice for the first time and operating out of the spare room at home it might seem surprisingly little, but as soon as he or she considers taking on staff the picture changes. Staff need working space and equipment, which inevitably means finding office premises and, if these are to be acquired and fitted out, for most young practitioners it means borrowing money. But how much?

The primary operational consideration in business is cash flow (liquidity), and cash flow needs managing. The problem is timing. An architectural practice's staff are its main cost (about half of total practice costs), and staff have to be paid every month come what may. By contrast, fee income cannot be relied upon to come in regularly even when a practice institutes stringent procedures for getting the money in, and in any case there is an unavoidable time lag between invoicing and payment. That time lag has to be financed.

The same considerations apply to an established practice that has decided to aim for an increase in turnover. More staff will be needed to cope with the additional work and will have to be equipped and paid. The practice will still have to find the extra finance to cover the period before the additional fee income materialises.

Before approaching any potential lenders it is important to seek financial advice and prepare a detailed financial plan so as to be prepared for the questions that will be asked about the practice's business objectives and its financial state of affairs. Lenders will want to know the likely costs of additional technical staff required to meet the workload envisaged and the increased overheads to support them. They will want to know the amount of partners' drawings, as opposed to the projected amount of profit, so that they can estimate how much can be ploughed back as working capital. However accurate the estimates are, it may be a long time before there is a sufficient cash flow to meet the anticipated monthly expenditure, and this must be reflected in the size of the loan sought and the terms for its repayment. It is essential to obtain sound financial advice.

B2.4 Raising money

Architects usually need to raise money to set up in practice. When established, they may need additional funds to allow expansion into larger premises or to refurbish existing, or to acquire some costly fixed asset such as a computer system. The usual route taken is to the bank to negotiate a loan or overdraft, but there are other ways of raising money. For example:

- by seeking venture capital from bankers, institutions or individuals;
- by using the office premises and assets to provide capital by sale and leaseback;
- by approaching an insurance company for a loan linked to a life assurance policy or pension;
- by converting a partnership into a limited company and raising capital by selling shares in the new company.

A primary reason for considering conversion to a limited company is that investors are less keen to lend money to a partnership where the only security is the personal assets of the partners, whereas in the case of a company, a loan is normally secured against a charge on all its assets. However, it is becoming more common for directors to be asked to give personal guarantees, thus largely negating this protected position.

Venture capital funding is the investment of long term risk equity to generate capital gain instead of interest or dividends. Venture funds are captive, ie linked to a bank or institution, or independent. The clearing banks all provide venture capital through their own fund vehicles, and so do merchant banks and various investment institutions. Merchant banks might seek to acquire an equity interest in the firm, but clearing banks are unlikely to be interested in acquiring equity stakes or providing unsecured loans.

There may also be government schemes and enterprise initiatives which might provide limited funding, or grants and development loans available locally and this should be investigated.

Any approach to a potential source of funds will need to be supported by adequate financial and general information about the practice and its objectives. This should be presented as the practice's Business Plan.

A Business Plan

In formulating a Business Plan it is important to consider who its readers will be, what form it should take, what it should say, and how it should be presented. These are the essential aspects of any form of business communication.

The Plan should be well presented and easy to read. Its purpose is to persuade an external source to risk lending a sum of money and to reassure that source that the practice's finances and prospects are healthy enough to be able to sustain and service the loan. The interest rate charged on the loan will reflect the lenders' view of the state of the market and their estimate of the risk involved. There will also probably be a charge on property or other assets as security. Repayment of the loan and the interest usually starts at once, on a monthly or quarterly basis.

The first thing financiers look for is evidence of good management. They seldom know much about architects and their work but they will not hesitate to make judgements about them as business people, the quality of the information they present and the attitude they demonstrate towards business matters. This they expect to be serious, well-informed and clear-sighted; any temptation to exaggerate the practice's prospects or abilities should be firmly resisted. They will also be impressed by the reputation and quality of the practice's business advisers, whose help will have been sought in preparing the Plan.

There are no rigid rules about the way to formulate a Business Plan, as this will depend upon the size of the practice and its reasons for seeking funds. The basic requirement is a summary statement which describes the practice and its objectives, how much it needs to borrow and when, and how it proposes to service/repay the loan. This summary will need to be supported by financial reports and statements and descriptive material about the practice's workload and personnel.

A suggested outline of contents is set out as Fig B2.3. As a general rule, the written information should be brief and the financial information presented in a form the potential lender will instantly recognise, typically a projected Profit and Loss Account, Balance Sheet, a cash flow forecast and, if appropriate, the firm's audited accounts.

Fig B2.3 Business Plan: outline of contents

1 **The practice**
A description of the firm, its personnel and premises
Its management structure
Its business advisers

2 **The service provided**
The type of work undertaken
The type of clients targeted

3 **The practice's position in the marketplace**
An evaluation of its present position
Its anticipated position

4 **The practice's business philosophy**
Its objectives
Its views about competition, quality, profitability

5 **Marketing effort**
Initiatives, controls, feedback, results

6 **Financial performance**
Past and current state of affairs
A résumé of work in progress

7 **Business management and controls**
How the firm manages its finances
How it manages liquidity
How it gets the money in

8 **The financing required**
The amount needed and its timing
How it will be used
How the loan will be serviced and repaid

Supporting material such as practice brochures, CVs of senior staff, financial statements, audited accounts, details of work in hand; project-related presentational material, videos.

The Business Plan for a large practice might adopt a report format with a contents list and the body of the report divided into sections; a small practice might confine itself to a summary statement and two or three key financial statements. All Business Plans will need to be supported by appropriate documents and material about the practice and its work; these can either be bound in as appendices or presented separately.

Before preparing the Plan for presentation it is essential to check for arithmetical errors and discrepancies and make sure that the written sections are well expressed and have been checked for spelling and typographical errors. Bankers and funds managers will have little confidence in borrowers who are incompetent communicators and whose numerical presentations are sloppy and inaccurate.

Attractive presentation is important. Depending on its length, the Plan can be presented as a spiral-bound report or loose sheets in a folder. Only a limited number of copies of the Plan should be prepared, and each copy should be numbered.

B2.5 Tax management

The tax situation changes from year to year, and needs to be kept under constant review. The taxation service provided by an accountant consists of tax compliance work and tax consultancy work. Tax compliance work is the service of preparing tax returns – typically the annual corporation tax return of a company, and the annual income tax returns of individuals. Tax consultancy work is the provision of advice on tax planning and management and is a highly competitive field. The accountant will aim to minimise a practice's tax liability making sure that any relief available is taken up, and giving advice about the least onerous way of meeting payments.

It is essential to have enough cash available to meet tax payments when they fall due. The various tax collectors have extensive powers of enforcing payment, and punitive interest is usually charged on unpaid tax.

The main taxes affecting architectural practice are:

- Income Tax (Schedule D, Classes I and II). Due in two half-yearly instalments.
- Schedule E (PAYE). Employers are responsible for deducting tax and NI contributions from wages and salaries.
- Corporation Tax (payable by limited and unlimited companies on their profits).
- Value Added Tax (payable on goods and services sold). VAT returns are usually made quarterly.

There may also be implications for Inheritance Tax and Capital Gains Tax in the case of some practices. It is also important to investigate taxes collected by the local authority, in particular those connected with rating business premises.

For a partnership, Income Tax is complex to calculate and administer and the advice of an accountant is essential. One of the advantages of conversion to trade as a company is that the income tax burden at least is simplified, as all employees, including directors, are subject to PAYE. From 1998, individual taxation will be based on self-assessment, which means it will be even more important to be meticulous about keeping records of all transactions.

Pensions for partners and directors

Whatever kind of pension provision is being contemplated, two things are essential: first, to obtain expert advice on the tax implications and, second, to set up pension arrangements as early in one's career as possible so as to build up an adequate sum for retirement. Actuaries are experts in pension matters, and although their advice is expensive, it is independent (ie not tied to an insurance company), and is likely to be a worthwhile investment.

Pension provision should be kept regularly under review (at least yearly).

B2.6 Making a profit

Profitability is not simply a matter of 'doing well' in the long term or achieving an increase in turnover; it should be seen as a quantifiable target for the performance of the business overall, as a target for each job in its own right and for each fee-earning person employed by the practice.

In times of high inflation, a practice that is breaking even on paper is, in real terms, operating at a loss; it follows that setting a level of overall profitability that relates realistically to the economic climate can be a matter of survival. In more stable market conditions, profitability is something that a practice might feel able to take a view about, in line with its character and philosophy.

The question of profit arises whenever a job opportunity materialises. On some jobs, costs can be reliably quantified and a profit margin set with confidence; others are less easy to evaluate. Sometimes it might be worth doing Job X and keeping the profit margin low because there is a good prospect of more work coming in from the client. It is questionable whether it is ever worthwhile taking on a job where it seems that the best outcome will be to break even – and in a period of high inflation, even more doubtful.

Profits can be eaten away by sloppy commissioning procedures. The income expected from each project should be established in the terms of the commission agreed with the client and described in a properly formulated written agreement. If the client subsequently asks for additional services, the client must pay for them: the commission must not be allowed to 'creep' into something more than what was defined in the agreement. Profits are also dissipated by overestimating the time needed to complete a job, and by allocating too much, or inappropriate, staff effort to it.

When assigning staff to projects a balance often has to be struck between skills, availability, and costs. On some jobs, the first question might be who is the best project architect for this particular job; on another, who can the practice afford to put on it; or simply who is available at the moment? If the answer is no one, then the question is whether someone should be got in on contract.

Setting realistic profit margins depends upon a precise knowledge of costs – the cost of running the practice overall; the cost of running each job, and the chargeable and actual cost of each of the people employed by the practice (see B3.5). Previous experience of a particular type of job will help to indicate what level of profit can be targeted, but even where the situation is unknown a figure should still be set, and job costs meticulously recorded.

Some jobs will be found to be less profitable than others and the reasons for this should be analysed. In some cases it may be the type of work involved, in others it may be the quality of the project team deployed – and there may be other reasons. It is important to read the signs and learn the lessons during a project as well as after its completion; if an unprofitable situation is revealed whilst a job is in progress it may be possible to take corrective action.

The varied and fluctuating nature of commissions does not permit architects to set a once-for-all pattern of costing that will assure profitability. Even if the arithmetic is sound, there is always the variability of human factors; key staff may leave or fall ill; there may be a disagreement on policy between partners, or a misunderstanding may arise with the client. Watchful and responsible management, supported and implemented by sound technical and financial procedures, will always be needed.

B2.7 Marketing

The Institute of Marketing has defined marketing as 'the management process responsible for identifying, anticipating and satisfying customer requirements profitably'. It is the process of exploring the market place and matching or developing skills and services to meet its demands.

Marketing opportunities

The market environment for the practice of architecture was analysed in the 1988 report by the then RIBA Market Research Unit. One of its most important findings was that many services that could have been performed by architects were being performed by other professionals (see Fig B2.4).

At the same time it identified areas of opportunity for architects, advising them to equip themselves with new skills and expertise, so that they would be in a position to:

- vigorously market their main and best-recognised strength – design quality;
- offer a complete package of services from inception through to maintenance of the completed building;
- be involved right from the start of a project: finding a site, assisting the client with early cost planning, and helping to develop the brief;
- offer operational building services such as advice on energy efficiency, environmental concerns, facilities management, running costs, life cycle planning;
- be involved with the operation and use of the completed building, advising the client on maintenance and accommodation needs.

Since then, other work opportunities have become available for architects as new legislation has been put in place. Following the introduction of the Health and Safety CDM Regulations 1994, architects can now act as Planning Supervisors under a separate appointment. The Party Wall etc Act 1996 presents opportunities for architects to provide special party wall services for clients whose projects are affected including, as appropriate, acting as party wall surveyors.

Practices need to keep aware of emerging market opportunities, and be prepared to acquire new expertise either by importing staff with the necessary skills, or by taking steps to train existing staff in-house, or enabling them to undertake the appropriate learning themselves.

Fig B2.4

Potential market for architectural services
as indicated by the RIBA MRU Report 1988

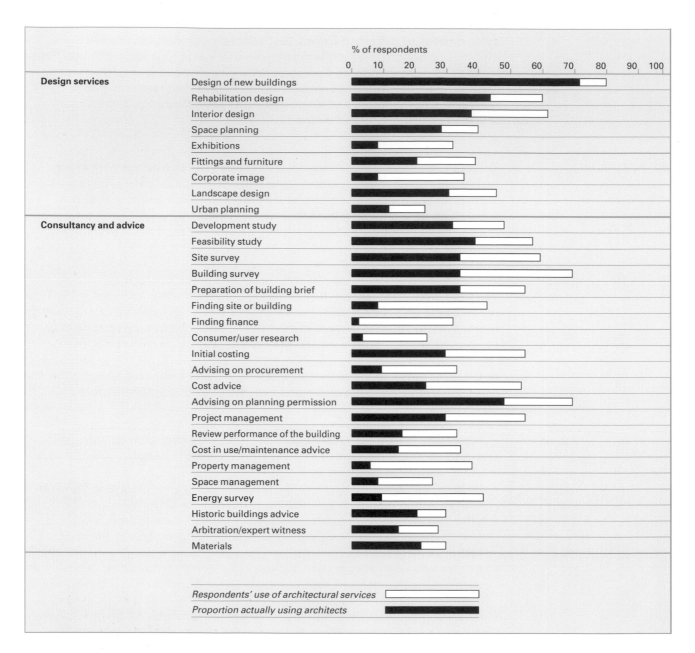

Approaching clients

The professional codes and standards are now relatively relaxed over what used to be referred to as the 'advertising' of professional services.

By the RIBA Code of Professional Conduct, members undertake:

- not to attempt to oust another architect;
- not to offer discounts, commissions, gifts or other inducements in order to secure an introduction;
- not to quote a fee without receiving an invitation;
- not to revise a fee quotation in order to undercut another architect.

The only direct reference to advertising is in an undertaking by the member not to allow his name to be used in advertisements for services or products associated with the construction industry. Presumably this allows architects to feature in advertisements for other products, and perhaps this wider exposure might serve to attract potential clients.

By the ARB Code of Professional Conduct and Practice, the Standard requires all advertising of professional services to be conducted in a truthful and responsible manner. It also requires that advertising conforms to the codes and standards of the industry (eg British Code of Advertising Practice, ITC and Radio Code of Advertising Standards and Practice) as relevant. Before any approaches to clients are made, RIBA members should take steps to establish that they have the necessary expertise, competence and resources, and that there are unlikely to be conflicts of interest.

There is of course no simple answer to the question of how best to attract work. However, there are many well tried approaches to clients, both direct and indirect, which might usefully be considered. Amongst these are:

By applying for entry to the RIBA Register of Practices

This is the database from which the RIBA Directory of Practices is compiled, and on which the Clients Advisory Service operates. To be listed, practices have to provide the following:

- evidence of adequate professional indemnity insurance;
- evidence of adequate practice management procedures;
- evidence of compliance with CPD and Code obligations;
- information about the practice, submitted to a prescribed format;
- an annual registration fee.

The RIBA Directory of Practices, published annually, is sent to some 5,000 clients or potential client bodies.

By paying for entries in the Yellow Pages (or equivalent) telephone directories, trade directories etc

Inclusion in the RIBA Corporate Boxed advertisement in Yellow Pages is normally handled on a regional basis and restricted to practices which are listed in the RIBA Register of Practices. Any entry in trade directories is likely to prove of limited direct benefit, but it might at least draw attention to the name of the practice. Architects should take a cautious view of any unsolicited mailshots inviting entries (usually for a considerable sum of money). In the UK, the Unsolicited Goods and Services Act 1971 controls such practices, but operators elsewhere in the EU are generally not so constrained.

By approaches channelled through the Clients Advisory Service, either from RIBA headquarters or regional offices

CAS helps clients to find an architect by providing a shortlist of practices suitable for the type, size and location of the project under consideration.

By approaches for inclusion on a register of approved consultants such as those held by the DETR, local government or other public bodies

Such lists are usually reviewed and updated annually. Inclusion in them is often a first stage to an invitation to bid for a professional engagement, an approach popularised by the US Brooks Method of selecting consultants.

By responding to press notices inviting interest in being considered for a specific commission

In such situations it is essential to obtain sufficient information about the proposed project in order to estimate the resources necessary, establish the client's requirements, and discover the extent of the competition.

By making direct approaches to prospective clients

This can be by telephone, fax, e-mail, or by letter. It is best done as a follow-up and not 'cold', and ideally targeted at a particular individual. Such a move might spring from a casual introduction or social conversation, or be generated by reliable intelligence reports, or simply be a routine follow-up to earlier commissions. A practice brochure, regularly updated and capable of being assembled with a particular interest in mind, is an indispensable marketing tool in such situations.

By approaches following the production of proposals for developing derelict or underused land, or finding new uses for redundant buildings etc

This could be a speculative move, which would create interest from firms known to have an interest in and sympathy with such initiatives (eg contractors, developers, conservation bodies). It might be a loss leader and would need to be kept under tight control, but it could generate some welcome publicity and spin-off benefits.

By approaches following the development of particular expertise in areas of topical concern

This could be in an operational respect (eg as energy consultants, planning supervisors, specialists in upgrading premises to health and safety requirements, specialists in adapting buildings for disabled access, etc). It could also be in respect of building types (eg health centres, housing association work, building conservation, community architecture etc), particularly where these accord with current political strategy or seem likely to feature in funding programmes.

By approaches to contracting organisations in offering a package approach – preferably design-led

Such a partnering could broaden the client base and catchment, but would need close control. It could also extend to working with construction management contractors.

By approaches to other construction professionals, lead consultants or project managers, to secure a subconsultant's role

This could result in longer term relationships. Simply working as subconsultants to another firm of architects might be expedient, but the work is likely to be unpredictable, needed at short notice, and accompanied by considerable pressures.

By taking part in competitions

Preferably not the informal type where an unscrupulous client seeks to obtain the maximum amount of free information. A competition should be regarded as unacceptable if it is not possible to elicit:

- the scope of the competition and a design brief;
- the terms and conditions of the competition;
- the conditions upon which the fee (if any) is based;
- the number of practices invited to take part;
- the time available for a stated (and reasonable) amount of design.

Under the RIBA Code of Professional Conduct, members undertake not to enter any architectural competition which the Institute has declared to be unacceptable. Current information on competitions, both UK and international, is held by the RIBA Competitions Office at 8 Woodhouse Square, Leeds LS3 1AD. It publishes a regular newsletter, *Competition Hotline*, available on subscription. The newsletter contains information about the briefing documents, submission requirements, and assessors for each approved competition.

All approaches to clients are based on the assumption that a practice has first put in place a marketing plan, and has developed appropriate marketing procedures and tools.

A marketing plan

A natural development of the practice's established business strategy will be the identification of a marketing plan and allocation of a marketing budget. Then the practice will need to choose the marketing methods that best suit its objectives and will reach the right people. However, it is important to remember that no matter what marketing goals are set, the priority is to maintain the flow of work in the immediate short term.

The first step in developing a marketing plan is to analyse the previous year's workload, broken down into three categories:

- carry-over work: commissions already in progress carried over from the previous year;
- repeat and referral work: repeat work for former clients, and work received by referral with little marketing effort;
- new business: work obtained by actively seeking it.

Carry-over work from existing commissions is likely to remain roughly constant as a percentage of turnover from year to year as completed commissions are replaced by new ones.

Fig B2.5   **Example of a composite marketing plan**
based on Weld Coxe's approach in *Marketing Architectural and Engineering Services*

		Health Service	Local Authority	General	Industrial and commercial
Markets	Present clients	21	5	80	1
	Potential clients (to be contacted)	–	3	–	50
Process	Message	Our track record	Our track record	We are local	We are better and cheaper
	Market method	Referral	Repeat and prospecting	Housing Association	Prospect
	Sales tools	Present brochure	Present brochure	Newsletter	New brochure
Organisation	Staff member	AB	CA	JB	BC
	Staff effort	4 hours/week	8 hours/week	12 hours/week	16 hours/week
	Direct costs £	2,500	800	5,000	7,000
	% of total effort	10	20	30	40
	% of total budget	10	10	50	30
Goal	Targeted income £	6 new / 250,000	75,000	100,000	2 new / 75,000
Long range plan	% of present workload	50	15	20	15
	Priority	3	4	2	1
	% of future workload	30	15	20	35

Repeat and referral work is a substantial part of most architects' workload, with repeat work from existing clients of particular importance. Although repeats and referrals are the result of the practice's successful previous work and good reputation, it is still essential to maintain contact with clients to make sure that this satisfactory state of affairs continues. Even though the requirements of such clients are likely to be well known, they should still be carefully targeted.

New business must be actively sought, both in familiar areas of work and in any new areas defined in the practice's business strategy. The plan adopted can aim at a single market, or target several. A single target plan aims at one market only, for example, healthcare projects or restoration work. It can be a way of introducing a new area of work into the practice in a limited way, or of concentrating effort on a single important market.

When a practice is undertaking a comprehensive review of several markets, a marketing plan will be needed for each; these can then be combined into a composite plan which allows comparisons to be made between the individual plans, and adjustments made to ensure that resources are used to the best advantage.

A framework for a composite marketing plan is given as Fig B2.5, while Fig B2.6 summarises the points for consideration when approaching the task.

Fig B2.6 Developing a marketing plan

Market
What types of client, types of project, and geographical location are to be covered?

Capability
What services and strengths can the practice offer?

Message
What particular message does the practice wish to convey; is it offering anything special?

Contacts
What past, present or potential clients have already been identified?

Methods
What methods will the practice use for research, lead-finding, courting prospects and presenting the firm's credentials? Will the approach be passive or aggressive?

Tools
What sales tools (promotional literature, publicity, advertising etc) will be appropriate?

Organisation
What tasks and roles will be required, and who will be responsible for organising the marketing initiative? What time should be allocated? What budget should be allowed?

Goals
What results are desired, and how will they be measured?

A marketing budget

The marketing budget will need to reflect accurately the effort the practice plans to put into getting work, and needs to be set in the early stages of drawing up the marketing plan. All direct expenses, and the amount of staff time expended, should be recorded on time sheets so that it is possible to monitor and assess cost-effectiveness. The budget should be kept under review and will probably need upgrading – the natural tendency is to underestimate the marketing requirement in the hope that the targeted work will soon come rolling in. It is important to maintain marketing activities through good times as well as bad, and the marketing budget should be regarded as a continuing commitment when planning the deployment of practice finances.

Managing marketing

Three important decisions to be made are:

- Who is to be in charge of the marketing drive?
- How is it to be organised?
- Who will carry it out?

Most architects have only limited experience of marketing, although some may have a natural flair for various aspects of it. Marketing expertise can be brought in, and firms of marketing consultants abound, although only a few have any special knowledge or experience of the needs of architectural practices. One of these could be briefed to carry out the whole marketing operation, find clients and 'deliver' them to the practice principals. Alternatively they could be used to support an in-house marketing effort, where practice principals and senior design staff play the leading roles.

If it is decided to institute and organise a marketing force in-house, careful consideration will have to be given to what level of effort is needed, whether the

Fig B2.7 Marketing roles and tasks

Lead finding

Task: explore the market, find out whom to contact, make contact, introduce to the practice.

Person: must know where to look, have a good nose for prospects, persevere although work can be tedious and unrewarding.

Development

Task: develop good understanding and convince client of practice's abilities.

Person: must be authoritative and carry conviction – probably a principal. Each principal could deal with a group of clients.

Success

Task: present the practice's proposal to client and win commission.

Person: a principal, with full authority and knowledge. Client may expect him/her to manage the project as well.

Co-ordination

Task: maintain marketing 'tools', put together publicity material, proposals and presentations.

Person: a full-time job if the practice has 15–20 staff. Should be well-organised, quick to respond, good writer.

Management

Task: to make sure it all happens.

Person: an appointed 'marketing director' or a principal responsible for directing the marketing drive. Could be a manager/ facilitator with an integrated support service.

---

practice has sufficient and appropriate resources, and whether this is the most cost-effective way of meeting its marketing needs.

A large practice might consider appointing a marketing director with a number of full-time staff, or a marketing manager with or without supporting staff. Smaller practices might make a member of staff responsible for marketing activities on a part-time basis, or one of the principals might devote some of his or her time to marketing.

The tasks involved in a marketing drive are various. In a small practice one person will probably have to carry them all out, but a larger practice may be able to match people to tasks and roles to which they are particularly suited (see Fig B2.7). This makes the best use of available skills, as well as spreading the load.

It should be remembered that a practice that embarks on a marketing exercise is asking to be assessed and evaluated in public, and it is bad for morale, as well as business, to be seen to fail. If the marketing effort is poorly executed, there is little hope of impressing clients about the quality of the professional service being offered.

Marketing tools and techniques

Once the marketing aims are clear and decisions have been made about who is to manage the marketing drive, the various tools and techniques needed have to be considered. It is important to channel effort and expenditure into the most cost-effective directions.

An expanded entry in the RIBA's *Directory of Practices* is sensible if the practice is looking for new work. Press releases about significant new commissions or completions may result in some valuable (and free) publicity in the locality. Placing an advertisement can sometimes be stunningly successful as a one-off 'impact' event, but advertising is relatively expensive and can seldom be afforded on a regular basis.

Marketing will make use of a wide range of documents and generate yet more. The collection could include:

- information about practice – its history, personnel;
- information about projects: job records, competitions and awards, photographs and slides;
- promotional brochures and leaflets;
- project brochures, presentations and models;
- press cuttings;
- market research and reports, directory entries etc.

There should be a database for recording details of clients and potential clients, and the production and issue of marketing material. Equipment will also be needed for printing and binding documents, for producing visual materials, and for storing files, photographs and slides, brochures, models and exhibition material.

In a small practice, whoever acts as librarian could be responsible for looking after such material. A large practice with a vigorous marketing department might consider making a special appointment.

Measuring performance

In simple terms, the success of a marketing plan can be quantified in terms of the commissions won and the fees earned. However, there are intangible benefits, such as 'potential' and 'goodwill', which are not directly attributable either to the excellence of the people involved in the exercise or to the accuracy of the targeting. Even if the only identifiable result of the whole operation is that the practice has become better known in the locality, it will not have wasted its energies entirely. That said, marketing activities must be monitored and judgements made about their effectiveness, so that corrective measures can be taken if necessary and money is not wasted.

As a matter of quality management, marketing operations should be audited at regular intervals to make sure that the plan is on target, being operated properly, and that any weaknesses are identified and corrected. The questions to ask are:

- Is the overall programme being maintained?
- Are the right staff, in the right numbers, being used?
- Are they performing their tasks effectively?
- Is the budget set at the right level?
- Are the promotional aids sufficient and of the right quality? Are presentations well prepared and executed?
- Have the right targets been identified?
- Is action being taken to address future needs?
- How effective are the marketing tools and techniques?
- What are the quantifiable results so far?

The long term implications of the results will need to be evaluated to allow forecasts of:

- future workload and staffing;
- any change in financial commitment;
- the kind of marketing required in the future.

B2.8 Quality management

An important objective for some practices will be to seek independent third party assessment and certification under the international quality management standard BS EN ISO 9001:1994, to give them a distinct marketing edge over their competitors. Clients are increasingly asking potential consultants for evidence of management capability, and a quality-managed practice, whether or not the full route to certification is to be followed, can offer assurance that it has achieved and intends to maintain a described level of quality, which it is able to demonstrate by means of well documented and regularly audited procedures.

When an architect sets up in practice, a business entity is born with a definable philosophy and character, and with its own objectives, skills and ways of working. As the workload and staff complement grow, it becomes necessary to describe these attributes and activities in some formal manner, so that everyone in the practice can be certain about the way things should be done, where authority resides, and who is responsible for what. Most practices meet this need by compiling an office manual for staff to refer to.

A quality management system is a structured development of the office manual (see C1.1) into a comprehensive description of practice activities in a format that is suitable for regular review and audit. It enables the practice's overall management and detailed methods of working to be monitored, controlled and, if necessary, corrected.

The first of the three components of the system, the Quality Manual, describes the practice itself – its aims and objectives (see below), management structure, main areas of work, and staff complement. It sets out the practice's quality policy (Fig B2.8), and explains how the quality system operates, who is in charge of it, procedures for review and audit, and methods for dealing with mistakes, inconsistencies and complaints. The two other components of the system are compilations of the detailed procedures connected with Design Management and Project Control, and Office Management.

It is important for a quality management system to be readily understandable and procedures properly codified so that everyone in the office is clear about their applicability and currency. The system should be lean, focused and effective; over-documentation should be avoided, or the system will become unwieldy and time-consuming to apply. Practices who do not feel confident about developing and instituting a system of their own devising can seek help

Fig. B2.8 A model practice quality policy

This Practice strives to provide a reliable and competent professional service to all its Clients and end users, and in its day to day relationships with professional colleagues and other members of the construction team.

This service is supported by a positive policy within the Practice towards staff training and continuing professional development, where individual aspirations and objectives are recognised, leading to the maintenance and improvement of personal and professional skills.

By means of the development and implementation of this Quality System the Practice demonstrates clear and controlled systematic working methods. This System which complies with the requirements of BS EN ISO 9001: 1994 is subject to regular review to ensure its continuing effectiveness and relevance to Practice requirements and to provide for continuing improvement.

Signed: .... Principal/Partners.

Date: ....

Example statement of practice aims and objectives

1 Provide a competent and comprehensive professional service to Clients based on principles of quality and integrity.

2 Further individuals' aspirations both within the Practice and in the context of their continuing professional development.

3 Encourage the enhancement of the environment by dedication to good architecture and design.

4 Maintain the development and implementation of quality management techniques.

5 Eliminate or minimise risks and hazards to health and safety, in construction and post completion maintenance, repair, cleaning and demolition by careful and considered design.

6 Manage the design and building procurement process to meet the agreed needs of Clients and end users.

7 Measure the efficiency of project information.

8 Develop lasting relationships between the Practice and its Clients.

9 Conduct the Practice's business in such a way as to meet its responsibilities to employees, Clients, end users, suppliers and the community as a whole.

10 Achieve the budgeted level of profit.

11 Encourage ideas for new and improved products and for new applications of technology.

(B2.8 *continued*)

from specialist consultants, or buy a ready-made system and customise it to suit their own needs.

Design professionals need a quality management system that is appropriate, effective and easy to set up and administer. The Quality Workshop model system published by RIBA Publications meets these requirements and has been well tried and tested in the construction industry. It is compatible both with this Handbook and with the *Architect's Job Book* (Sixth Edition).

After salaries, premises are usually the most significant outlay in any organisation, often taking up to 20% of a firm's revenue. The adequacy and suitability of premises should therefore be a policy matter which is kept under regular review.

Organisations constantly change and develop, and as a result there may be a need to increase accommodation or use space more efficiently. Furniture and equipment rapidly becomes obsolete, and the effectiveness of environmental control may need improving. It is essential to make one person in the practice responsible for the review and management of all matters relating to premises.

Suitability

A number of interrelated factors need to be considered when evaluating the suitability of premises as follows:

- *The size of the practice* (eg the number of permanent and temporary staff both at present and in the foreseeable future); whether the office is headquarters or a branch office; whether the office is a self-contained unit, multi-disciplinary or part of a consortium; whether IT-related work arrangements such as outsourcing, hot-desking or telecommuting should be catered for; whether all work stations are planned to be occupied all the time.
- *The form and nature of the practice* (eg sole principal, partnership, company or collaborative); the range of activities and equipment to be accommodated, and the support spaces likely to be needed.
- *The organisation and structure of the practice* (eg hierarchical, functional or egalitarian). This might influence the space planning and standards to be followed; it might determine the appropriate ratio of open plan to cellular layout.
- *'Fit' and 'feel good' factors.* What is the preferred shape of the premises relative to the optimum space requirements of the practice; the ratio of dead or unusable space to usable area (at least 85% of the area available should be usable); whether a layout will be compromised by the position of structural members, existing services and other elements; and whether there is likely to be flexibility for subdivision of areas with minimal reorganisation.
- *Adjustment.* The amount needed to bring premises into line with modern standards and current legislative requirements, eg the Workplace (Health Safety and Welfare) Regulations 1992. This will particularly apply to ventilation, lighting, minimum room dimensions, planning of work stations, workers' access to windows, opening and safe cleaning, washing and sanitary conveniences etc.

Location

Modern working methods and communications in the electronic age of the lap-top, mobile phone, fax machine, e-mail and networking, in one sense make the location of the office less critical. Working from home might be a satisfactory initial or permanent arrangement given efficient electronic backup and accessibility, but it requires a disciplined attitude and a methodical approach to ensure that all business is conducted in an environment free from domestic interruption. This is more likely where the office can be located in a dedicated area (eg converted outbuildings or a purpose-built studio) with a separate entrance for visitors and all necessary support services separate and self-contained.

Otherwise the location of a practice should be a prime consideration, not only in terms of image and identity but also for the sake of accessibility and convenience for staff and visitors. Ideally there should be good public transport links with shops, restaurants and other amenities.

Where a suite of offices is located within a building, it is important for access to be direct and obvious, the entrance well signed and close to car parking for delivery services and also for visitors. Any staircase or lift to the particular floor should enhance the approach and not be perceived as a barrier. The front door – the point where the design philosophy of the practice becomes clear – should open to the main point of contact, ie the reception area and desk. First impressions are all important.

Requirements

Any schedule of office accommodation will include the usual requirements for cellular offices, work stations layouts, conference and interview areas etc. Other matters for consideration might be:

- *Adjustments to the physical features of the premises*, if this is a duty of the employer under Section 6 of the Disability Discrimination Act 1995.

- *Library, information and research area*. Even with electronic and microfiche systems, hard copy is still needed. This could be invaluable when seeking to establish the 'state of the art' on some future occasion.

- *Archive arrangements*, whether completely or partly in-house. These should be conveniently placed to allow for the orderly deposit and retrieval of key material. Access might be needed for up to 20 years, and lawyers prefer original documents.

- *Appropriate amenity areas for staff*, eg hot and cold drinks machines, kitchen facilities, rest and first-aid area, changing rooms and showers, parking for cycles etc.

- *Smoking areas*. If premises are designated as non-smoking, facilities for smokers are best planned to be unobtrusive as well as convenient. The sight of desperate smokers loitering outside a main entrance does not give a businesslike impression.

- *Adequate storage*. For equipment, including survey and site visit gear, materials samples, office supplies and stationery etc. Difficult to quantify, but often underestimated.

Requirements relating to premises which arise from legislation include the following.

Occupiers Liability Act 1957
The long title of this Act refers to 'the state of the property or to things done or omitted to be done there', and Section 2 requires that the premises be 'reasonably safe'. This is a provision which could apply to landlords and their tenants.

Fire Precautions Act 1971
A fire certificate might be necessary depending on the number of staff employed, and where they are placed within the building.

The Workplace (Health Safety and Welfare) Regulations 1992 These deal with space allocation, environmental conditions, circulation and sanitary provisions. Note in particular:

Reg 6 Suitable and effective ventilation, natural or mechanical;
　　7 Reasonable temperature during working hours, normally at least 16°C;
　　8 Suitable and sufficient lighting, natural or artificial. Also refers to fittings, switches etc;
　 10 Sufficient floor area, height and free space at work stations. Allow volume of at least 11 cubic metres per person;
　 15 Position and operation of opening windows and roof lights, so as not to endanger occupants;
　 17 Organisation of traffic routes, both for people on foot and travelling in vehicles;
　 20 Number of sanitary conveniences, accessibility, lighting and ventilation;
　 21 Number and suitability of washing facilities;
　 22 Provision of 'wholesome' drinking water;
　 25 Suitable rest facilities, including where relevant, suitable places to eat meals.

Requirements relating to furniture and fittings arise from the Health and Safety (Display Screen Equipment) Regulations 1992. These concern the use and position of VDU screens and minimum requirements (including environmental) for work stations.

Fixtures and fittings are usually a major item of office expenditure. At the time of writing, the cost can be set against capital tax allowance, with 25% recoverable in the first year and 25% of the balance recoverable at each subsequent year. As with all tax or revenue matters, it is essential to check the current situation with the firm's accountants. This concession applies only to mobile items or systems including screens and partitions. If anything is permanently fixed, then recovery will not be possible. In this respect, work stations will usually be mobile, either an assembly or stand-alone items or units in an integrated system. While the latter has attractions, the choice often brings a measure of inflexibility and commits the user to continued use of the same system.

If consideration is being given to taking on a lease on existing premises, requirements should include ensuring that accurate records and plans of the area are available and that there is evidence (eg copies of inspection reports) that:

- passenger lifts have been properly maintained at regular intervals;
- electrical equipment and installations have been properly maintained, comply with legislation, and have sufficient capacity for intended loads;
- water systems and water heating installations have been properly maintained.

In addition, it would be advisable to check whether a current Fire Certificate is held (if relevant), and whether a Health and Safety File is deposited in respect of any recent work.

It can sometimes be a good move to bring in an outside firm of architects where a practice needs to remodel premises for its own occupation. An outside firm is likely to take a more objective view and be well removed from any of the influences and constraints often generated by internal politics. The outcome may be both more effective and more economic overall.

The acquisition of premises will have a considerable impact on practice finances. The main considerations are the type of tenure and any associated terms of availability or restrictions on the use of the building; the cost of acquisition; the condition of the building and the extent of liability for its maintenance and repair; and costs in use. The basis for rating buildings used for business purposes varies according to the local authority involved. The amount to be paid may be considerable, and it is wise to discover at the outset what it is likely to be.

Whatever method of acquisition is considered, legal and financial advice should always be sought.

Leasing

The most common method of acquiring premises is to lease them for a short, medium or long term. Normally, leasing payments are met out of income, but some capital outlay may be needed if a premium is required or if fixtures and fittings have to be purchased or provided. These costs can sometimes be recovered upon relinquishing the tenancy. There may also be opportunities to sublet at a profitable rental or to assign a lease for a lump sum consideration.

Occupiers of business premises are given some protection in law, but nevertheless a landlord has the right under certain circumstances to obtain repossession. Leases should be carefully drafted, and a solicitor's advice should always be sought.

Restrictions on use of premises are often introduced in a lease. These should be looked at carefully in the light of future development, because even a change of legal persona or a consortium could be prohibited. Such restrictions could make it difficult to dispose of the lease in mid term.

Also, the conditions under which a lease may be disposed of before its term has run may be limited by the lease itself. The longer the lease the more important it is to have the ability to dispose of it with reasonable freedom. The principal ways in which this may be done, some or all of which may be permitted, are as follows:

- *Assignment*, ie getting another party to take over the unexpired portion of the lease. It may be possible to take a premium. The right to assign may be subject to certain restrictions and may be prohibited entirely. It is certainly likely to be difficult to find a taker for a leasehold interest with less than five years to run.

- *Subletting*, ie retaining an interest in the lease but finding a tenant to occupy all or part of the premises and pay a rent. The holder of the lease is still responsible to the landlord. Subletting may be specifically prohibited or may be subject to restrictions. In any event, the landlord's consent will usually be required.

- *Break clauses*. Certain leases permit one or both parties to determine the lease at certain fixed points during the term. The effect of this is that the lease, instead of running for its full period, ends at the earlier date. It is important to be aware whether the landlord has this right. If he has, it is useful to regard the lease as being for the shorter term with the possibility of extension.

Restrictions on hours of access may be introduced in the lease, particularly where circulation includes common areas where the one building is divided between several lessees.

Leases of more than six years usually have a rent review clause, under which rent is to be renegotiated at certain points. New rents are usually adjusted in line with market values, but in some leases the chance of a downward shift is specifically excluded.

Leases should state clearly and precisely the obligations on the lessee concerning repair, maintenance, and insurance. Full repairing terms in a lease should be regarded with caution, and never entered into without an agreed schedule of condition.

Buying or building

Instead of renting or leasing, premises can be bought. If capital is available, the property can be purchased outright. Alternatively, funds may be borrowed. However, it is not always wise to tie up capital in such a way, and buildings are not necessarily a good investment. Professional advice should always be sought on the merits of a particular course of action at a particular time.

Building brings the obvious attraction of accommodation customised to the needs of a practice. It might also be possible to secure income by letting part of the premises, perhaps to another construction professional.

Sale and lease-back

Having purchased or built new accommodation, the asset may then be sold subject to the granting back of a lease. This permits the release of invested capital and may also offer a capital gain. The vendor may try to incorporate terms in the lease favourable to himself; if so, the sale price may have to be lowered.

Sale and lease-back is sometime attempted purely for an initial profit, but it may also be a useful method of raising capital.

Managing the premises

Efficient management of the premises can make an important contribution to the economic as well as the smooth day to day operation of a practice, and it must be the responsibility of a nominated person in the practice. It is essential for someone to have an overview of the operation of the building as a whole.

The operating cost of premises is the total cost of running and maintaining fabric and services. The key cost elements are:

- energy consumption;
- cleaning;
- maintenance;

- security;
- insurance;
- renewal.

Offices in urban areas also often incur heavy service charges, which will add significantly to running costs. With these in mind, attention should be paid to each of the above elements.

Energy consumption
This should be monitored. Devices can be introduced to reduce wasteful consumption of energy, and staff should be informed of the levels appropriate to particular tasks and circumstances and be encouraged to observe them. Demands on installations change over time, and obsolete or worn fittings can often reduce efficient consumption. It is sensible to establish a policy for regular checking and replacement.

Cleaning

Responsibility for cleaning arrangements can be a testing task for the office manager. Reliability on the part of the operatives is essential. The alternatives are to contract a professional cleaning service, which can be costly, or rely on a more informal service. The essential consideration is the trustworthiness of the personnel involved, since the office manager must be sure that people coming into the premises outside normal working hours are not a security risk.

Programmed maintenance

The cost of ad hoc repairs to the fabric should be distinguished from routine maintenance costs. If the condition of the building is causing excessive expenditure, a major rethink about the viability of the premises might be indicated, whereas increasing operational costs within the office are often connected with staff requirements, and might be reduced by better space planning or by replacing obsolete equipment.

Security

A contract can be arranged, or personnel can be hired. Insurers may ask for information about the arrangements made.

The cost of providing and maintaining a special security system, which might be a priority in some urban areas, will be a significant one-off cost commitment and special financial provision should be made for it. It is advisable to seek advice on security from a specialist firm, or from the local police.

Staff must be clear about procedures for locking up at the end of the day, for setting alarms and systems, and for entering the premises outside normal working hours. It is important to make staff security-conscious; many practices have a signing-in book and require all visitors to provide identification and wear a lapel badge.

As well as the building and access to it, various items on the office premises need to be kept secure. These include:

- equipment;
- personal belongings;
- project drawings and documentation, some of which may be commercially sensitive;
- accounting and personnel records.

Computer equipment is likely to be particularly at risk and items should always be security marked.

There should be adequate insurance cover against risks. The advice of an insurance broker should be sought. The practice's policies should be scheduled and reviewed regularly to make sure they remain relevant and adequate, that the level of cover is sufficient, and that any requirements by insurers for security procedures and fireproof storage are being met.

Fig B2.9 Schedule of office insurance policies

1 Commercial combined
Material damage
Theft
All risks
Money
Glass

2 Liability policy
Employers' liability
Public liability

3 Travel policy
Medical and additional expenses
Public liability
Personal accident
Baggage and personal effects
Personal money

4 Computer policy
Fire and theft
Accidental loss or damage

5 Business interruption

6 Motor cars

7 Fires and extended perils:
building

8 Liability for property overseas

B3.1 The function of accounting

At various times a practice needs to be able to communicate to its investors, creditors, advisers and managers information about its profitability, liquidity, financial viability and the soundness of its business strategy. The function of accountancy is to generate and present that information in a suitable form.

Day to day accounting procedures allow the activities of an enterprise to be compiled, recorded and analysed. Transactions are identified, measured in monetary terms, classified, and entered in a book-keeping system. They are subsequently summarised in financial statements presented in a form appropriate to the needs of the user. The process of financial management is illustrated in Fig B3.1.

Financial statements are used by Government, in the shape of the Inland Revenue (for income tax purposes), and Customs & Excise (for VAT). Company accounts are filed at Companies House, where they are inspected for the purpose of levying Corporation Tax. Otherwise, the users of financial statements fall into three major categories: investors, creditors and managers. Architects could find their accounts reviewed by all three categories.

Investors are those who have a financial stake in the business, whilst creditors may be suppliers of goods who extend credit, or lending institutions such as banks. In addition there are those who advise the business, or have a direct interest in it (eg staff, unions). Practice managers also use financial statements, together with various other reports compiled specifically for management purposes.

The different users of financial statements evaluate the information presented according to their particular needs. Investors or owners are primarily interested in trying to predict a return on their investment and in assessing the risks involved in that investment. They will concentrate on evaluating the firm's past performance and estimating its future profitability and overall financial strength. They will compare it with their other investments.

A creditor's primary concern is that the business should be able to repay its obligations (a concern that an architect might share when considering a potential client's financial status). Long term creditors are therefore concerned with the company's long term financial performance and strength; short term creditors are more concerned with the solvency of the business in the near future, and tend to focus on its immediate liquidity.

The practice manager will analyse the information about the firm's past to evaluate its present results so that corrective or other action can be taken.

The key factor in the analysis of financial information is comparability, because unless the present performance of the business can be compared with previous, or with the results of similar enterprises, or with budget, a financial statement by itself is of limited informational value. Comparing results from previous years may reveal trends and provide a yardstick for evaluating current performance and financial strength. It is important to establish that the accounting policies and methods used remain constant over the relevant period. The value of the monetary unit fluctuates (with inflation, for example) so that only a rough comparison can be made year on year.

For architectural practices who trade as companies it will be particularly relevant (and easy) to compare their financial results with those of others.

Fig B3.1 Financial management: the process

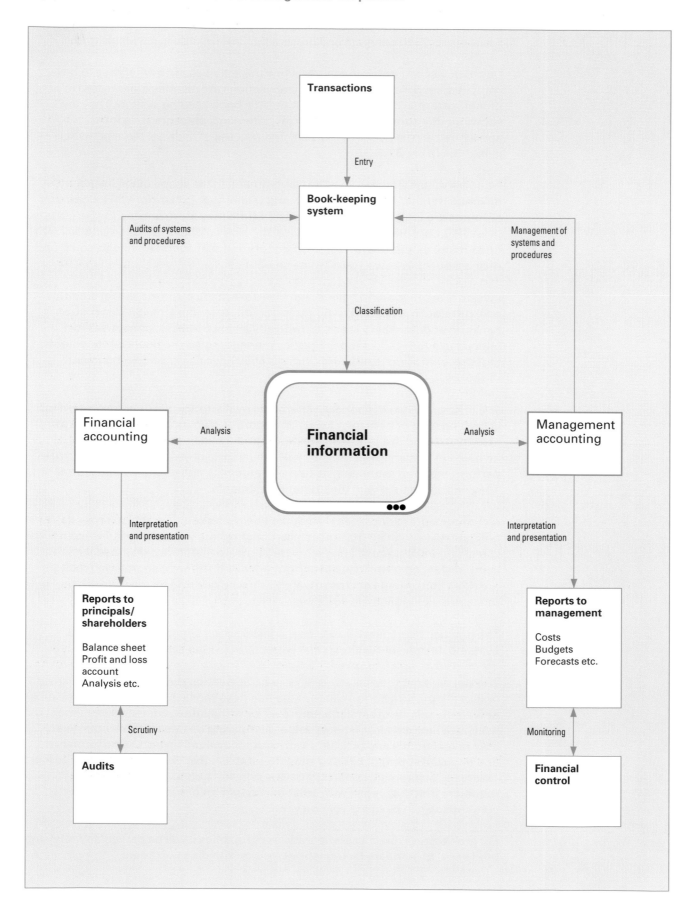

B3.2 Accounting principles

In accountancy, as in all professions, certain principals and conventions have been drawn up to establish norms and a consistent basis for operation. Accountants conduct their work in accordance with Statements of Standard Accounting Practice (SSAP).

Principles

There are four principles which need to be understood by anyone attempting to interpret financial statements:

A going concern
Valuation is always based on the assumption that the firm is going to continue indefinitely. An entirely different valuation would be made of a firm's resources and position if its break-up value was being assessed.

Consistency
The same accounting methods are used each year and throughout each year. Any change in this respect has to be stated in the accounts.

Prudence
Accountants are often accused of taking a depressing view of events, but in financial statements they are required to exercise caution and restraint in calculating profits in order not to mislead the users of these statements.

Matching
The fundamental principle of accounting is to match expenses against revenues. Thus if a cost occurs in one year but the revenue does not materialise until the next year, the cost is 'carried forward' and shown in the next year's accounts.

Accounting entities

An accountancy entity is not the equivalent of a legal entity. For example, in the case of a sole practitioner there no distinction in law between the business and its owner – the owner is responsible for all debts incurred by the business regardless of how much he or she has invested in it. However, for accounting purposes there is a distinction between the sole practitioner's business and personal financial activities: the business is held to be an accounting entity separate from the owner.

In English law, a partnership is not an entity or persona, but in accounting it is recognised as a business entity distinct from the private financial dealings of the individual owners.

A company, on the other hand, requires no such splits of personality for accounting purposes: it is a legal entity incorporated under the Companies Act 1985 and operated according to the Statement of Standard Accounting Practice (2) issued by the Accounting Standards Committee. It has an infinite life until and unless action is taken to dissolve it, regardless of whether its directors, managers or shareholders sell their shares, retire or die.

B3.3 Standard financial reports

Standardised formats for financial accounting reports have been developed by the accounting profession. A set of statements for an accounting entity would cover:

- its financial position at the end of a period (the Balance Sheet);
- its revenue and expenses for the same period (the Profit and Loss Account);
- Its investments by and distribution to owners during that period (the Appropriation Account);
- its funds flow for the period;
- its statement of accounting policies;
- its auditors' report.

The two key statements are the Balance Sheet (Fig B3.2), and the Profit and Loss (P & L) Account (Fig B3.3).

The Balance Sheet shows the financial position of a firm at a given point in time, whilst the P & L Account shows its revenue and expenditure over a period. In the case of a company, the P & L Account will also show the amount of profit that is re-invested in the company, the dividends that are paid to shareholders, the accumulated net profits from the previous year's trading, and the tax liabilities. In the case of a partnership, it will illustrate the amount of profit that has been transferred to the appropriation account (which shows how the profit is distributed between the partners), what has been drawn, and what remains as capital.

The Balance Sheet

The Balance Sheet is made up of assets, liabilities, capital and reserves.

Assets
Assets are used to help generate, either directly or indirectly, future revenue for the firm. They can be tangible (fixed), like buildings and equipment, or intangible (current), such as money owed to the firm or work in progress. However, to be included in the Balance Sheet the value of every asset must be measurable in monetary terms.

Liabilities
Liabilities are debts, ie what the firm owes. They are claims by the creditors on the firm's assets. A creditor is someone who has provided an asset to a firm in exchange for future reimbursement, usually in the form of cash. Trade creditors in the Balance Sheet represent the amount owed to suppliers of goods and services. Other liabilities will be to the Inland Revenue, and will include bank loans and/or overdrafts.

Liabilities are split into current and non-current. Current are expected to be met and satisfied within one year; non-current after one year.

Capital and reserves
In a partnership this will be represented by the partners' capital account, which shows the profits distributed to them from the P & L Account, less any withdrawals that have been made. In a company's Balance Sheet this would be reflected in two principal items: share capital, and reserves.

Fig B3.2 Balance Sheet: typical structure

Sparrow & Grebe Ltd: Balance Sheet as at 31 December 1990

	£000s	£000s
FIXED ASSETS		
Land and buildings		100.0
Office equipment		60.0
		160.0
CURRENT ASSETS		
Stock, and work in progress	20.0	
Debtors	140.0	
Cash at bank	40.0	
	200.0	
Less		
CURRENT LIABILITIES		
(due within 1 year)		
Creditors	60.0	
		140.0
Net Current Assets		300.0
Less		
LONG TERM LIABILITIES		
(due after 1 year)		
Bank loan		100.0
		200.0
CAPITAL AND RESERVES		
Share capital		60.0
Reserves		140.0
		200.0

Prepared February 1991

The Profit and Loss Account

The P & L Account enables a firm's past financial performance to be evaluated. Whereas the Balance Sheet reflects its financial position at a point in time, the P & L account shows the in-flows and out-flows of resources over a period, expressed as revenues and expenses.

In architectural practice, revenues are earned by providing services to clients. Expenses are costs incurred by the practice in the process of generating those revenues. All the revenues and all the expenses are added up to show the net result of the practice's operations over a period, ie its profit.

Published P & L accounts usually add all the operating expenses together, whereas those accounts used for internal management purposes analyse the operating expenses in greater detail under a range of budget headings (Fig B3.4).

Fig B3.3 Profit & Loss Account: typical structure

Sparrow & Grebe Ltd: Profit & Loss Account
for year ending 31 December 1990

		£000s
Sales		640.0
Less: Cost of Sales		347.0
Office equipment	Gross Profit	293.0
Administrative expenses		192.2
	Operating Profit	100.8
Bank loan interest payable		23.8
	Net Profit before Tax	77.0
Tax		25.0
	Profit for Year	52.0
Dividends payable		30.0
		22.0
Plus: Reserves b/f		118.0
Reserves c/f		140.0

Prepared February 1991

Management accounts comprise the information provided by the ledgers and cash book presented in a way that enables decisions to be made about practice planning and operation. Their presentation and timing are determined by the needs of the practice and will relate to its size and the nature of its work. The function of the management accountant is to interpret and extrapolate information to monitor and control the direction and profitability of practice finances. The main aspects of his or her work are budgeting, and financial control – in other words, where the practice is going, and how to keep it on course.

B3.4 The annual budget

The annual budget should represent a realistic forecast of total income and expenditure for the coming year. It is used to set targets for the level of fee income anticipated, staff salaries and other direct costs, logistical support, office overheads, and, ultimately, profit for the year. It indicates how much money has been made available for marketing, training, new systems, furniture, equipment and books etc.

The annual budget consists of a series of agreed budget headings (Fig B3.5). The amount of fee income budgeted will represent the commissions expected to materialise during the year ahead. Direct costs include technical salaries, consultants' fees, drawing office materials and other recoverable expenses. Overheads (indirect costs) include all the costs of running the business that are not directly associated with projects. They typically consist of fixed or recurring charges (many of which are known in advance or can be realistically adjusted)

Fig B3.4 Profit & Loss Account: management accounts

Sparrow & Grebe Ltd: Profit & Loss Account for year ending 31 December 1990

	£000s	£000s)
Income		
Fee		640.0
Other		nil
Total:		640.0
Direct costs		
Technical salaries	(297.0)	
Consultants' fees	(25.0)	
Other expenses	(25.0)	(347.0)
GROSS PROFIT		293.0
Premises expenses		
Rent, rates, insurance	42.0	
Utilities	11.0	
Repair and renewal	5.0	(58.0)
Administrative expenses		
Staff salaries	52.1	
Staff training	4.5	
Staff pensions	4.2	
Cars	12.4	
Office equipment	16.6	
Printing, stationery	7.0	(96.8)
Financial expenses		
PI insurance	20.0	
Professional advisers	10.0	
Bank charges	3.2	
Bad debts	4.2	(51.4)
TOTAL EXPENSES		192.2
OPERATING PROFIT		100.8
Less: Bank loan interest payable		(23.8)
NET PROFIT BEFORE TAX		77.0

Prepared February 1991

Fig B3.5 Annual budget: budgeted Profit & Loss Account

<u>Sparrow & Grebe Ltd: 1990 Annual Budget</u>

	£000s	£000s)
<u>Income</u>		
Fee		600.1
Other		<u>2.9</u>
Total:		<u>603.0</u>
<u>Direct costs</u>		
Technical salaries	(260.0)	
Consultants' fees	(20.0)	
Other expenses	<u>(20.0)</u>	
GROSS PROFIT		<u>303.0</u>
<u>Premises expenses</u>		
Rent, rates, insurance	42.0	
Utilities	12.0	
Repair and renewal	<u>6.0</u>	
<u>Administrative expenses</u>		
Staff salaries	50.8	
Staff training	9.0	
Staff pensions	4.0	
Cars	12.4	
Office equipment	17.6	
Printing, stationery	<u>6.2</u>	
<u>Financial expenses</u>		
PI insurance	21.5	
Professional advisers	10.0	
Bank charges	3.5	
Bad debts	<u>5.0</u>	
TOTAL EXPENSES		<u>200.0</u>
OPERATING PROFIT		103.0
<u>Less:</u> Bank loan interest payable		<u>(23.5)</u>
NET PROFIT BEFORE TAX		<u>79.5</u>

Prepared December 1989

(B3.4 *continued*)

such as rent, rates, utilities. Of the costs remaining, some can be estimated on the basis of previous expenditure, deducting any abnormal items and adding any known additional commitments.

The budget is set once a year, but the assumptions and forecasts on which it is based may well change in the course of the year, so that at strategic intervals it will be necessary to review and revise the budget to take account of any actual or expected changes.

The annual budget is the key control document for assessing overall profitability, and it can be used as the basis for quarterly or monthly analyses of income and expenditure. Any overspending on budget can be identified and corrected; conversely, if budget targets are not met for some particular initiative or commitment (staff training, for example) the reason should be investigated. It is important for accounts staff to be clear about who is responsible for authorising expenditure under the various budget heads, and they in turn should make sure that those with such authority are kept informed of the position each month.

The annual budget of a small practice can be broken down into monthly elements and supported by cash flow forecasts; a large practice will need more detailed information, which might include overhead costs analyses, performance indicators, forecast balance sheets and funds flow statements.

A level of overall profit will also be budgeted. A primary decision is how much is to be retained in the business as working capital and how much is to be distributed to partners or shareholders.

B3.5 Financial control

The second and crucial aspect of management accounting is financial control – of cash flow, time and costs.

Controlling cash flow

Cash comes in to the firm in several ways, such as payment received against invoices; money invested in the firm; bank loans; and proceeds from the sale of the firm's assets. Cash goes out from the firm to pay staff, creditors, and to reward partners or shareholders.

In the section about profitability (B2.6) and the capital requirement (B2.3) it was noted that the principal difficulty in architectural business is coping with the time lag between doing the work and being paid for it so as to maintain equilibrium in the bank balance, ie solvency. How can this situation be managed? It stands to reason that the best positive action is to be properly funded in the first place, and to control the factors that are capable of control, and the best defensive action is to anticipate the worst situation and know what to do if it arises.

Payments out
As far as outgoings are concerned, there are many peaks and troughs of expenditure that can be levelled out. It is often possible to arrange to pay annual bills such as rates in monthly instalments; the same applies to gas and electricity bills. Non-urgent orders for books, stationery, drawing office and computer supplies can be placed when the cash is available.

Payments in

Getting the money in is far more difficult. A basic business practice that architects are traditionally diffident about is establishing the creditworthiness of prospective clients. Discreet inquiries of professional contacts is often the most reliable indicator, but using a credit reference agency is inexpensive and anonymous and is certainly better than nothing. Checking creditworthiness should be done as a matter of routine with new clients, or where large additional costs are agreed when work is in progress.

There are certain disciplines that will help to get the money in regularly. An important one is to insist that clients pay on a monthly basis. Every appointment should clearly specify terms of payment, and these should always be recorded in writing. The arrangements agreed should suit the practice's accounting procedures and financial situation as well as the client's convenience.

Unfortunately, in business there are always some consistently late payers and a few who never pay at all. Practices need to establish a policy for dealing with both these situations and agree a cut-off point for work in the event of non-payment (say, three months). It is wise to put in place chase-up procedures to deal with late payers so that the problem does not become large-scale; unless the money comes in, the solvency of the practice will be threatened. Repeat work for bad or slow payers should be carefully considered and only undertaken if more effective controls can be put in place – or the job priced accordingly.

The cash flow situation

As well as establishing basic controls of this kind, the general cash flow situation should be constantly monitored, and this is done by means of cash flow forecasts (Fig B3.6). One is usually prepared based on the annual budget to show the likely position at the end of the new accounting year and to serve as a check on the budget, and again at regular intervals throughout the year. It will highlight any surpluses or shortfalls, allowing decisions to be taken about possible investments or whether an additional loan or overdraft will need to be negotiated.

The manager of a small practice might produce a cash flow forecast every three months. Larger practices usually need the interval to be shorter – probably monthly. Cash flow forecasts can relate to the practice's running costs and to its expected fee income. These can be combined to give an overall picture of liquidity over the year or be broken down to show the situation over shorter intervals.

Fig B3.6 Cash flow forecast

Sparrow & Grebe Ltd: 1990 Annual Budget

	Jan–Mar £000s	Apr–Jun £000s	Jul–Sep £000s	Oct–Dec £000s
Receipts				
Fee income	125.0	132.8	181.2	149.3
Other	0.1	1.7	0.3	1.2
	125.1	134.5	181.5	150.5
Payments				
Capital expenditure	nil	nil	(15.6)	(24.2)
Salaries	(72.2)	72.1)	(84.6)	(95.8)
Fees	(14.7)	(3.2)	(15.3)	(14.9)
Rent & rates	(17.0)	(7.0)	(17.0)	nil
Stationery etc	(2.8)	(1.0)	(3.0)	(1.7)
Insurance	nil	(1.5)	(30.0)	nil
Other	(10.4)	(5.7)	(42.0)	(21.9)
	(117.1)	(90.5)	(207.5)	(158.5)
NET CASH MOVEMENT	8.0	44.0	(26.0)	(8.0)
Plus: Opening balance	17.0	25.0	69.0	43.0
Closing balance	25.0	69.0	43.0	35.0

Prepared December 1989

Notes

1 Cash at the bank at the start of the year is £17,000.
2 Cash receipts in Jan–Mar are £125,000.
3 Cash payments in Jan–Mar are £117,000.
4 The net cash receipts are £125,000 less £117,100 = £8,000.
5 Add the net receipts (£8,000) to the start of year cash (£17,000) and the total is £25,000.
6 At 31 March the balance is £25,000.
7 This process is repeated for each quarter in the year.

Bracketed figures are outgoings from the bank account.

Putting a price on time

Architects often have to make fee quotations in competition with others and have to know exactly how low they can bid without sacrificing profits. This means that, whatever the fee basis for a job is, they have to be able to assess and measure, with precision, its work content and the related staff effort needed to service it. It is essential for financial survival that the price charged for providing the professional service required by the client takes into account all the costs involved, direct and indirect.

The only element of a professional service that can be measured is the time taken to provide it. This has nothing to do with the quality of that service or the competence of the people involved in its provision; these are things that have to be judged and assessed – they cannot be measured. Even where there is a tangible product such as a feasibility study or investigative report, the client pays for the time taken to produce it, not for the aptness or excellence of its recommendations. The intangible, but priceable, commodity of the service that architects provide is time.

The direct costs of a job arise from the amount and level of staff effort allocated to it. The time of an experienced job architect is considerably more expensive than that of a student on Professional Training, although both may expend the same amount of time on the same job. Failure to get the experience–inexperience balance right can reduce efficiency and, ultimately, profitability.

When a job comes in, it is necessary to calculate how much staff time will be needed to complete it, and to put a price on that time. The crucial management tool in job costing is the time sheet.

The time of a full-time architect is spent in five principal ways:

- in carrying out project work;
- in looking for new business;
- in management and administration;
- in training and development;
- in legitimate absence.

Time spent on promotion and advertising would be included under new business, and CPD activities under training and development. Sickness, holidays and other legitimate absences have to be included in the reckoning.

All staff, non-technical as well as technical, should be asked to complete time sheets and hand them in each week. To allow time expenditure to be analysed, time sheets can be divided into the five major time categories described above, with individual projects listed under Project Work and identified by job number and work stage where appropriate (Fig B3.7). It must be made clear to everyone exactly what counts as 'project time', and what is the smallest unit of time that is to be recorded.

Time spent on project work is directly chargeable to each project, but time under the four other categories is not. The question therefore arises of how the cost of that other time is to be recovered. All the hours in the working day have a price; there is no 'free' time – salaries have to be paid and the costs of running the business have to be met.

Fig B3.7 Example time sheet

| Sparrow & Grebe Ltd Time Sheet | | Name: _____ | | | Week _____ | | |
| Date completed _____ | | | | | Signature _____ | | |

Projects		Monday	Tuesday	Wednesday	Thursday	Friday	Total	Overtime
Partner i/c	Job no.	hrs	hrs	hrs	hrs	hrs	hrs	hrs
JR	927	5	3	6			14.0	
CJ	641		2.5		3	6	11.5	
Promotion/ business development					·5	1·0	1·5	
Management/ administration			2	1·5	·5	·5	4·5	
Training/ development		2·5					2·5	
Personal/ absences					3·5		3·5	

Notes
1 Working day is 7½ hours.
2 Minimum unit of time to be recorded is 15 minutes.
3 Overtime work to be agreed beforehand with project partner.
4 For job costing purposes, it is important to take into account agreed overtime rates.

Senior staff may spend about half their time on non-chargeable work: partners often as much as 80%, and junior staff only 10–15% (Fig B3.8). If 70% of a job architect's time is fee-earning, the remaining 30% has to be recovered by the price put on the job. If the ratio of chargeable to non-chargeable time can be improved, profitability should similarly improve. This ratio should be closely watched.

It is never easy to persuade staff of the need to complete time sheets, which is often seen as a tiresome chore imposed on busy people who consider they are already doing their best. Staff are more likely to comply if care is taken to explain why time sheets are needed – particularly if it is pointed out that they are a mechanism used to improve efficiency and profitability, which will bring benefits for the staff themselves.

The time of non-technical staff can sometimes be charged as a direct project cost, such as special research and secretarial back-up, computer time, or information provided by in-house specialists, but more often it cannot and in any case this is a matter that should be agreed with the client. However, it is still important for non-technical staff to complete time sheets; this often provides valuable information about the underlying costs of providing a professional service.

Calculating realistic hourly rates

A small practice will need to identify for each fee-earning member of staff an hourly rate that both recovers all the costs of employing that person and includes a margin for profit. For a larger practice it may be more appropriate to work out an average rate for each grade of staff.

The first step is to calculate the number of fee-earning hours available in a year (Fig B3.9). Other information needed is:

- the percentage of fee-earning time given in Fig B3.8;
- details of staff salaries;
- the direct employment costs of each staff member;
- the practice budget .

The method of calculation* is given as Fig B3.10, and the explanatory notes included should be read. Taking time sheet data as its base, this approach enables the total cost of employing each grade of staff to be seen, the cost of each fee earning hour and, adding on an appropriate margin, the annual fee-earning potential of each grade. The point of the exercise is for architects to be able to know the real costs of employment each time they are required to put a price on a commission so as to be sure that these costs are going to be recovered. The RIBA published fee scales and hourly rates are only indicative and do not remove the need for sound arithmetic based on up to date cost information for each new project.

Typically, the larger a practice becomes, the more time partners need to spend on management and looking for new business, and the less time they spend on direct project work. However, sooner or later the question will arise of how to rationalise in a job costing system the relatively high salary of a partner with the relatively low percentage of his or her time that may be charged directly against the project. It may be more realistic to regard the non-chargeable element of a partner's time as a practice overhead. In the calculation, it would then be absorbed evenly by the other grades and is shown as indirect costs in column 4 of Fig B3.10.

It must be stressed that the method demonstrated is only one way of approaching the arithmetic, and it is based on various arbitrary assumptions. It does not take into account the many variations in skill, seniority, efficiency and appetite for work between individual staff. Time spent on a job can be measured, but arithmetic says nothing about how effectively that time has been spent. The human factor should not be ignored.

Managing the workload

Calculating the practice's fee-earning potential has an important application as a strategic control in managing the practice's existing and expected workload. This requires a realistic forecast of fee income to be kept under review, so that action to recruit additional design or other staff can be taken as necessary.

*As advocated by Jonathan Lucas of Gray Lucas Management Consultancy, to whom the editors are indebted.

Fig B3.8 Analysis of time expenditure by grade of staff

	Projects	Promotion/ business development	Management/ administration	Training/ development	Personal/ absences
	%	%	%	%	%
Principal	45	20	25	3	7
Associate	60	10	20	5	5
Senior professional	70	5	15	5	5
Professional	75	nil	10	10	5
Junior professional	85	nil	3	7	5

Notes

1 Read this Figure in conjunction with Fig B3.7 Example time sheet.
2 The percentages assume a working week of 5 days, and a working day of $7\frac{1}{2}$ hours.

Fig B3.9 Calculating the number of fee-earning hours

			Hours
Assumptions	A 5-day working week		
	A $7\frac{1}{2}$-hour working day		
	Paid annual leave: 20 days		
	Paid public holidays: 8 days		
Total hours	Per year ($52 \times 5 \times 7\frac{1}{2}$)		1,950
	Minus		
	Public holidays ($8 \times 7\frac{1}{2}$)	60	
	Paid holiday ($20 \times 7\frac{1}{2}$)	150	
	Sick leave (say)	40	
		250	250
Fee-earning hours	Number of fee-earning hours per year per full-time member of staff:		**1,700**

Fig B3.10   Calculating the employment costs of fee-earning staff

Column 1	2	3	4	5	6	7	8	9	10
	Basic salary £	Other direct employment costs £	Indirect costs £	Total cost of employment p.a. £	Fee-earning percentage of time %	Fee-earning hours hrs	Cost per fee-earning hour £	Add 20% margin £	Fee-earning potential p.a. £
Principal	40,000	9,000	20,000	69,000	45	765	90	108	82,620
Associate senior professional	30,000	5,000	20,000	55,000	60	1,020	54	65	66,300
Senior professional	25,000	3,000	20,000	48,000	70	1,190	40	48	57,120
Professional	20,000	2,000	20,000	42,000	75	1,275	33	40	51,000
Junior professional	15,000	1,000	20,000	36,000	85	1,445	25	30	43,350

Notes

Column

All figures given are purely illustrative and should not be taken as a realistic guide.

3   Direct costs apart from salary include payroll costs such as bonus, employer's N.I. contributions, and benefits (car, pension, private health etc). These will vary with the grade of staff.

4   Indirect costs ('overheads') include salaries of administrative staff, PI insurance and all costs of running the business that are not specifically project-related. They are divided equally amongst the five categories of staff (and see (6) below).

5   Column 2, 3 and 4 are added together to give column 5.

6   These are the assumed fee-earning percentages shown in Fig B3.8. In practice, the figure for principals will vary widely, and might be a low as 20% – even lower in some cases. In such cases it might be more realistic to redistribute all or part of principals' non-chargeable time as an overhead (ie included in column 4).

7   The column 6 percentages of assumed total available hours per year (ie 1,700, see Fig B3.9) are converted into hours.

8   The cost per fee-earning hour is calculated by dividing total employment costs (column 5) by the number of fee-earning hours (column 7).

9   The figures in column 8 with a 20% weighting. Obviously, the appropriate profit margin will vary according to the particular job.

10   The potential fee income for the grade of staff is calculated by multiplying the number of fee-earning hours (column 7) by the profit-weighted hourly rate (column 9).

(Managing the workload *continued*)

The forecast could take the form of a schedule of all committed work, ie all commissioned projects and any prospectives that are judged likely to materialise. The best way to monitor and control variable data of this kind is to use a computer spreadsheet. There are many add-on packages that work in conjunction with accounting software to forecast fee income on a monthly basis and record fees invoiced and received. In this way a running check can be kept on the status of each project and its performance against target. This allows fine tuning to be done if a lean period is indicated or a possible overrun means there may be a shortage of key staff to start on a new job. If similar information is compiled relating to the actual expenditure of practice overhead costs against budget, a picture of the overall liquidity and profitability of practice finances can be produced.

Speculative work

Carrying out work before a commission has been formalised is obviously risky, although most jobs start off as 'prospectives', to be converted to 'in progress' status when commissioned. In some cases, of course, the project does not proceed and the work done proves abortive. This is of no great consequence if it amounts to a few sketches and the odd meeting, but there must be a defined cut-off point for such 'free' work. Records should be kept of the amount of time spent, and at the cut-off point each should be given a prospective job number and budget. It will then at least be possible to assess the cost of the job realistically and, if it proceeds, even to recover the cost of some of the preliminary work.

Job overruns

As soon as a job overruns, its profits begin to be eroded. The reasons for the overrun must be stringently investigated. The fee quotation or time estimate may have been unrealistic, or the balance of staff assigned to the project may have been inappropriate or their performance inadequate. It may be that work additional to the original commission has 'crept' in. Whatever the reason, the lessons must be learned.

Day to day control

The practice's bank balance must be kept under constant review, so that credit is not exceeded or unnecessary loans maintained. Surplus funds should not be allowed to lie idle, and automatic transfer into an interest-earning account should be considered. Three monthly reviews are suitable for small practices; for larger firms they will need to be more frequent.

It is essential to know exactly where the money goes. A great deal is often lost by careless administration at a day-to-day level. Book-keeping records should be studied and analysed; they will often reveal where waste is occurring and economies can be made, or where stricter control is needed.

An important management consideration is to identify who is responsible for authorising expenditure. Accounting procedures simply expedite the decisions of others; it must always be absolutely clear where the authority for expenditure lies, what limits there are, and to whom the authorising person is accountable.

Accountancy software

There is a wide range of accountancy software, and it is essential that the staff who will be using it have, or acquire, a working knowledge of the basic principles of day-to-day financial accounting, ie book-keeping (see Fig B3.11). Although most accountancy software programs are easy to use, those using them must understand what they are trying to produce and for what purpose. To use computing vernacular, what goes in as garbage will come out as garbage.

The same general caveat applies to all systems, manual or electronic: however sophisticated and time-saving they are, they do not remove the need for sound judgement and thoughtful management.

Fig B3.11 A summary of book-keeping duties

Book-keeping duties are carried out daily, weekly, monthly, quarterly, and annually, and can be summarised as follows:

Daily
Deal with banking, petty cash.
Deal with items received in the mail.
Make appropriate entries in double entry system.
Raise invoices.

Weekly
Verify the situation at the bank.
Review petty cash activities.

Monthly
Send out fee accounts.
Prepare wages and/or send out salary notifications.
Deal with PAYE adjustments.
Settle month end accounts.
Pay office bills.
Compile, record and pay staff expenses.

Prepare financial statements as required for management accounting purposes. These might include:

- cash flows
- profit and loss matched against budget and previous year
- fees outstanding and amounts owing
- bank reconciliation

Quarterly
Prepare VAT return.

Annually
Prepare annual accounts ready for audit by accountant.
Put away the year's files and prepare new.
Compare profit and loss with annual budget.
Prepare annual budget.
Prepare revised budgets (forecasts).

Communication

In offices, oral and written communications often have to pass through various people and processes, and can easily become distorted in transit. If they are not clearly formulated at source and properly directed, they will have little chance of being received and understood, let alone acted upon. In management, it is essential to be certain:

- what information is needed;
- who needs it;
- what form it should take;
- that it will be understood.

Instructions should always be transmitted along designated and recognised channels of authority. If the proper route is bypassed, authority is undermined, the validity of the instruction is in question, and the result is uncertainty and confusion. Whatever the style of management, the procedure for transmitting instructions must be clearly defined and must be followed at all times.

Information tends to proliferate in offices, much of it trivial and unnecessary, and unless priorities are identified and pursued, channels of communication can become overloaded, resulting in delay and frustration. Principals need to keep the situation under constant review, otherwise they may find themselves talking to everyone but failing to communicate with anyone.

C1.1 Office manual

When an architect sets up in practice, a business entity is born with a definable philosophy and character, and with its own objectives, skills and ways of working. As the workload and staff complement grow, it becomes necessary to describe these attributes and activities in some formal manner, so that everyone in the practice can be certain about the way things should be done, where authority resides, and who is responsible for what. Most practices meet this need by compiling an office manual for staff to refer to.

Apart from its crucial role as the base document for developing a quality management system, the office manual is an excellent management tool in its own right, in that it provides support and guidance for staff, clarifies policies and responsibilities and ensures that working procedures and methods are coordinated and effective.

An architect starting up in practice can gradually compile a set of standard policies, formats and procedures, developing these as time goes by into an organised and authoritative collection of facts about the emerging firm and the way it operates, with statements about its aims and objectives and general philosophy. The contents could be arranged looseleaf with card thumbguide dividers to demarcate sections; it is important to be able to update and revise the contents easily so that they remain current. Larger practices are likely to need several manuals covering the firm's activities and may well seek to implement a full quality management system (see B2.8).

Compiling and keeping the office manual up to date is time-consuming and should be someone's designated responsibility; a principal or other senior member of the practice should be in overall charge of it. One or more copies should be kept available for reference by all staff.

A well-organised and informative office manual is an excellent vehicle for communication and an authoritative point of reference. In addition, it saves a great deal of management time by providing ready answers to a multitude of routine queries from staff at all levels. An outline contents list is given as Fig C1.1.

Fig C1.1 Outline contents for an Office Manual

1 **The practice**
Organisation and structure
Aims and objectives
Responsibility and authority
Training and CPD

2 **Office management procedures**
Computer
Post
Correspondence
Filing
Library
Measuring equipment
Archiving and storage

3 **Appointments procedures**
Terms of engagement
Speculative work
Design team appointments
Reports and advisory work

4 **Design management procedures**
Design and production information
Specification writing
Design change control
Health and safety

5 **Job administration and Plan of Work procedures**
Work stage checklists
Health and safety
Permissions and approvals
Cost plans and monitoring
Architect's meetings
Reports to client
Job information records
Site visits

6 **Building contract procedures**
Standard forms
Contract correspondence
Instructions and certificates

7 **General procedures**
Corrective and preventive
Document control
Audits
Feedback

C2.1 Dealing with the post

It is important for this to be handled systematically. One person only should open all the post and deal with it as appropriate. There should be a set of procedures drawn up for receipt and distribution and these should be complied with by all staff. They should be set out in the office or quality management manual, and regularly audited to make sure they remain effective (Fig C2.1).

In small practices a principal usually opens the post, but in larger practices the task may be delegated to a practice administrator. Whoever is responsible must be capable of identifying important and urgent items that need immediate attention. Professional practices get inundated with letters and literature of all kinds, much of it speculative, and it is important that whoever deals with the daily post is not sidetracked by irrelevant items and can be relied upon to discard time-wasting rubbish.

Fig C2.1 Dealing with incoming and outgoing mail

Incoming
Procedures should be put in place to ensure that:

- letters, packets, parcels etc are opened, date-stamped, and recorded;
- items are marked for action and distributed as appropriate;
- drawings received are entered in the appropriate register;
- courier deliveries are signed for and logged, with receipts retained, and recipients alerted about arrival;
- faxes are photocopied and the originals destroyed;
- items marked 'personal' or 'confidential' are given unopened to addressees, but are returned for logging etc if practice-related;
- invoices are passed promptly to accounting staff.

Outgoing
Procedures for controlling outgoing mail should ensure that items:

- are checked and signed by originators;
- have the right enclosures or attachments;
- are correctly franked or stamped;
- are collected for postal or courier transmittal as appropriate;
- achieve intended delivery dates and times.

C2.2 Writing letters

The conventional wisdom that letters require a beginning, a middle and an end is based on sound commonsense. Each element has a distinct and proper function. Fig C2.2 is a checklist.

Letters should be dated correctly, include the relevant references, and give the name and full address of the intended recipient. Informal letters begin *Dear Ms/Mr Jones* and end *Yours sincerely*. Formal letters begin *Dear Sir/Madam* and end *Yours faithfully*. It is important to check that the addressee's name and title are correctly spelt; if in doubt, ring up their office and ask, or consult the relevant directory.

All letters should have their subject headings typed in capital letters or bold so that they can be quickly identified, and to make filing and retrieval easier. The heading can include the in-house job number. Avoid using *Re* before the heading: this is old fashioned and unnecessary.

Fig C2.2 Elements of a letter

Date

Your ref
Our ref (*may include project number*)

(*Name*)
(*Address*)

Dear ...

(*Name of project*)

(*Beginning of letter*)
Thank for letter of (date)
State context of request)

(*Middle of letter*)
Reply as requested, or
Make request for information, state action required

(*End of letter*)
Sum up
Restate view, request
Final greeting

Yours ...

(*Your name and title*)
Encs (or Atts) ...

Copies to: ...

The preferred style of layout is blocked to the left of the page, ie there are no indented paragraphs (see the specimen letters in this section). Punctuation is not included in dates and addresses. Where a choice is available, use a clear typeface such as Times Roman or Univers (like this Handbook) for business correspondence. Be sparing with *italic* script: it is not easy to read in quantity and is best used to emphasise or highlight words, phrases and short items.

Check through the letters after typing or processing and make sure that all enclosures or attachments have been prepared for posting, and appropriate copies made and marked up. Fig C2.3 is a checklist. A compliments slip with the name of the intended recipient should be attached to copies that do not show the office address and other details. Note that compliments slips should not be used where transmittal needs to be recorded, particularly in the case of drawings. The issue, description and despatch of drawings should be carefully recorded in the appropriate register.

Fig C2.3 Checklist before despatch of letter

---

1 Does it include
correct title, name, address of recipient
references (theirs and yours)
job number, date?

2 Is the mode correct
formal/informal?

3 Have I referred correctly to their letter
date, heading?

4 Have I said what I wanted to say clearly, concisely and appropriately?

Will they know
what I am talking about?
what they have to do now?
whether I expect a response and, if so, when?

5 Should I remind or reassure them about anything before I sign off?

Is the final greeting correct and appropriate?

Have the proper enclosures been added?

Has the letter been copied
to the right people?
at the right addresses?

6 Has the letter been properly laid out?
Is it pleasing to look at?
Has the spelling been checked?
Have necessary corrections been made?

7 Is the file copy exactly the same as the despatched version?

8 Have I signed the letter and initialled the copies?

After signing the letter, initial all the copies including the file copy. This is always advisable with formal correspondence and is a good habit to cultivate as a matter of risk management. The writer's name and status should be typed under his or her signature. Lastly, read through the letter and consider it from the recipient's point of view.

- Is its purpose clear?
- Is it well expressed?
- Will they know what action, if any, they should now take?

C2.3 Responding to letters

An incoming letter marked for attention should be read, initialled and date stamped, and a decision made whether it needs immediate action, whether it can or should wait, or whether it can be filed.

When replying to letters, the first rule is always to respond promptly, even if this is only by way of acknowledging receipt while considering how to respond. Preprinted acknowledgment cards are not recommended for use by professional practices: they give an impression of remoteness, tend to get lost or ignored, and are awkward to file.

Fig C2.4 Reminders

Letter one: (Heading)
We do not seem to have received a reply to our letter of (date) about this matter/enclosing our invoice etc. Would you please confirm that you have received it and that you are giving it your attention?

Letter two: (Heading)
We refer to our letters of (date) and (date). Would you please let us have your reply by the (date)/end of the week?

Letter three: (Heading)
We are sorry to note that you have not replied to our letters of (date), (date) and (date). In such circumstances, our standard practice is to withdraw service/credit/instruct solicitor etc. We are reluctant to do so in your case, and hope that your immediate response will make such action unnecessary.

Fig C2.5 Letter to newly appointed clerk of works

Our ref.: BL/HM/Appts97/F
26 June 1997

Mr B Finch
72 Old Common
Wargrave
Berks RG2 8PJ

Dear Mr Finch

APPOINTMENT OF CLERK OF WORKS:
'Treetops' Estate, Chorley

We are pleased to tell you that the employer, (name), has instructed us to confirm your appointment on the terms agreed at interview and as described in the enclosed contract of employment and description of your duties and authority as clerk of works.

Please read these documents carefully and then sign, date and return the contract to us in the enclosed envelope. If there are any matters that you would like to discuss further before signing the contract, please telephone us.

So that you can familiarise yourself with the project, we enclose a set of drawings, bills and specifications as issued to the main contractor.

There is to be an initial project meeting on (date), which you should attend. An agenda is attached. You will see that your duties and responsibilities as clerk of works are to be discussed under (items x and x).

On your first day, please report to the project architect, (name), at this office, and collect a pad of weekly report forms, a daily diary, and a pad of Directions.

We hope that you will enjoy your work on the 'Treetops' project and look forward to your joining us on (date).

Yours sincerely

(name)
Encs
Copy to: (employer)

The second rule is to reply politely – even when the writer seems rude, or is 'fishing', or trying to exert pressure for whatever reason. The temptation to respond to rude people with 'put-down' one-liners should be resisted; a bland reply is often more deflating. Similarly, a fishing letter is best dealt with by a little exposure, such as, *I suspect that what you are really asking me is . . . and, if so, I am afraid I can't help you . . .* A letter refusing some product or service should be firm and unequivocal, otherwise a long and time-consuming correspondence may ensue.

It is good practice to have a standard procedure for issuing reminder letters, such as the set of examples given in Fig C2.4. After sending the third letter, give them a few days' grace, and then be sure to take the action threatened.

A formal letter of appointment should refer to the firm as 'We'. It should confirm the discussion and agreement reached at interview, and may have attachments such as a contract of employment or a statement of working conditions. As examples, two specimen letters connected with the appointment of a clerk of works are given as Figs C2.5 and C2.6.

Fig C2.6 **Letter of refusal**

Our ref.: BL/HM/Appts97/neg
26 June 1997

Mr B Finch
72 Old Common
Wargrave
Berks RG2 8PJ

Dear Mr Finch

APPOINTMENT OF CLERK OF WORKS:
'Treetops' Estate, Chorley

Thank you for coming in for an interview yesterday. I am sorry to tell you that your application has not been successful.

However, we were impressed by your knowledge of the building industry and your interest and enthusiasm, and we will keep you in mind when and if other appointments are being made.

Yours sincerely

(name)

C2.4 Contractual correspondence

Letters, AIs, site meeting minutes and notes of inspections connected with contract works are part of the history of that contract, and if there is any subsequent court action, they will be part of the evidence. Therefore it is crucial for them to be clearly expressed and unambiguous. Many disputes arise simply because letters and instructions are misunderstood. Fig C2.7 is a checklist.

Fig C2.7 Checklist for contractual correspondence

Use a formal style
Letters connected with contractual matters are always formal. Start and end them *Dear Sir – Yours faithfully*. Be sure to refer to yourself as *We*, not *I*.

Get the references right
The main heading will be the name of the contract works and any project number. Always date the document as the date of issue, not the date it was drafted.

State the relevant clause in the contract
Quote the clause number in the contract that relates to the subject of the letter or AI with the name of the form of contract under which the works are being carried out. (*This request is made in accordance with Clause . . . of IFC 84.*) Check that you have got it right.

Quote drawing numbers correctly
It is equally important to quote drawing numbers and their titles exactly and fully.

Refer to events precisely
State the relevant date and where necessary the location.

Keep sentences short and language simple
Contract provisions are often expressed in a convoluted way and this tends to creep into the rest of the correspondence. Write as clearly as possible.

Remember to send copies to all the relevant parties
Some architects believe in copying all job-related correspondence to the client as a matter of course. You *must* copy all contract-related correspondence to the client.

Consult your solicitor
Be sure to do this whenever a situation arises where there may be legal repercussions; he or she will advise you in the light of the particular circumstances.

Advise your insurers
Similarly, you must advise your insurers immediately of any circumstances likely to give rise to a claim. Failure to notify in good time can be a valid reason for their refusing to indemnify you.

Don't ignore claims
Respond if claims or allegations are made, but always take legal advice about the form of your reply.

'Powers' and 'duties'
Under a building contract, the architect has 'powers' and 'duties'. Make sure that you know the difference between them. A power is usually expressed as *the architect may;* a duty as *the architect shall*.

'Without prejudice'
It is a common misconception that heading a letter 'Without Prejudice' in some way protects the author from its contents. *It only does this in certain, special circumstances.* For the purposes of business correspondence, always assume that it does *not*. Again, consult your solicitor.

There has been an information explosion over the last 20 years, evidenced by:

- new primary information in the form of regulations, standards and codes, technological developments and products;
- new secondary information to explain it all, eg official guidance, textbooks and research reports, manufacturers' literature;
- new information systems, to allow organised access to this vast body of information.

The paperless office confidently predicted some years ago remains an attractive theory. The popularity of the paper product continues because it is available, portable, and can be circulated round the office. Its use does not depend on special equipment. That said, some practices now have most of their practice database information in electronic form and make use of on-line access to external information, and some have fully integrated management information systems which can be accessed by everyone in the organisation.

An architect setting up in practice will be primarily concerned with the need to manage and maintain reference material, files and records, publicity material, archives, and quality management documents.

C3.1 Library services

The library will be the source of most of the technical, practice and legal information needed by staff working on projects. It will be in constant use, and information must be adequate and up to date. It must be properly resourced, both in terms of budget and, where appropriate, staff. It must be clear who is responsible for maintaining library information; if there is no dedicated librarian, an appropriate member of staff should be put in charge.

Libraries do not run themselves: there are tasks to be carried out on a day to day basis such as ordering, accessions, periodicals, classification, microfilming and indexing. Someone will need to spend a good deal of time monitoring construction industry events and information, dealing with manufacturers' representatives and, as necessary, undertaking research. It may also fall to the 'librarian' of a small practice to compile the practice's brochure and other publicity material such as press releases, advertisements, directory entries, practice newsletters and so on (see B2.7). Another designated activity might be the storage and labelling of manufacturers' samples and yet another the compilation of computer databases. A checklist of library contents is given as Fig C3.1.

Library space and layout should be considered in relation to the practice's size and the nature of its premises. Accessibility is important and so is the provision of adequate shelving, bearing in mind that even the best-managed libraries expand – they never contract. Where possible, working space should be provided, so that activities connected with cataloguing, publicity material and archiving can be carried out within the library area. Space may also be needed for computers to allow access to on-line information services, practice databases, and for microfilm and microfiche readers. Adequate user space must also be provided for browsing and reference.

Classification

An appropriate classification system should be used in the practice library. CI/SfB is in general use in the construction industry, but is likely to be replaced in the long term by Uniclass, which was developed for the Construction Project Information Committee (CPIC) and was published in 1997. Uniclass is more comprehensive and flexible than CI/SfB and is able to cover the many new categories of information which have developed since CI/SfB was introduced more than 30 years ago. An example table from Uniclass is included as Fig C3.2.

Fig C3.1 Checklist of library contents

Quick reference collection
Items in constant use or of broad application, such as:
– CI/SfB manual/Uniclass manual
– Barbour Compendium
– RIBA Product Selector
– RIBA KeyFile Library
– dictionary
– telephone directories

Non-trade literature
Books
Pamphlets
Official publications
British Standards
Journal extracts/cuttings/research

Trade literature
Manufacturers' catalogues
Product data sheets

Samples
Materials, eg
– glass types
– timber species
– others
Products, eg
– bricks
– ironmongery
– others

Periodicals
Current (on display)
Back numbers (shelved)

Maps

In-house information
Central collection of the practice's own literature:
– promotional brochures
– office manual
– standard specification
– preferred details
– approved contractors lists
– technical data and feedback
– in-house magazines

Stock of standard forms
RIBA contract administration forms
In-house standard forms

Computers
Computers, modems and terminals for:
– internal indexes and databases
– RIBA disc
– CD-ROMs from external sources
– external on-line information systems
– internet access

Microfilm
Microfilm and fiche reader/printers for:
– commercial micro-file systems
– own archives

Visual aids
Wallcharts, posters etc
Slide sets
Films
Videos

Fig C3.2 Uniclass table

Management Concise Table

C1 Management theory, systems and activities

C11 Corporate strategy
C12 Quality management
C13 Security, industrial espionage, trade secrets
C14 Objective setting
C15 Decision making
C16 Problem solving
C17 Co-ordination
C18 Appraisal, assessment
C19 Other

C2 Management personnel

C21 Top management, directors, partners
C22 Other levels of management

C3 Type of business/organisation

C31 Organisations by scale and location
C32 Private enterprises
C33 Mixed enterprises and partnerships
C34 Government and related organisations
C35 Public enterprises
C36 Non-profit-making organisations, charities
C37 Industrial and commercial associations
C38 Construction industry
C39 Other types of organisation

C4 Specialist areas of management

C41 Management of office services
C42 Marketing, selling
C43 Research and development
C44 Finance and accounting, business economics
C45 Personnel management and industrial relations
C46 Management of computing, information technology

C5/C9 Management of construction activities/project management

C50 General techniques/information

C61 Inception/procurement
C62 Feasibility
C63 Outline proposals/programme preparation
C64 Scheme design/costing
C65 Detail design/costing
C66 Production information
C67 Bills of quantities
C68 Tender action

C71 Construction preparation/project planning
C72 Construction operations on site
C73 Completion

C81 Occupation/facilities management
C83 Feedback
C84 Refurbishment and recommissioning

C91 Decommissioning
C92 Demolition etc.
C93 Redevelopment

RIBA Office Library Service

Few practices can afford to employ a full time librarian in house, but the RIBA Office Library Service is used by numerous practices to maintain and update their library of product literature, and the OLS can provide the latest information on publications, products and other services available from the RIBA and RIBA Companies. For a very small practice it may be more economic to use a freelance librarian from time to time. The Construction Industry Information Group (CIIG) can provide a directory of freelance members.

External reference sources

Practices should also take full advantage of the many outside information services that are available, some of them on-line. The professional institution libraries, notably the RIBA's British Architectural Library, are excellent sources of information in their respective fields, as are the libraries of large specialist institutions and government bodies. Access to non-members is often available, sometimes by arrangement, and it may also be possible to borrow books and other material.

British Library

BL is the foremost copyright deposit library and its coverage is unequalled. Its lending division is the British Library Document Supply Centre at Wetherby in West Yorkshire. It has a collection of more than 7 million journals, theses, books, conference proceedings and reports. It provides loan and photocopying services and orders can be processed on-line. It will loan documents not normally lent from other libraries, such as directories, whole journal issues and British Standards. It also has an Urgent Action service.

Annual audit

An annual review of practice library services should be carried out, and the principal questions to be asked are:

- Is the practice being provided with the scope of information it needs?
- Is the information provided relevant, adequate and up to date?
- Are staff clear about who is in charge of library resources and activities?
- Is the library budget sufficient?

C3.2 Files and records

A systematic approach to filing is essential if an office is to run smoothly and efficiently. It is important to set up a filing system that will serve the practice over a long period and can be expanded as its workload grows.

Administrative

Administrative documents are typically produced in-house and will be mainly to do with practice organisation, finance, staff matters, publicity, and premises management. There will be a wide range of miscellaneous topics and related paperwork which may need temporary filing and which should be ruthlessly pruned out of the system if and when they become redundant. An alphabetical checklist for administration files is given in Fig C3.3, together with an indication of how CI/SfB or Uniclass might be used to provide a classified arrangement.

Project records

Project records usually consist of paper items (correspondence, contract documents, forms, reports, instructions), and drawings, photographs and models. Some of these items are bulky and/or need special storage, and Fig C3.4 demonstrates a classified arrangement of project files that takes account of this.

Fig. C3.3 Filing arrangements for administrative documents

Administration filing:
Framework based on CI/SfB Table 4

Practice organisation
Communications
Preparation of documentation
Public relations
Controls and procedures
Personnel
Education, training, CPD
Research and development, O & M
Accommodation
Secretarial activities
Copying, photocopying
Filing
Finance
Projects

Administration filing:
Framework based on Uniclass

C1	Management theory and systems	C45	Personnel management
C11	Corporate strategy	C452	Recruitment
C12	Quality management	C453	Training/CPD
C123	Quality assurance	C454	Communication
C19	Other	C455	Industrial relations
C193	Awards	C456	Conditions of employment
		C457	Remuneration
C2	Management personnel	C458	Working conditions
C4	Specialist areas of management	C5/C9	Projects
		C50	General techniques/ standard procedures
C41	Office services		
C411	Switchboard		
C412	Reception	C81	Facilities management
C413	Security	C811	Premises
C414	Secretarial	C812	Space management, equipment
C415	Mail management		
C416	Reprography	C813	Contract office services
C417	Records management	C814	Premises services
C4171	Documentation/filing	C8141	Catering
C4172	Stationery, forms	C8145	Transport/company cars
C4173	Library/archives		
C42	Marketing	C8146	Communications/ mobile phones
C423	Promotion		
C4231	Advertising	C815	Maintenance and operation
C4236	Press releases		
C4237	Promotional publications	C8153	Cleaning
		C8159	Health and safety at work
C43	Research and development		
C44	Finance and accounting	C816	Emergency procedures

Administration filing:
Categories of financial documents

Original documents
Books of original entry
– day books
– cash books
Ledgers
Trial balances
Final accounts
Forecasts
Assessments
VAT records
Tax records
Administration
Reference*

*useful data such as interest rates,
research notes, checklists

Administration filing:
A–Z checklist of subjects

Administration
Archives
Classification
Commissions
Communications
Computers
Drawing office practice
Education, training, CPD
Equipment
Finance
General administration
General office routines
Information system
Institutes and associations
Insurances
Library
Management
Marketing
Office organisation
People, roles
Petty cash

Post room
The practice
Practice control
Practice development
Practice philosophy
Practice structure
Premises
Project control
Project planning
Publicity
Purchases
Quality assurance
Quality control
Reprographics
Secretarial practice
Staff
Subscriptions
Technical procedures
Transport
Travel

Fig C3.4 Filing arrangement for project documents

PART 1
CORRESPONDENCE AND
PAPERS
(mainly filed)

0   GENERAL
0.1   General

1   CLIENT
1.0   General
1.1   Project manager
1.2   ...
       (subdivide by
       departments as
       appropriate)

2   DESIGN TEAM
2.1   Design team meetings
       and programme
2.2   Project manager
2.3   Architect
2.4   Quantity surveyor
2.5   Structural engineer
2.6   Building services
       engineer
2.7   Mechanical engineer
2.8   Electrical engineer
2.9   Lift engineer
2.10   Drainage engineer
2.11   Civil engineer
2.12   Windows consultant
2.13   Lighting consultant
2.14   Acoustic consultant
2.15   Interior designer
2.16   Landscape architect
2.17   Perspective artist
2.18   Modelmaker
2.19   Photographer
2.20   Planning Supervisor
2.21   Principal Contractor

3   STATUTORY
      CONSENTS, NOTICES
      AND CONSULTATIONS
3.0   General

Client-related interests
3.1   Ministry
3.2   Landlord etc
3.3   Funder
3.4   Insurers
3.5   Users, tenants,
       community
3.6   Adjoining owners

Planning and
construction
3.7   Building regulations
       and byelaws
3.8   Disabled access and
       facilities
3.9   Drainage
3.10   Fire
3.11   Health and safety
3.12   Highways
3.13   Means of escape
       Party walls
3.14   Public health
3.15   Town planning

Miscellaneous
3.16   ...

4   PUBLIC SERVICES
4.0   General, co-ordination
4.1   Electricity
4.2   Gas
4.3   Post
4.4   Refuse
4.5   Sewer connection
4.6   Street lighting
4.7   Telephone
4.8   Water
4.9   Work on public
       highways and
       pavements

5   MAIN CONTRACTOR
5.0   General
5.1   Touting from
       contractors
5.2   Pre-tender enquiries
5.3   Tendering
5.4   Main contractor

6   SUBCONTRACTORS
      AND SUPPLIERS
6.0   General
6.1   Touting from
       subcontractors and
       suppliers (SCs and Ss)
6.2   Enquiries and
       quotations
6.3   Surveys and advance
       contracts
6.4   Bulk quotations/bulk
       purchase/direct supply
6.5   Nominated SCs and Ss
6.6   Named SCs and Ss
6.7   Domestic SCs and Ss
6.8   Works contractors
6.9   Independent works
       and supplies

7   CONTRACT
      ADMINISTRATION
7.0   General

Meetings and progress
7.1   Briefing meetings
7.2   Site meetings
7.3   Programmes
7.4   Progress reports

Site staff
communications
7.5   Clerk of works reports
7.6   Clerk of works
       correspondence
7.7   Site staff
       correspondence
7.8   Site visits and
       inspections

Instructions
7.9   Clerk of works
       directions
7.10   Site instructions and
       draft instructions
7.11   Contractor's
       confirmation of verbal
       orders (CVOs)
7.12   Architect's instructions
7.13   Drawing issue notes

Quality control
7.14   Sample notes and test
       results
7.15   Defects schedules
       (pre-handover)
7.16   Handover and defects
       records
7.17   Making good defects
       records – buildings
7.18   Ditto – services
7.19   Ditto – landscape

Cost control
7.20   Cost control reports
7.21   Dayworks and
       overtime records

Claims
7.22   Claims records

Certificates
7.23   Valuations and
       certificates for
       payment
7.24   Certificates –
       extension of time
7.25   Ditto – practical
       completion
7.26   Ditto – making good
       defects
7.27   Ditto – others

Other
7.28   ...

8   WORKING PAPERS
8.0   General
8.1   Brief and client's
       instructions record
8.2   Surveys and
       investigations
8.3   Specification notes
       and schedules
8.4   Quantities information
8.5   Calculation sheets
8.6   Information for
       maintenance manual
8.7   Data on project
8.8   Costing
8.9   Ceremonies
8.10   Awards
8.11   Publicity
8.12   Press cuttings
8.13   Internal memos
8.14   Miscellaneous
       correspondence
8.15   Miscellaneous
       meetings
8.16   Miscellaneous reports
8.17   Miscellaneous papers

9   LATE ADDITIONS AND
      SPECIAL EXERCISES
9.0   General
9.1   Post-completion filing
9.2   Specific claims,
       arbitrations etc

PART 2
SPECIAL DOCUMENTS
(mainly bulky)

10   GENERAL
      DOCUMENTS
10.1   Job book/building
       record
10.2   Drawing register

11   LEGAL DOCUMENTS
11.1   Agreements
       (consultants)
11.2   Contracts (contractors)
11.3   Collateral warranties

12   PROJECT
      DOCUMENTS
12.1   Soil report
12.2   Design reports
12.3   Job literature (eg trade
       catalogues, official
       publications)
12.4   Specifications
12.5   Bills of quantities and
       priced schedules
12.6   Site records
12.7   Weather records
12.8   Maintenance
       manual/tenant's
       handbook
12.9   Health and safety file
12.10 Final account
12.11 ...

13   DRAWINGS
13.0   General
13.1   Site survey
13.2   Sketches
13.3   Design set
13.4   Special presentation
       or publicity drawings
13.5   Perspectives
13.6   Consents sets
13.7   BQ/tender set
13.8   Contract set
13.9   Site records
13.10 As-built sets
13.11 Drawings by others
       (sub-divide by
       originator and then
       subdivide as above or
       keep in numerical
       order)
13.12 CAD records
13.13 CAD disks

14   PHOTOGRAPHS
14.0   General
14.1   Site
14.2   Design drawings
14.3   Model
14.4   Progress
14.5   Defects
14.6   As built
14.7   Publicity
14.8   ...

15   MODELS
15.1   ...

Many disputes arise simply because there are inadequate written records. Good records, systematically stored and easily retrievable, are an essential part of risk management.

Records should be made and kept of all meetings, the advice given by consultants, including the architect, and of the considerations which influenced the many decisions taken during the design process. Architects constantly have to make difficult judgements and consider compromise solutions, and must be able to justify their decisions on the basis of contemporary records. Job and office diaries should be compiled legibly and systematically and kept with other project records for as long as the practice retains any liability for a project.

Databases

In-house computer databases for the storage and retrieval of information are widely used for job lists, job records, lists of clients, lists of contractors, indexes (of reports, files), library catalogue etc. They may be part of an integrated management information system but it must be made clear who is responsible for their compilation and maintenance.

External databases can be accessed via various commercial on-line services or purchased CD-ROMs. Reference databases include bibliographic information, sometimes with abstracts; catalogues of library stock or library network; and directory information, eg names and addresses of organisations. Source databases contain the original source material in machine-readable form, eg newspaper stories, statistical surveys, company annual reports.

Promotional material

The items which will need to be collected and developed are considered under B2.7. In a small practice, responsibility for publicity and PR will need to be designated and may be included as part of library duties. Whatever the arrangement, there should be a separate budget allocation, and cost-effectiveness should be kept under review.

C3.3 Archives

The storage of records that are no longer active needs special consideration. A policy should be developed as to how this is to be done and for what time period, and who is to be responsible for making such decisions. Some may need to be kept for a specified period for reasons of liability; some may be intrinsically valuable and need carefully preserving, perhaps by donating them appropriately – to the British Architectural Library, for example, or to CIRCA (Construction Industry Resource Centre Archive).

Storage is always a problem for architects, because each project generates a large quantity of documentation – drawings in particular, which are large and unwieldy. Most practices are short of storage space, and consideration may need to be given to storage out of house, or on computer, or on microfilm. There are many specialist firms offering secure storage, although they tend to be expensive. Storage on computer will suit some items, but duplicate hard copies will often be needed, and should be stored well away from the computer area in a fire-proof container.

From the management point of view, it is essential that archived material can be accessed without difficulty when and if it is needed. This means developing clear procedures for indexing and the accessing and return of material. If the practice has no librarian, someone senior must made responsible for controlling this important activity. Procedures should be set out in the office Quality Manual and audited regularly.

It should be clear to all participants why a meeting is necessary and what it seeks to achieve; in architectural practice, meetings are typically called to review progress and get decisions approved. The people who attend should have the appropriate authority to act in accordance with the decisions taken.

All meetings should have a proper structure and most will benefit from an agenda, sent out in good time before the meeting. This not only focuses the minds of the people attending on the issues to be discussed but provides a framework of control for the meeting itself. A model general purpose notice and agenda is given as Fig C4.1.

The meetings that job architects normally call, chair and minute include:

- the initial design team meeting;
- the initial project team meeting;
- any site inspectorate briefing meeting needed;
- the architect's regular progress meetings.

Fig C4.1 Specimen notice and agenda

NOTICE OF MEETING AND AGENDA

Name of project   **Job no.**

Type of meeting   **Meeting no.**

This meeting will be held at Sparrow & Grebe's offices at (*time*) on (*date*). It is expected to end at (*time*).

There will be a (*forty minute*) break for lunch/A sandwich lunch will be provided during the meeting.

Apologies, names of replacements should be notified to (*name of architect or secretary*).

AGENDA

1 Minutes of last meeting

2 Matters arising

3 (Item for discussion)

4 ditto

5 ditto, etc.

6 Any other business

7 Date of next meeting (*if any, with details of time and place*)

Distribution: (names of people or organisations invited/expected to attend)

Date: (agenda was issued)

C4.1 Taking meetings

It is essential to keep control, otherwise the purpose of the meeting may be defeated and a great deal of time wasted. Confining discussion to the points at issue usually requires good humour and diplomacy, but it may sometimes be desirable to allow grievances to be aired and to encourage the less articulate and self-confident to have their say. If it is appreciated that the chairperson is prepared to be reasonable and considerate but will not tolerate time-wasting and pointless argument, the meeting is more likely to run smoothly.

Meetings should start on time, with the chair calling the room to order firmly but pleasantly. Then he or she should identify those present, introduce newcomers or replacements, ask for apologies for absence and mention any already received. The minutes of the last meeting should then be accepted, with any agreed corrections noted. Their acceptance as a fair record of the previous meeting is usually recorded as item 1 of the new set of minutes. In the case of formal meetings it is important to follow these procedures so as to achieve a true and agreed record which can subsequently be referred to with confidence.

It is then usual to take *Matters Arising* from the previous minutes. Discussion of these should be strictly limited, and any attempt to introduce a new topic or an agenda item at this stage should be resisted – new items should be raised under *Any Other Business* at the end of the meeting, and agenda items should not be discussed out of sequence. A note should be made of any important points made and these should be included in the next set of minutes under *Matters Arising* with their previous numerical references.

Agenda items should be taken in their set order, only departing from this if there is some cogent reason for doing so. It is useful to sum up at the end of each item, especially if discussion has been lengthy, and to repeat the decisions made and actions to be taken. If the chair is also taking the minutes, time should be allowed to check that an adequate note has been made before taking the next agenda item. When these have all been properly dealt with, new issues may be raised under *Any Other Business*.

Lastly, the chair should thank those present for attending, make sure that notes taken are in good order and that he or she has a copy of anything tabled at the meeting in preparation for writing up the minutes.

C4.2 Minuting meetings

Minutes are a written record of the significant items of business transacted at a meeting. They have a number of important functions:

- they record why the meeting was called, what it achieved, and what further actions are needed;
- they provide a record by which future progress can be measured;
- they are a means of reporting the proceedings to interested parties;
- they constitute a record which may be relied upon in the future.

Architects, especially in their early years of professional life, often have to chair meetings and minute them, and many find this difficult and worrying. Fortunately, minuting is a skill that improves with practice, although it always needs a high degree of concentration. If the meeting itself is run competently, minuting it will be that much easier.

It is important to draft minutes while the meeting is still fresh in one's mind. The primary decision to be made is what to include and what to exclude, as a full record is rarely appropriate. The art is to identify priorities. It is essential to record some things (decisions, actions to be taken) and relevant to record others (changes in situation, strongly opposing views). It may be desirable to include some parts of the remaining proceedings – and equally desirable to exclude others. This is where discretion must be exercised.

When writing up minutes, care should be taken to link people with views expressed and actions to be taken. An *Actions* column running down the page to the right of the text is a good way of focusing the attention of recipients on follow-up actions. Formal meetings are written in 'reported speech', ie events are put into the past and the style is observational. Although many of the meetings connected with architectural practice are informal or semi-formal in character and will not require stringent grammatical attention, it is no less important for them to provide a well expressed and unambiguous record that can be relied on in the future.

The aim should always be to issue minutes within a few days of the meeting, and in any case well in advance of the next, if this is a series of meetings. The sooner the minutes are issued, the more time people will have to take the action or obtain the information required of them and the more likely they are to make a satisfactory contribution to the next meeting.

For more detailed guidance about practice correspondence and minuting, refer to *Writing Matters* (RIBA Publications).

C4.3 In-house talks and seminars

Practices may consider holding occasional, or even a series, of in-house talks or seminars to disseminate project or research information, or as a matter of continuing professional development. These need to be well managed, and consideration should be given to the following:

- the structure and content of the programme overall, and who is expected to attend or participate;
- who is to be responsible for the programme overall and each event on the day;
- the likely costs and what budget should be allowed;
- the timing of events;
- finding a suitable venue with adequate facilities;
- identifying speakers or presenters with the appropriate expertise and knowledge;
- ways of promoting the programme so as to attract speakers and ensure a good attendance.

Fig C4.2 is a checklist. Any kind of learning programme may be intrinsically useful and valuable to the participants, but it will only be of real benefit when the lessons can be applied while they are still clearly in mind. With in-house events, this should be relatively easy to achieve because the participants will probably be dealing with topics which are of immediate concern to the practice. Otherwise, every effort should be made to capitalise on newly acquired skills, information and interests. If this is left uptapped for too long, the real impact and benefit may be lost.

Fig C4.2 Organising an in-house event

1 **Who is it for?**
Students, mid-career architects,
management, non-technical staff

2 **What are the options?**
Do it yourself
Collaborate with other practices
Bring in external organisers

3 **What kind of programme?**
The approach: reactive, proactive,
anecdotal
The event: talk, workshop, forum,
video etc

4 **Organisation and planning**
Decide who is to be responsible
Set a budget
Decide timing and venue
Plan necessary publicity
Assess what clerical and catering
support is needed
Approach speakers, presenters

5 **Running the event**
Make room booking, hire equipment
Prepare questionnaires for feedback
Brief the chair about speakers,
timetable
On the day:
Prepare and check the venue
Check that equipment functions
properly
Do a dry run of the event

6 **The role of the chair**
Introduce the event
Manage speakers and audience
Keep to the timetable
Wind up

7 **How did it go?**
Issue questionnaires to participants
and audience
Evaluate the event as a whole
Report the event as appropriate
Learn the lessons for next time

Job architects spend a great deal of their time engaged in writing project reports of various kinds. A client who is kept properly informed and involved will be able to deal promptly with report recommendations and give appropriate instructions. Prior to design development, reports normally fall into two main categories: surveys, and feasibility studies. Once a full architectural service has been commissioned, there will be regular reports to be made to the client at the completion of work stages.

C5.1 Surveys

Surveys commonly undertaken by job architects will be to do with the land or the site and/or existing buildings. The subject is well covered in the *Architect's Job Book*, to which reference should be made. The advice included on conducting and reporting a survey of an existing building is given here as Fig C5.1.

Specially commissioned surveys such as those for prospective house purchasers, building societies, commercial enterprises and church authorities may also be undertaken, but these often carry risks for architects which should be properly understood (see F5).

Fig C5.1 Guidance on surveys of existing buildings

It is essential that the architect personally walks through every room in the building to be surveyed, regardless of whether the survey is being done by in-house personnel or by a surveying firm. It is important to perceive the architectural character of a building and the way it has been constructed.

The measured survey drawings might show:

- plans, sections, elevations;
- elevational features, eg plinths, string courses, openings;
- precise levels at floors, datum, thickness and construction;
- levels of external ground;
- details of decoration, profiles, false columns etc;
- finishes and colours;
- loose equipment, landlord's fittings etc.

A written report might include information that cannot be shown graphically, such as:

- structural and other defects and their causes;
- dry rot, damp penetration, condensation;
- infestation by rodents, beetles and other insects;
- recent repairs and decoration;
- settlement cracks, mis-shapen openings, gaps at skirtings and windows;
- walls that are misaligned or have bulges;
- sagging roofs, defective roof coverings;
- deflection of beams or lintels, cracks at beam bearings.

The architects/surveyors should state whether or not they were able to see inside the structure of the building and how much they were able to see. It is important not to infer the state of the whole building from sight of one part of it. A statement on the following lines should appear at the end of the relevant part of the report (as stipulated in most professional indemnity policies):

'It has not been possible to make a detailed examination of the floor or roof construction except at the positions described because material damage would have been caused in gaining access. It is therefore impossible to make any statement about the condition of the unexamined structure.'

Where appropriate, the client should be advised to call in specialists, eg mechanical, electrical, timber treatment, and should be asked for instructions regarding any fees, expenses and inconvenience arising from their investigations.

C5.2 Feasibility studies

The Stage B project feasibility report is especially important, since the client's decision whether or not to proceed will be based on what it says.
Depending on the project's complexity, feasibility may need investigating by means of various and sometimes numerous exploratory studies. These can range from simple assessments of possibilities to sophisticated and extensive research into social, industrial and economic factors. Only some of these areas will be within the average architect's expertise. It is important to recognise one's limitations and not try to take on unsuitable work which could overstretch the practice and even put it at risk.

In broad terms, the Stage B report will consist of:

- a statement of its purpose;
- its findings;
- its proposals and recommendations;
- the decisions required from the client;
- any supporting material.

C5.3 Design development

At the completion of each of Work Stages C, D and E a report will be sent to the client advising progress and seeking approval to proceed to the next stage. It will summarise the present position on the brief, site matters, consents and approvals, and relevant contractual matters (see Fig C5.2).

Fig C5.2 Stages C, D and E reports

Stage C
At the close of Stage C, the report to the client might:

- summarise the design work so far;
- present outline proposals;
- make recommendations including an approximation of cost and an outline programme for the project;
- suggest a method of procurement;
- append relevant supporting information and drawings;

Stage D
At the close of Stage D, the report to the client might show the development of the scheme in respect of:

- planning permission;
- the appearance of the building;
- materials and methods of construction;
- services systems;
- outline specifications;
- special features as required;
- a cost estimate and a programme for the project.

Stage E
The report at the close of Stage E might:

- confirm completion of the detailed brief in line with the outline specification and agreed materials and methods of construction;
- describe how the client's specific requirements for plant, equipment, services, layouts, and the fitting out of special areas are to be met;
- report on statutory approvals;
- include revised cost estimates and a programme for the project.

Reports to client should be clear, concise and well presented. It is important to pursue a consistent structure and format and maintain it throughout the series of reports. A judgement should be made about the client's level of technical knowledge and explanations included as necessary. Each Stage report should have a covering letter requesting the client's written approval of the report and its proposals, and asking for instructions to proceed.

C5.4 Work in progress

Once site operations commence, the client will expect to be kept informed about the progress of the work, usually in the form of a report at regular intervals with a detailed statement of expenditure, an appraisal of the current position and a forecast of total costs. Cost reports are normally prepared by the quantity surveyor, but where no QS has been appointed (eg for minor works), these may have to be prepared by the architect. A specimen financial report to client is given as Fig C5.3.

The client should always be sent a copy of the minutes of architect's progress meetings and copies of correspondence relating to notices of delay and the award of any extensions of time. Similarly the client should be kept informed of any problems concerning materials and workmanship where it becomes necessary to issue architect's instructions. He should also be advised in good time about such matters as maintenance contracts and any need to instruct staff about the operation of installations.

C5.5 Site inspection reports

The purpose of site visits is to observe and comment. Checks of a general nature might include:

- whether quality complies with the provisions of the contract;
- whether progress accords with the contractor's master programme;
- whether essential parts of the design have been or are being carried out in accordance with contract provisions.

Reports of site visits are not usually sent to the client, but they should be prepared to a consistent format and written up as soon after the visit as possible. Record photographs (dated), notes and sketches should be attached and carefully filed. Fig C5.4 is a specimen site visit report form.

Fig C5.3   Specimen financial report to client

Job no: Job title:

Financial report to client

To end of (month) (year)	Savings £	Extras £	£
Financial approvals Contract sum as adjusted			
Additional approvals to date of last report			
Total approvals to date of last report			
Adjustments Contract sum as adjusted including contingencies			
Cost adjustment on PC sums ordered			
Cost adjustment on provisional sums			
Value of AIs issued to date			
Changes of work anticipated			
Contingencies Original contingencies sum £			
Estimated proportion £ absorbed to date			
Estimated remainder £			
Cost of works Estimated cost of works £ including contingencies sum			
Reconciliation Variations instructed by the employer since last report			
(a) [addition] estimated cost			
(b) [omission] estimated saving			
Additional approvals to last report			
Final estimate Estimated final expenditure on present information			
Not included in assessments: VAT, fees, other works (eg piling, landscape, advance orders)			

Fig C5.4   Specimen site visit report

Job no: _____   Job title: _____

Site visit report

Date _____   No. of visits scheduled _____

Visit by _____   Visit no. _____

Purpose
_____
_____
_____
_____
_____
_____
_____
_____
_____

Observed
_____
_____
_____
_____
_____
_____
_____
_____
_____
_____
_____
_____
_____
_____
_____
_____

Checked   **Recorded**

Samples _____   Photos _____

Verification of tests _____   _____

Vouchers _____   Video _____

Records _____   Other _____

Summary   ☐ Work properly executed   ☐ Proceeding in workmanlike manner

☐ Materials properly stored and protected   ☐ Progress to programme

At some time in their professional lives, most architects will be required to present a formal commissioned report and need to know how to tackle what is often a demanding task.

Reports commissions are formally accepted in writing and their cost is negotiated and agreed, usually on a time-charge basis. Their contents are the property of the commissioning person or organisation and are kept confidential. This may be important for commercial reasons, or the report may concern an investigation into alleged defects which could give rise to litigation. Such work is often unexpectedly time-consuming, and should only be taken on after fully considering the implications in terms of staff effort and availability and what repercussions there may be on other work in progress.

C6.1 Report structure

All reports have a basic structure and rationale, regardless of the complexity or otherwise of their content. As can be seen in Fig C6.1, a formal report consists of a main text preceded by introductory items, and followed by supporting material.

Formal report writing

Fig C6.1 Outline report structure

	Title page
	Summary of report
	Contents page
	Glossary
1.0	**Introduction**
1.1	The brief
1.2	Background
1.3	Scope of report
1.4	Methodology
2.0	**Findings**
2.1	Site
2.2	Buildings etc
3.0	**Conclusions and recommendations**
3.1	Conclusions
3.2	Recommendations
4.0	**Remedial proposals**
4.1	Options available
4.2	Costs
4.3	Recommendations
	References
	Appendices
	Bibliography

C6.1.1 Preliminary items

Title Page
This should show the report's title and job number, status (draft, interim, final etc), date, and the name and address of the client. Report covers can become detached with handling or during storage and may be lost. As a result, the report may be difficult to identify, particularly if a considerable time has elapsed since it was written or if it was one of a series. Therefore as well as giving full details of origination on the title page, this should be repeated at the end of the report after the appropriate signatures.

Summary of Report
A separate summary of findings, conclusions and recommendations is sometimes attached to the front of the report immediately after the title page. This can be useful where the report is lengthy, makes numerous recommendations, or is for the use of a committee. In the very rare case of the report's findings being newsworthy, such a summary could be used as a press handout, and can be written in the manner of a news item.

Contents List
All the contents of the report should be listed, including any appended items.

Glossary
When a report contains numerous specialist or technical terms, it is sensible to include a glossary to explain them. It is most helpful if it appears at the front of the report, usually just after the contents page. List the items alphabetically and make sure that the explanations are clearly given in plain English.

C6.1.2. Main text

Introduction
The introductory section establishes the terms of reference for the report, gives relevant background information to put it in context, defines its scope and describes the way the investigation has been tackled.

The Brief
The instructions from the client constitute the terms of reference for the report. They will state:

- who the report is for;
- why it has been commissioned;
- what it is about;
- when it will be completed;
- who will be writing it.

There may also be instructions about the way it should be presented.

It is usual to include an account of the commissioning process in this section, on the following lines:

On [date] we were instructed by Mr E C Jay, Estates Officer for ABACUS (UK) Developments Ltd to carry out an investigation of ... ... and present our findings as a draft report to be submitted to the Corfield Housing Committee on [date]. We accepted this commission by letter on [date], saying that the investigation would be made by CJ Perrin DipArch and WC Lea DipArch.

Where desirable, copies of the exchange of commissioning letters may be included in an appendix.

Background Information
This section is sometimes called *History of the Project*. It contains information about why the report has been commissioned, so that it can be read in proper context. For example, the subject of the report might be an unpopular housing estate where there had been a long history of vandalism and neglect and where many attempts had been made to mitigate its problems. It would be relevant to say what those problems are or were, what solutions were tried out, by whom and to what effect. It might be appropriate to include a map of the locality.

Scope of Report
For example:

The report covers all the two-storey terraced dwellings in Phases 1 and 2 of the development, but excludes all the 3-storey dwellings in Phase 2. It was agreed [with the client] that the extensive condensation observed in many of the flats should be the subject of a separate report.

The report may have been commissioned in stages. There may need to be a preliminary report and then an interim report, both to be superseded eventually by a final report. The preliminary report may just state the findings, the interim may discuss the options available and explore cost alternatives, while the final report will review the situation in the light of the client's reactions and the latest cost estimate and make final recommendations.

Methodology
This section relates how the investigation was tackled. For example, three visits to site may have been made. Describe them in chronological order, saying who was present at each, what actions the reporter(s) took, whether tests were made and if so why, where and by whom. Add whether any supporting research (for example, into local history, social conditions, climate, water table etc) was carried out. If any appendices are included, say why and in what respect they may be useful to readers.

Then briefly describe how the material in the report has been organised.

This report consists of four main sections. In Section 1 we describe the events which led to this commission and the way we have tackled the work. Section 2 records our findings, and Section 3 sets out the conclusions we deduce and our recommendations for action. In Section 4 we discuss the remedial solutions available and compare and cost the proposed options. We conclude this Section with recommendations. The appendices contain items and information which support and validate our findings and recommendations.

Findings
The findings should be a clear statement of facts; any temptation to comment or draw early conclusions or propose solutions should be firmly resisted.

This section of the report will go into some detail, breaking down the inspection of a building into, say, an element-by-element description (preferably illustrated). It will say who was present during the survey, what the weather conditions were then and had been recently (eg heavy rain the night before). It will record in detail any opening-up procedures, borescope inspections, dye or spray tests and so on. Some photographs may be included, but if they are numerous it is probably better to present them in an appendix.

Because of the technical detail included it is useful to conclude the section with a summary and to illustrate the material wherever possible. One good illustration can give the reader more information than several pages of text.

Conclusions and Recommendations

After analysing the situation, draw conclusions and then, if asked to do so in the brief, suggest a course of future action, explaining the salient aspects of various alternatives and the financial and other implications.

Set out conclusions clearly as itemised points. State the options available as *(a)*, *(b)*, *(c)* etc so that they can be referred to thereafter as *Option (a)* etc without having to recapitulate them extensively.

Some investigative reports end at this point. Where the brief asks for proposals for remedial solutions, another part is added.

Remedial Proposals

The options described, costed and compared will have been chosen because of their suitability within the context of any budget set. Recommendations must be performable as well as cost-effective, and it is essential at this stage to draw attention to any limitations or disadvantages of the remedies proposed.

C6.1.3 Appendices etc

References

Publications or sources of information are often referred to in the body of the report. Each item should be given a number (superscribed or in brackets), and a related list of numbered references should follow immediately after the main text. It may be convenient to use footnotes for references while drafting the report, but in the final version the convenience of the reader is paramount, and a separate list is generally more useful.

Appended material

Although nothing crucial to the theme should be banished into an appendix, it is important not to allow the main text to become clogged with extraneous material. In some reports it may be necessary to include copies of relevant correspondence, notices, extracts from codes and standards or related literature – even translations of foreign research papers on occasion. These can all be appended items.

Appendices should be listed on the contents page at the front of the report. Each should have its own title page and number and its own internal page numbering. Paragraphs should be numbered in a similar style to the main text.

Bibliography

In the context of report writing, a bibliography is a list of sources of information consulted by the author in the course of preparing the report. It is a category of information in its own right and should be kept separate from appendices. Sometimes more than one kind of bibliography is appropriate: for example, a selected bibliography to support the main text, and a detailed bibliography for a topic discussed in detail in an appendix. Reports which have required extensive literature searches or which are research based must have full bibliographies to validate them.

Index
Technical reports rarely need an index because their scope of enquiry is relatively limited. If an index does seem desirable, it should be the very last item included in the report.

6.1.1.4 Content and style

It is important to assess the recipient's level of knowledge accurately. If it is underestimated, some at least of the content of the report may be superfluous, which will probably irritate the reader; if it is overestimated, the report may be largely unintelligible, which will doubtless infuriate him. It is best to steer a middle course, particularly where the client is a committee consisting of, say, members of various professions, local authority officers, and lay people. Whatever mix of readers is expected, it is good practice to sum up at the end of sections in the main text, particularly where the subject matter is complex or technical.

As to writing style, in report writing special efforts have to be made to achieve a style that is clear and unequivocal, businesslike, free of subjective judgments, reactions and comments, and suited to the disciplined structure of the report format. The linguistic peccadilloes and inelegances that sometime characterise practice correspondence will not be overlooked or forgiven if they appear in reports. They will erode the validity of the opinions expressed and do little to reassure the client of the excellence of the writer's professional judgment. Fig C6.2 contains some guidance for report writers.

Fig C6.2 An appropriate writing style

Be businesslike

Your tone should be consistently helpful and pleasant, neither chatty nor clinically remote. Do not lecture your readers. Decide how to refer to yourself as the author of the report. The safest advice is to use *we*, meaning your firm.

Be concise and accurate

Remove weak modifiers such as *quite, rather, somewhat, about*. To say that *the bricks were rather/somewhat/wet* tells the reader nothing about the *degree* of wetness, just that the bricks were wet. Similarly, prune out monitoring phrases such as *as it were, so it seems, all things being equal, to all intents and purposes, more or less*. These can weaken or actually defeat what you are trying to say.

Be specific

Generalities such as *Flashings generally blow off in bad weather* are not helpful and will make you look foolish. Beware of making value judgments, such as *This is a good way to fix tiles, The contractor made a bad decision*. In reports in particular, statements should be validated.

Be relevant

Do not include superfluous or distracting themes and details. As a check, re-read the brief at the end of each section and ask yourself whether what you have written is useful and relevant. Keep to the point.

Be intelligible

If you cannot avoid using technical or specialist terms, make sure that you add explanations where necessary, and sum up frequently in plain English. If necessary include a glossary of terms at the front of the report.

Be digestible

The more difficult a subject is to grasp, the more important it is to present material in appetising chunks by making paragraph breaks at logical points in the argument or discussion. Paragraph headings relieve the monotony of a long text and help readers find specific topics. Make sure that they are relevant and keep them short.

Rephrase

Many linguistic knots can be untied by rephrasing sentences (or whole passages) instead of trying to find a precise change of word or construction. You can 'free' a dense sentence by introducing more clauses and sentence division.

Example:

(a) *Built in 1932, Hoopers Park, a Tudor-style development with houses arranged around a central courtyard, was recently designated a Grade II listed building.*

(b) *The Hoopers Park development was built in 1932. The houses, which are Tudor-style, are arranged around a central courtyard. Hoopers Park has recently been awarded Grade II listed building status.*

C6.2 Checking the report

Checking should be carried out at three stages:

First check
Before the report is processed, the writer should revisit the brief and check that all its requirements have been understood and met and that the response to it is adequate and comprehensible. Reading the text out loud to a colleague can be a good test of intelligibility and will expose any lack of coherence and clarity of expression.

Second check
Before photocopying and binding, check:

- for typing and spelling errors;
- that the report looks well presented;
- that the contents list corresponds with the actual contents, paragraph numbers and headings, and that page numbers are correct;
- that all the items to be included are assembled in the proper order;
- that the report has been signed, dated and referenced.

Reports must always be signed and dated by the writer and countersigned by a principal, who is thereby assumed to have read the report and approved its contents. It is essential that this happens: it has been known for a practice to be separately commissioned to present expert advice on behalf of opposing parties and for this only to have been picked up at the time of that crucial final reading.

Third check
Before despatch, check:

- that the right number of copies has been prepared (remembering the requirements of the library, filing system etc);
- each copy has been correctly collated, with no skewed or defective pages included;
- that the necessary identifying information has been included and is clearly visible;
- that the report handles well;
- that any separate items have been properly prepared and are clearly identified.

Whatever the pressures of work and time, this final check must be thorough.

C6.3 Reports for litigation

Architects are increasingly being retained as expert witnesses in construction disputes. From the management point of view, it is important, when asked to undertake such a commission, to consider what impact this will have on one's own and the practice's workload. Acting as an expert witness, particularly if the technical matters at issue are complex, can be extremely time-consuming. Expert reports may need to be revised and redrafted many times, there may be numerous meetings with lawyers and with experts from the other side to agree matters pre-trial. Then there can be many days spent in court, some of them simply in an advisory capacity. While this kind of work is usually lucrative and enhances a firm's credibility, its uncertain timescale may well have unwelcome repercussions on the work of the practice as a whole.

The function of an expert witness is to assist a court or an inquiry to arrive at fair and just decisions. In Britain, the expert witness is not an advocate for the client: he or she has been retained to give independent and objective evidence. To be accepted by the court as an expert witness able to deal with the particular issues in question, an architect has to be able to demonstrate special authority derived from qualifications and experience.

An architect's involvement in litigation often starts with an instruction to report on the condition of a building, and this can be done using the report format already described. In addition, he or she may be asked to give an opinion about the attribution of responsibilities.

On the basis of this advisory report, a client may decide to initiate legal proceedings and ask the architect to act as an expert witness. The case will often be heard in the Queen's Bench Division of the High Court and will be Official Referee's business. The judge will have special jurisdiction to hear cases which involve complex technical matters.

An expert report is not to be confused with a Proof of Evidence. This is a formal written statement in which someone sets out facts and matters which he or she can swear are within his or her personal direct knowledge. By contrast, the expert report is evidence of opinion.

Writing the expert report

Lawyers may have a view about the way the expert report is to be structured and presented, but will usually leave this to the discretion of the writer. It is likely that the draft report will be revised a number of times before a final version is agreed. The report should be validated by supporting documentary evidence, such as copies of extracts from codes or standards or relevant manufacturers' or other literature.

Reports by expert witnesses are usually written in the first person and signed by that person only, as the expert recognised by the Court. Therefore countersigning by a practice principal is not appropriate and may even call into question the expert's claim to exclusive authorship.

Professional standing and experience add weight to the expert evidence given. At the beginning of the report the expert has to declare who he or she is and state relevant qualifications and experience. This preamble is usually written in the first person.

I am Cecilia Brown, partner of Smith and Brown, architects and party wall consultants, of [address]. I am retained as expert witness on behalf of . . .

Then give a résumé of qualifications, work experience and anything else of particular relevance to the action being brought.

The report will be structured formally, beginning with details of the brief, background information and a description of the way the investigation was tackled. Then items of claim and response are listed in the order they appear on the Scott Schedule (if there is one) and comments given, followed by comments on the remedial work required and the related costs. Lastly the expert sets out his or her conclusions. A further report may be required later, after the expert has studied the other side's reports.

C6.4 Presentation of reports

Reports may be an important element of a firm's output and an important aspect of its public image. The way reports are organised and presented will be influenced by the firm's house style. Details may be set out in its office manual.

Reports must handle well and all the contents must be easily visible. This means that lefthand margins must be particularly generous if the report is to be tightly bound at the spine. Spiral binding is generally suitable for reports, but poses problems where frequent redrafting is likely, as the product has to be pulled apart and reassembled. However, usability is excellent, as spiral-bound documents can be opened completely flat , and illustrative material such as photographs can be seen properly. Any items difficult to bind into the report could accompany it in a separate folder or large envelope. Some can be put in a plastic wallet and bound into the report as an appendix. Ring binders and lever arch files are convenient where large texts need frequent redrafting and the hard covers give durable protection.

Some practices invest heavily in facilities for producing and binding reports, brochures and booklets to achieve a high quality finish and businesslike image for all the firm's output. An alternative is to put this kind of work out to a printer or one of the many firms that offer drawing office services.

Processing

Use double spacing whenever the report has draft status, or is likely to need redrafting by any of the parties involved. Reports commissioned by the legal profession should always be double-spaced, and paragraphs numbered throughout in sequential whole numbers. The final version of a report can be presented single-spaced with the pages backed up.

C6.5 Feedback

As a practice develops, so its library of reports will develop. It is often forgotten that this collection of researched information is a valuable asset which all professional and technical staff should be encouraged to share and study. In the course of preparing and researching a report an architect may encounter some new state of the art information or discover a fresh perspective on solving some problem, or be faced with some aspect of design which they had never considered before.

None of this information should be allowed to disappear from the collective memory of the practice, which should develop an effective system for disseminating as well as gathering information. Reports should be circulated to suitable staff as a matter of continuing professional development, and some of the topics covered might also be taken as the subject of an in-house talk or seminar (see C4.3).

Working with staff

Salaried architects are employed under a contract of service. Formerly the terms of this contract were left entirely to negotiation between the parties, but in recent years there has been a substantial increase in employment rights created by Acts of Parliament, and these mainly benefit employees.

Full-time staff members have a statutory right to the following:

- a written statement giving the terms of their appointment;
- an itemised pay statement;
- a minimum period of notice;
- not to be dismissed unfairly or made redundant without compensation;
- to be given reasons for dismissal;
- maternity leave or maternity pay;
- not to be discriminated against;
- to join or not join a trade union.

Employment legislation has been brought together in the Employment Protection (Consolidation) Act 1978 as amended by the Employment Acts 1980, 1982 and 1988. Also relevant are the Equal Pay Act 1970, the Sex Discrimination Acts 1975 and 1986, the Race Relations Act 1976, the Wages Act 1986, and the Pensions Schemes Act 1998.

Employers may be tempted to encourage staff to become self-employed in an attempt to avoid some of the statutory controls attached to contracts of service. It should be understood that it is a matter of law whether a person is an employee or self-employed, not just a change of name in the relationship. There might be certain tax advantages in being self-employed, but rights relating to unfair dismissal and redundancy can only be claimed by employees. On the other hand, protection under the Sex Discrimination Acts 1975 and 1986 and the Race Relations Act 1976 extends to the self-employed as well as to employees.

D1.1 The contract of employment

A contract of service or employment arises from the time that an offer has been made and accepted. Acceptance may be oral or written, but if oral the acceptance should be confirmed in writing.

The terms of the contract will be those stated at an interview or set out in a letter. They should be fully and accurately presented, because additional and amended terms cannot be introduced once the contract is made without the agreement of the other party.

A contract of employment may be of the normal open-ended variety or for a fixed term. An open-ended contract will continue until the employee resigns or is dismissed or made redundant.

The length of any probationary period required to confirm suitability must be stated in the contract of employment. When it has been satisfactorily completed, the employee should be notified in writing that the employment is now confirmed. For the purpose of calculating annual leave allowance, bonus, pension and other entitlements, employment will be deemed to have commenced at the beginning of the probationary period.

All full-time employees, ie those working 16 hours a week or more, must, not later than 13 weeks after the commencement of their employment, be given a written statement or a fuller written contract of employment. This should also apply to part-time employees (ie those who work at least 8 but fewer than 16 hours a week) after they have completed 5 years' service.

The difference between the 'contract' and the 'statement' is that:

- the contract contains all the terms of the agreement reached between the employer and employee;
- the written statement is a document required by statute, but does not necessarily contain the full terms and conditions of employment.

The employer may, in the written statement or the contract of employment, refer the employee to another document for certain detailed provisions, stating where it can be inspected. The practice's office manual could contain the information required by statute and any additional policy statements. It must be readily accessible, properly incorporated by reference, and always kept up to date.

If the contract of employment contains all the information required by law, then a written statement is not required as well. However, it may be good practice to attach a summary sheet to the written contract, listing the ways in which the statutory obligations are met.

D1.2 Written Statement

A written statement of terms must be issued to a full-time employee as soon as possible and not later than 13 weeks after the date on which employment commenced. Even when the contract of employment is straightforward, the following information should be included:

- the name and address of the employer;
- the name of the employee and the address of the site of employment;
- the date employment starts;
- the title of the job;
- rates of pay and the intervals at which payment will take place (ie the right to an itemised pay statement);
- normal hours of work (days of the week, starting and finishing times, overtime arrangements, lunch break allowance);
- entitlement to paid holidays (including bank/public), and how such entitlement is calculated;
- details of paid leave for sickness or injury;
- details of disciplinary procedures, or an indication of where these can readily be found, and the name and job title of the person whom an employee can approach if dissatisfied with a disciplinary decision;
- an explanation of the employer's grievances procedure or an indication of where this can be found, and the name of the person with whom the employee can raise a grievance;
- details of any pension scheme provided and whether the employment is contracted out for the purposes of the Pension Schemes Act 1993;
- details of any period of notice binding on both parties if the employee's contract is terminated.

The employer is obliged to issue the Written Statement only to all full-time employees (ie those who work more than 16 hours per week), or to part-time employees who have worked for the same employer for more than 5 years. However, it is good practice (and usual in office-based employment) to issue a Written Statement to all employees.

An employee who has not received a statement, or who has not been supplied with particulars of any changes within the specified time (ie one month), may complain to an industrial tribunal. A complaint may also be made if a statement received is incomplete. The tribunal may confirm the particulars as they exist, amend them, or substitute new ones. There is no fine or award of compensation.

The Employment Protection (Consolidation) Act 1978 (and as amended by subsequent legislation) also refers to recognition of annual leave, time off for public duties, sick leave, and rights for the expectant mother. It specifically states that if there are no agreed particulars under any heading, that fact must be stated.

Annual leave

There is a statutory obligation for the leave granted by an employer to be included in the employee's Written Statement. The majority of private practice employees receive 20–24 days annual leave.

The leave year usually runs from January to December or follows the financial year, April to March. It is reasonable to expect employees to take the majority of their leave allowance within the stipulated year, with some leeway for carrying over a few days into the early part of the new year. It is not good management practice to agree that carried over days can be paid for instead of taken; employees (particularly those with managerial responsibilities) should be encouraged to take their full leave allowance. This is in the interests of the practice as well as the employee.

The employee's Written Statement should state that the final salary cheque on leaving the practice will include, as appropriate, the financial equivalent of any annual leave not taken by the termination date, or a deduction for any excess annual leave taken prior to it.

The holiday commitments of new employees should be honoured where possible, and it is sensible to ask if there are any at the initial interview. Leave arrangements should in any case be discussed as early as possible to make sure that there is no conflict between employees' proposed holidays and their work commitments.

In addition to their annual leave entitlement, employees should receive the recognised national or bank holidays.

Leave for public duties

The Employment Protection (Consolidation) Act 1978 (and as amended by subsequent legislation) refers to employees who are:

- Justices of the Peace;
- members of a local authority;
- members of any statutory tribunal;
- members of a Regional or District Health Authority in England and Wales or, in Scotland, a Health Board;
- members of the managing or governing body of an educational establishment maintained by a local education authority in England or Wales or, in Scotland, a school or college council or college of education;
- members of a water authority in England and Wales or, in Scotland, a river purification board.

Under this legislation an employer is required to permit reasonable time off for any of the duties of a Justice of the Peace, or duties deriving from membership of any of the bodies listed above, viz:

- attending meetings of the body or any of its committees or sub-committees;

- performing duties approved by the body necessary to discharge its functions or those of its committees or sub-committees.

The Act does not require employees to be paid while carrying out their official duties.

Under the Juries Act 1974 all eligible persons summoned for jury service are obliged to attend any jury to which they are allocated. Jurors may claim from the Court travel, subsistence and other costs, as well as loss of social benefits. There is no obligation under the Act to reimburse loss of earnings in full, although a practice may consider including an undertaking in the employee's Written Statement to continue to pay his or her salary to compensate for any shortfall.

Sick leave

Employers are responsible for paying Statutory Sick Pay (SSP) to their employees for up to 28 weeks of sickness in a tax year. SSP will be treated like wages in that it will be subject to PAYE income tax and to National Insurance (NI) contributions, although periods of entitlement no longer relate to the tax year. Employers are able to reclaim the NI contribution which they pay for an employee in respect of SSP.

It is a statutory requirement that all periods of absence (including holidays) are recorded, and those relating to sickness identified.

Many employers supplement SSP to bring it up to employees' normal salary level. For example, the SSP of established staff could be fully supplemented for the first three months of absence, followed by three months at half salary.

Maternity leave

Under the Employment Protection (Consolidation) Act 1978 (and as amended subsequently) and the Social Security Act 1986, employers are required to pay Statutory Maternity Pay (SMP), recouping this by deducting the amount from NI contributions.

To qualify for SMP, employees must have been continuously employed by the existing or associated employer for at least 26 weeks, ending with the 15th week before the expected week of confinement. Their average weekly earnings during the last 8 weeks of the qualifying period must not have averaged less than the lower earnings limit for payment of NI contributions.

SMP is payable for a maximum of 18 weeks. It is paid at the earliest from the 11th week, and at the latest from the 6th week, before the expected week of confinement. There are two rates: women who have worked 16 hours or more a week for their current or associated employer for at least 2 years (or have worked between 8 and 16 hours a week for a minimum of 5 years with their present employer) will receive the higher rate of SMP, ie nine-tenths of normal weekly earnings; women with at least 6 months' but less than 2 years' service the lower (current) rate.

Maternity pay must be paid in the same way as salary (ie weekly, monthly etc) in accordance with the employee's contract. The employee is entitled to SMP whether or not she intends to return to work.

Although an employee can leave work up to 15 weeks before the expected date of confinement and claim SMP, if she wishes to secure her right to return to work after the birth, she must not leave work sooner than 11 weeks before the expected date of confinement and must have worked for at least 2 years with her present employer.

The employee has the right to return to her original job (or equivalent if her original job is genuinely no longer available) up to 29 weeks after the week in which her baby was born. If she is ill, she still has the right of return for a further 4 weeks, provided she produces a medical certificate, and provided that the qualifying rules governing continuous employment are still observed.

The employer may postpone her date of return by up to 4 weeks from the notified day, but must inform the employee of the new date and give reasons for the postponement. The employer may write to the employee within the 29 weeks of her expected return asking her to confirm her intention to resume work.

Childcare provision

In Britain, about 40% of women with dependent children do not work. An Equal Opportunities Commission report has concluded that about half a million mothers would return to work if current demands for childcare were met. It is often deplored that women architects are a small proportion of the practising profession, and it is clear that more practical initiatives are needed to help young women architects cope with the often conflicting demands of family and profession.

Architectural practices are unlikely to have the resources to provide childcare facilities in-house, but they might consider other kinds of support, such as agreeing flexible working hours or making a contribution if employees want to pay others to look after their babies so that they can return to work

This kind of help should be offered to non-technical as well as technical staff; the administrative and secretarial staff are often the backbone of a practice, and should not be forgotten.

Other leave (non-statutory)

Compassionate leave
Most practices readily grant compassionate leave in cases of urgent domestic distress or upheaval, but may view with less enthusiasm frequent requests to attend the funerals of unusually prolific families. Each case should be judged on its merits, fairly and sympathetically.

Leave for continuing professional development (CPD)
In upholding the Standard of Professional Performance, RIBA members undertake to 'fulfil CPD obligations and when employing other members on a full-time basis to allow them reasonable time to do likewise'.

It is in the interests of architecture that architects participate in activities which relate to the profession, such as serving on RIBA committees. There should be a policy about allowing leave for these pursuits, whether it is to be paid leave, and whether a certain number of days per year should be specified for it.

Extra leave for long service

Some practices grant extra leave for long service. It could be calculated as (x) number of additional leave days each year for each additional year served (over and above a certain period of service).

Unpaid leave

Some practices do not allow unpaid leave to be taken at all; some deal with it on a discretionary basis; others specify the amount that may be applied for. The best course is to have a policy about this and make it known to employees.

D1.4 Disciplinary and grievance procedures

The Employment Protection (Consolidation) Act 1978 requires that an employee's Written Statement should include details of the disciplinary and grievance procedures available.

An office operates more smoothly and effectively if importance is placed on maintaining an atmosphere of trust, confidence and mutual responsibility between employer and employee. However, even in the best-managed offices differences may arise which, if fundamental, may need to be handled more formally. Grievance and disciplinary procedures should be regarded primarily as a means of avoiding unnecessary damage to the employer–employee relationship rather than as a last resort when all else has failed.

A disciplinary code is needed to maintain standards and to ensure fair treatment of the individual, but it is also a means of indicating acceptable patterns of behaviour. The code should be in writing, and should specify:

- to whom it applies;
- procedures for dealing with the matter quickly;
- what disciplinary actions may be taken and by whom;
- a right of appeal.

The Written Statement should indicate the person whom an employee with a grievance can approach. This may be their immediate superior, or someone with responsibility for personnel. Employees who consider that they have not received a satisfactory response should have the right to appeal to a practice principal.

D1.5 Termination and redundancy

Termination

Under the Employment Protection (Consolidation) Act 1978, after one month of continuous employment an employee must give a period of notice of not less than one week, although the contract may specify a longer period. The employer must give not less than one week's notice for each year of continuous employment, up to a maximum of 12 weeks' notice. However, most contracts reflect agreement that an appointment may be terminated at 4 weeks upon notice in writing by either party.

An employee has a statutory right not to be dismissed unfairly, or made redundant, without compensation – and has the right to request written reasons for dismissal.

An employer has the right to dismiss an employee without notice on the grounds of gross misconduct. Examples might include extreme cases of indiscipline, drunkenness, dishonesty, or fundamental breaches of the contract of employment.

Redundancy

The legislation governing redundancy is the Employment Protection (Consolidation) Act 1978. Redundancy payments are due if:

- the employee has been continuously employed for at least two years at the date of termination of contract, and
- has not unreasonably turned down an offer of alternative employment, and
- a male employee has not reached the age of 65; a female employee the age of 60.

D1.6 Other statutory rights

Sex discrimination

Under the Sex Discrimination Acts 1975 and 1986 discrimination on grounds of sex or marital status is unlawful. Discrimination may occur in recruiting staff, selecting them for training, or assessing their promotion prospects.

Discrimination is direct or indirect. Direct discrimination occurs where, given similar circumstances, a person is treated less favourably than another on the grounds of sex. Indirect discrimination would occur if, say, a requirement were imposed on all employees which effectively excluded considerably more women than men.

The requirements of this Act also apply to job advertisements. As with the Equal Pay Act, employees have rights under this Act however short a period they have worked for an employer.

Racial discrimination

The Race Relations Act 1976 makes it unlawful to discriminate against a person, directly or indirectly, in the field of employment on grounds of race.

Direct discrimination is treating a person less favourably than others are or would be treated in the same or similar circumstances. For example, segregating a person from others on racial grounds would constitute less favourable treatment.

Indirect discrimination consists of applying in any circumstances covered by the Act a requirement or condition which, although applied equally to persons of all racial groups, is such that a considerably smaller proportion of a particular racial group can comply with it, and it cannot be shown to be justifiable on other than racial grounds. Possible examples are:

- having a rule about clothing or uniforms which disproportionately disadvantages a racial group and cannot be justified;
- a requirement for a higher standard of language than that needed for the safe and effective performance of a job.

The requirements of this Act also apply to advertisements for job vacancies. As with the Equal Pay and Sex Discrimination Acts, employees have rights under this Act however short a period they have worked for an employer.

Trade union membership

Under the Employment Protection (Consolidation) Act 1978, employees have a statutory right to belong to a trade union and to take time off to participate in its activities. Agreement has to be reached between the employer and the union representative that the latter represents the employees at that place of work.

D1.7 Other relevant legislation

Disabled persons

Employers' obligations towards the disabled arise out of the Disabled Persons (Employment) Acts 1944 and 1958 and the Disability Discrimination Act 1995. The legislation applies to firms of 20 or more employees.

Immigration

The employment of citizens from outside the United Kingdom is regulated by the Immigration Act 1971, and the European Communities Act 1972. This area of employment law is complex, and reference should be made to current guidance available from the Department of Employment.

The principles governing the legislation are these:

- Commonwealth citizens who can prove that a grandparent was born in the UK may apply for an entry clearance from the British Embassy/Consulate. There is no restriction on such people working or residing in the UK;
- a Commonwealth citizen who is the son, daughter or wife of a citizen of the UK and colonies does not need a work permit, but must possess a certificate of patriality issued by the Home Office or British Embassy/Consulate;
- EU residents may work in the UK without a work permit, but require a residence permit, available from the Home Office;
- other Commonwealth citizens and aliens must obtain a work permit before entering the UK unless they are overseas students studying in the UK, in which case they can apply for a work permit when resident.

D2.1 Duties of both parties

Once a contract of employment has been entered into, certain duties are imposed on both the employer and employee. The relationship is largely, but not entirely, covered by legislation.

The employer has a duty to pay the agreed wages, and to pay expenses reasonably incurred by the employment. He or she has a duty to ensure that staff are reasonably safe, and shown appropriate respect and consideration.

The employee has a duty to render faithful service so as not to damage an employer's interests. This means making sure that self interests do not conflict with those of the employer and that no secret profits are made. These, together with a duty not to compete with the employer, could be important where an employee undertakes private work and uses the firm's resources for it. Further complications could arise where the copyright in such work rests with the employer. Employees also have a duty to obey lawful and reasonable instructions, and to carry out all duties with reasonable care.

In general, employers assume a vicarious liability for the actions of employees, provided that the employees are doing what they are employed to do – however bad or negligent their performance of it. This vicarious liability will not normally extend to independent contractors, who are free to decide their own methods of working, nor would it extend to employees who indulge in frolics of their own outside the scope of their employment.

D2.2 Professional responsibilities

Architects and other professionals have responsibilities of an ethical nature which arise from the rules and standards imposed by their professional bodies.

The ARB Code of Professional Conduct and Practice, and the RIBA Code of Professional Conduct and Standard of Professional Performance, impose obligations which relate to employment in the architect–client context and to architects who are employers or who are employed.

It is to be regretted that some architects fall short of being model employers. At the time of writing much concern is being expressed by the RIBA at the plight of architecture students who are contracted on Schedule D contract terms so that the contracting practice can avoid the financial effects of employing staff with proper PAYE (ie Schedule E) status and entitlements. The resultant savings in wage bills are then used to slash fees and undercut competitors, thereby damaging and depressing the market for architectural services generally. In such situations students who undertake Professional Training, whether as part of an academic course or prior to the Part 3 examination, are unlikely to have a planned programme of experience or receive supervision and guidance as advised under the RIBA Professional Training Scheme. They could also find themselves outside the protection of the practice's professional indemnity insurance cover.

This is a senseless and vicious spiral, and it is a disgraceful practice. However, it has to be said that students should realise that by accepting such conditions they are not only casting aside the protection of employment law for themselves but are also driving wages down for others and exacerbating the deterioration in employment conditions.

Self-employed persons have few rights against unfair dismissal and redundancy, and are only rarely given any entitlement to holidays, sick and maternity leave, and a proper period of notice. There is no statutory definition of 'employment', although the Inland Revenue's criterion is that where a person works in return for payment a contract must exist. The IR publishes a leaflet, *Employed or Self-Employed*, to which reference should be made.

D2.3 Health and safety

The legislation

The Health and Safety at Work etc Act 1974 is the principal legislation. Under it, Parliament has also introduced Regulations, including:

- Workplace (Health, Safety and Welfare) Regulations 1992;
- Manual Handling Operations Regulations 1992;
- Health and Safety (Display Screen Equipment) Regulations 1992;
- Personal Protective Equipment at Work Regulations 1992;
- Provision and Use of Work Equipment Regulations 1992.

Section 3(1) of the Health and Safety at Work etc Act 1974 says:

'It shall be the duty of every employer to conduct his undertaking in such a way as to ensure, so far as is reasonably practicable, that persons in his employment who may be affected thereby are not exposed to risks to their health and safety.'

Under the Act the employer has a statutory duty to provide a safe system of work, and not to expose employees to risks that could be foreseen by a reasonable person. The employer will be liable for all reasonably foreseeable consequences (such as injuries and loss of earnings) if he fails to meet this requirement. All employers have to be insured against claims by injured employees, and have to display a certificate confirming this insurance.

An employer of five or more employees must have a written statement of health and safety policy and details of how it is implemented. An employer must appoint or agree to the appointment of a safety representative in the firm, if requested to do so by one or more employees who are members of a trade union recognised in that place of work.

Employees have a duty to work in such a way as to maintain a safe system of work, but despite this duty the employer can be liable for the negligent acts of employees which cause injury to fellow employees in the course of their employment.

Architect–employers should refer to *Model Safety Policy with Safety Codes* (RIBA Publications 1996).

The model policy statement follows the advice given in the HSE publication 'Writing a policy statement – Advice to employers', but each practice will need to analyse its own activities, identify the hazards that could arise both in the everyday running of the business and in emergency situations, such as a power cut or equipment failure. It is important to consult staff at all levels and take account of their views. The model safety codes included in the booklet can be adopted by practices as they stand, or modified to suit individual circumstances. Some practices may find it more appropriate to create their own code or codes.

Local authorities are responsible for health and safety inspections (usually by the environmental health department) of the office environment. They may be prepared to offer advice about specific safety issues, but responsibility for the developed policy statement rests with the practice itself.

Hazards in the office

Although at first sight architects' offices might not seem to be particularly dangerous places, there are potential hazards. For example:

- the removal of a duct cover for inspection;
- temporary obstruction of a fire exit;
- a paper guillotine;
- an ammonia dyeline machine;
- model-making machinery;
- heavy parcels or items of equipment which have to be moved.

Staff should be trained to use equipment correctly and advised of any operational hazards. All equipment should be regularly inspected and properly maintained, and this should be the responsibility of a nominated person.

Hazards outside the office

Visits to building sites, unoccupied buildings and construction operations are potentially dangerous. The likely hazards should always be kept in mind. Staff should be issued with a safety code and be required to follow it.

Every office should have an inflexible rule which requires staff to give details of where they go when leaving the office on business, and when they expect to return. Someone at the office should know the whereabouts of all staff at all times. Safety codes are given here as Fig D2.1.

First aid

To comply with Health and Safety legislation, practices must make provision for first-aid. This means that:

- first-aid equipment must be available;
- someone must be appointed to take charge in the event of an accident;
- in cases of special hazard or practices employing more than a certain number of persons, some staff must be trained and qualified as first-aiders;
- all these arrangements must be known to all the office.

Practices must also maintain a logbook for recording and reporting accidents.

Health and medical

Most people who work in offices are at risk from repetitive strain injury (RSI), eyestrain, and exposure to video display units (VDUs). There may also be problems connected with reactions by staff to the internal environment.

It is prudent to have available at reception a list with the telephone numbers of the local hospital casualty department, the ambulance service, and a local doctor. A copy should also be kept somewhere where it can easily be found after normal working hours. This information should be included in the written health and safety policy.

Many practices encourage, and some arrange, periodic medical check-ups for senior and key members of staff.

Fig D2.1 Safety codes for visiting building sites

1 Occupied building sites

The contractor is responsible for the safety of persons lawfully on site. Do not enter sites or buildings without permission, and immediately report to the person in charge. Comply with all requests from the contractor, his representatives or other supervisory staff. See the contractor when you arrive and when you leave the site.

Wear suitable clothing, in particular protective headgear (a hard hat) and stout shoes or boots. Do not wear thin-soled or slippery shoes. Avoid loose clothes which might catch on an obstruction.

Check that ladders are securely fixed and that planks are secure. Beware of projections overhead, scaffolding and plant, and proceed with caution. Particular care is needed in windy, cold, wet or muddy conditions. Keep clear of excavations and beware of openings in floors etc. Do not lean on guard rails, scaffolding etc. Do not interfere with any temporary barriers, guard rails or lights. Beware of ladders on which the rungs may have rusted or rotted, and never climb a ladder which is not securely fixed at the top.

Do not touch any plant or equipment. Keep clear of machinery and stacked materials. Watch out for temporary cables, pumps, hoses and electrical fittings.

Report to the contractor anything that comes to your notice on the site as being unsafe.

2 Unoccupied buildings and sites

As a general rule do not visit an empty building or unoccupied site on your own. Make sure that someone knows where you are, and at what time you expect to return.

Do not take chances. Do not visit an empty building if you think it unsafe. Do not visit an unoccupied site if you think it dangerous. Anticipate hazards. Common dangers include:

- the possibility of partial or total structural collapse;
- rotten or insecure floors and stairs;
- hidden pits, ducts, openings etc;
- fragile construction, eg asbestos or plastic sheets on roofs;
- space which has not been used or ventilated for some time;
- live services;
- contamination by chemicals or asbestos;
- intruders who may still be around;
- contamination by vermin or birds, or poisonous substances put down to control them.

Plan the visit and make sure that you take with you appropriate equipment and protective clothing. Remember that unoccupied buildings can be dirty, damp, cold and dark. Go prepared.

Familiarise yourself with the plan of the building, particularly the exit routes. Make sure that security devices on exits will allow you to reach safety quickly.

Look for defects in the floors ahead, eg wet areas, holes, materials that might be covering up holes.

Walk over the structural members (eg joists, beams etc) whenever possible; do not rely on floorboards alone.

Check on protection when approaching stairwells, lift shafts, roof perimeters etc.

Do not assume that services (eg cables, sockets, pipes etc) are safe or have been isolated.

If you suspect the presence of gas, inflammable liquids, dangerous chemicals or free asbestos fibre, leave the building immediately.

3 General

Do not walk and look around at the same time. Keep one hand free at all times when moving. Make sure that you are in a safe and balanced position whenever making notes or taking photographs or measurements.

If you sustain cuts, penetration by nails, or other serious injury, seek immediate medical advice. Consider an injection against tetanus (available from your medical practitioner).

Always heed these three golden rules:

- Do not rush
- If uncertain, do not proceed; seek advice or assistance
- Do not smoke or use naked flame

Smoking at work

Many staff object to others smoking at work and are concerned about the dangers of passive smoking. The practice can try to improve matters by:

- improving ventilation;
- segregating smokers from non-smokers;
- designating certain areas as non-smoking.

It is best to consult all staff before instituting a non-smoking policy which means that smokers are excluded from the main work areas. New staff should be made aware of the policy at interview, so that they are forewarned.

Refreshments

Eating and drinking at the work station is not something to be encouraged. It gives a poor impression of the practice to visitors, and can cause hazards if there is spillage on to floors or desks, particularly in the vicinity of electronic equipment. For example, a cup of coffee spilt over a computer keyboard will cause a malfunction immediately, and the subsequent cleaning operation will be very costly and is not likely to be covered by a maintenance contract.

If possible, an area should be designated for eating and drinking, and for making tea and coffee. If a vending machine is thought more appropriate, it should be sited at a suitable distance from work areas. Again, spillages are likely to be frequent nearby, making the floor surface slippery.

D2.4 Insurance

All practices have to face the possibility of financial losses arising from unexpected events. The alternatives are to carry the risk themselves by setting aside adequate financial reserves to meet the unknown, or to pay someone else to take the risk – in other words, to insure.

All the risks to which the practice may be exposed should first be identified and evaluated. The schedule of insurances given as Fig B2.9 is intended as a helpful starting point, but the nature and level of risks will vary from practice to practice. It is always wise to seek the advice of an insurance broker.

A practice's risks should be re-evaluated regularly, preferably every year.

Employers' liability insurance

Under the Employers' Liability (Compulsory Insurance) Act 1969 and the relevant regulations, it is compulsory for every employer carrying on business to have employers' liability insurance. Without this cover, employees with a valid claim against an employer could find that the firm had no resources to satisfy that claim. The Act only protects employees who work under a contract of service.

Under the Act, all employers (except local authorities and statutory bodies) must insure with an authorised insurer and maintain insurance currently for a minimum indemnity of £2 million in respect of claims which it is legally obliged to meet relating to any one or more employees, including employees temporarily overseas on the firm's business, arising out of any one occurrence. The Certificate of Insurance issued under the Act must be displayed in a position accessible to all employees.

Insurers will only pay out where a claim is one for which the employer has a legal liability. Only incidents arising 'out of and in the course of the employment' are covered, but claims may be brought for:

- death, personal injury and/or industrial disease, and may include pain and suffering, and out of pocket expenses;
- legal costs;
- loss of earnings.

Claims may also be made if the employee is unable to resume the same type of occupation and thereby suffers loss of earning capacity.

Employers' liability insurance does not extend to third parties. It is not compulsory for employers to insure against this type of liability, but public liability insurance is something that should be considered, always depending on the nature of the work that the practice undertakes.

Personal accident, life and sickness insurance

In the course of employment, an employee may die, or become incapacitated by accident or sickness. The employer has lost the services of someone who may have to be replaced at considerable expense and at short notice.

The employee may have lost earning capacity permanently or temporarily. In the case of an accident, if the employer is not legally liable, even though the incident may have occurred while the employee was travelling to or from work or was engaged in the employer's business, then the employee may have to look elsewhere for redress – to a builder, for example, if the incident happened on site and the contractor is liable.

It might be prudent to consider arranging personal accident policies for selected employees or for the entire staff. These cover death, permanent total disablement, and temporary disablement, and may be extended to cover sickness. Premiums are based on the payroll and on the level of capital benefits to be provided, which may vary with the seniority of staff.

Lump sum benefits are usually payable in the event of death, loss of limbs and/or eyes or total permanent disablement, and on a periodic basis in the event of partial or temporary disablement.

A practice might consider a voluntary scheme whereby it arranges the insurance on behalf of staff who wish to participate and then recovers the premiums from them.

Business travel

If employees have to travel frequently, particularly overseas, it would be wise to consider cover for:

- curtailment and cancellation expenses;
- medical expenses;
- emergency hotel and emergency baggage expenses;
- baggage, money and personal liability;
- personal accident.

Temporary life cover would be established separately.

For overseas postings longer than three months, special packages should be considered which cover medical and repatriation expenses. The needs of each case should be discussed with the insurers.

Cars used for the firm's business

Cars owned and insured by the firm will be covered for business use.
If employees use their own cars on the firm's business, their insurance will not be valid unless the policy is properly endorsed. It is wise to inspect the insurances of those who are to use their cars on the firm's business and if necessary pay an additional premium for the appropriate business cover.

Permanent health insurance

If employees fall sick and are away from work for long periods, the practice may wish to continue making some payments to them. Permanent health insurance can be a relatively inexpensive add-on to pension packages. It will pay a proportion of a person's salary, after a qualifying period (usually three months) up to normal retiring age if necessary and will continue payment of the employee's pension contributions.

Personal belongings

A practice's contents policy does not cover loss of or damage to employees' personal belongings or clothing. Employees' own household policies may include all risks cover for certain valuable articles temporarily removed from the house.

D2.5 Staff training and development

A practice that actively works to realise the potential of its staff will be both meeting its professional obligations and enhancing its own calibre and effectiveness.

Training and development should not be regarded as something that stops once professional qualifications are obtained. Continuing professional development (CPD) is now an obligation in most professions, and it is not sufficient just to pay lip service to the requirement. Where students on Professional Training are employed, the Record Sheets should include entries on any training or development events in which they have been participants or observers.

In a small practice where everyone is well known, it is relatively easy to plan career development for each staff member. In a larger practice, principals may have to be guided by their senior staff. Monitoring the performance of individuals is an important part of planning career development. This will help the staff partner to build up new teams as necessary with the appropriate known skills and experience.

As a practice develops, new areas of operation, skills, equipment and procedures may be needed, and to introduce them someone who knows the field in question might have to be recruited. Alternatively, the necessary expertise could be developed in-house. If new methods are to be effective they will have to be accepted by everyone; therefore their introduction, particularly by an 'outsider', needs careful handling.

Training can take the form of attending seminars and courses arranged by a commercial organisation, or as part of a CPD programme. Staff may be encouraged or detailed to attend those relevant to their own career development or to the needs of the practice.

For reasons of cost, it may only be feasible to allow one or two people to attend such events, so it is important to disseminate the information gathered at them. Conference papers and delegates' reports should be placed in the office library. Feedback from the event could be incorporated into the practice's in-house CPD programme, where the new knowledge or ideas could be considered in the practice context and proposals for follow-up developed if appropriate.

In-house training should be aimed primarily at:

- new staff, to familiarise them with the way the practice works;
- students in both periods of Professional Training, as part of the practice's training obligation;
- existing staff who need their knowledge and skills refreshing and updating.

For reasons of competence, sound practice and quality management, it is essential that proper time and care is given to this activity. In terms of cost benefit and educational effectiveness, the in-house approach to training has much to commend it.

The sessions should be at regular times and places when everyone can and will want to attend, and should be organised as a planned programme of events. Staff with particular interests or experience should be encouraged to develop exploratory sessions in their areas, while all staff should be encouraged to prepare case studies of current work for feeding into the programme. An occasional fun session or competition could be included.

It is important to monitor the results of a training programme. The questions to be asked are these:

- Are new ideas being tried out in the practice?
- Are people making fewer errors, is there less wasted effort?
- How are individuals developing? Are they wiser, better motivated, more competent?

Individual study

From time to time staff may wish to undertake part-time courses of study, such as in landscape, conservation, urban design or business administration. This may mean day or block release, and it will inevitably divert some attention from the work of the practice. The individuals may also request sponsorship from the practice, as it may be assumed to benefit in the long term.

In all cases, it is important to consider whether the person is qualified to embark on the course proposed; whether he or she will still be able to give proper attention to the practice's work; and whether following the course is likely to be of direct benefit to the practice. Given the right circumstances, the office might well encourage this personal initiative and even consider financial help.

Recruitment can be a lengthy process. A minimum programme, where an advertisement is placed in the technical press, might entail six weeks from decision to advertise to making an offer; from offer to start date, up to three months. Contracts may have to be completed, notice worked, or relocation arranged. For some posts, it may be appropriate to have a two-stage interviewing process.

New staff can be recruited in a number of ways. The most usual is to advertise for them in the technical press or, if time is short, to use an architectural agency. For younger staff a school of architecture could be approached or, for special talent or expertise, some discreet head-hunting might be appropriate.

Advertising

Advertising is expensive, so it should be effective. Most architects looking for a job scan the technical press first, although they may also approach practices directly, or use the services of an agency.

A job advertisement should contain:

- the name, address and telephone number of the practice, and a name to ask for;
- the title of the job, a brief description of it, and where it is based;
- what attributes a successful applicant is likely to have;
- salary and benefits package, or whether this is negotiable;
- information about how to apply and whether to enclose a c.v. and details of portfolio.

The text should be succinct and should contain all the essential facts about the job being offered. Graphics are important in reflecting the practice's image and in giving the advertisement impact. Advertisements have a considerable PR value: they may be seen by prospective clients; by other practices; by other professions in the building industry; and by the practice's own staff, who will like to be seen as employees of a successful, high quality business.

Staff agencies

Using an agency can often produce a quicker result than placing an advertisement, and is useful when additional staff are needed at short notice. Agencies usually only expect to be paid if a candidate is appointed following an introduction by them. However, their fees are often high, and it is important to check the amount in advance, as conditions vary. The RIBA operates its own employment agency, which is open for business during normal working hours.

Employing students

Students from schools of architecture or colleges of technology sometimes seek casual work during vacations or because they have been advised to gain office experience before re-taking a part of their course. In such cases the student will approach the practice direct and the terms of employment will be entirely a matter of agreement.

Students undertaking training in accordance with the rules of the RIBA Professional Training Scheme can be very useful to an office, but it should not be forgotten that the work they do is part of their educational process. Programme, salary and other conditions should be established with this in mind. The placing of students still largely depends on students' own initiatives. Some schools of architecture have developed strong links with certain practices over many years, and maintain preferred lists for placings.

Students are normally required to undertake 12 months' professional training after three years' education, and a further minimum of 12 months after graduating and before attempting the examination in Professional Practice (the Part 3). Applications to offices are usually made during the Easter vacation, and availability starts in July. When taking professional training students, enquiries should be made about any special requirements concerning assignments, recalls for school seminars, etc.

Some offices maintain links with particular schools, and this kind of continuity can bring advantages. It should certainly be worth establishing a personal contact with the Professional Training Adviser from any school involved. Off the record information on an applicant's potential is usually available, and in the event of the placement not proving satisfactory, a hotline can be useful. Many schools visit students during Professional Training, and this will provide further opportunities for contact.

Offices wishing to bring job opportunities to the notice of students should contact the Professional Training Advisers in good time, sending details of the vacancies in a form which can be displayed on the school's practice noticeboard.

Job descriptions

Job descriptions are useful for reference and comparison and one should be written for each post, non-technical as well as technical. Most jobs shift in scope or emphasis over the years, and the job description should be regularly reviewed so that it remains true and accurate and any necessary adjustments to wages and salaries can be made. The description can also be a point of reference if there is any dispute or grievance.

The job description should record the title, duties and responsibilities of the post, any special assignments or responsibilities relevant at the time of appointment, to whom the incumbent is accountable and the limit of any financial authority. The details should be updated each time there is a new appointee. Fig D3.1 shows the essentials.

A job description should not be confused with the Written Statement (required under the Employment Act) of the main terms and conditions of employment which has to be issued to all full-time employees after they start the employment (see D1.2).

D3.2 Interviewing applicants

Someone should be nominated to receive written enquiries and field telephone enquiries. He or she should be welcoming, firm where necessary, and discreet. Telephone callers should be asked to send in a written application. Application forms (if available) and job descriptions should be sent out as necessary.

All applications should be acknowledged immediately, and those that are obviously unsuitable should be rejected at once. At the end of the stated period for receiving applications, the designated selection panel should consider all replies and make a shortlist of candidates for interview, keeping a few reserves in

Fig D3.1 Specimen job description form

JOB TITLE .... Job No. ....

Office/Department .... Base ....

Summary of duties ....

....

....

Detailed duties ....

....

....

....

Special skills/experience needed ....

....

....

Special responsibilities ....
(*for staff, budget, etc*)

....

Accountable to ....

(This part for adminstrative records)

JOB TITLE .... No ....

Holder of post ....

Salary .... Start date ....

Any special agreement, review? ....

....

How was post filled?

(1) by advertisement in ....
on (*date*)

(2) by ....
on (*date*)

hand. The selection panel will normally consist of the staff partner or director and the post's immediate superior. If the post is senior, it usual to have more than one principal on the panel.

A practice with a good reputation tends to receive a steady trickle of uninvited applications and will keep on ice any that indicate genuine talent until a vacancy occurs, when it can invite re-application.

The interview

A job interview is essentially a two-way exchange: the practice's primary objective is to gather enough information about an applicant to enable a judgment about him or her to be made, while the candidate has the opportunity to ask questions about the practice, its work, and the post in question. Notes should be taken discreetly during each interview, and developed afterwards into a form which can be kept on file. There are advantages in devising a standard record of interview form which can be used for all recruitment interviews.

The conduct of the interview should be planned in advance and agreed by all the members of the selection panel. Each should be clear about the part he or she is expected to play. If more than one person is conducting the interviews, a strategy should be agreed beforehand. The same structure should be adopted for each interview to ensure that all relevant areas are explored and that the results for each candidate can be compared within a consistent framework.

However experienced, interviewers should prepare thoroughly for each interview. There is nothing more disconcerting for applicants than to become aware that little thought has apparently been given to something that is of great importance to them and their future careers. Notes on the post advertised, and on the applicants, should be read again before the interview and questions or topics prepared which can be introduced to stimulate discussion. The relevant job description should be kept at hand, together with the c.v. and any other information supplied by the candidate.

The environment in which interviews are held should be free of distractions for the interviewers and encourage candidates to feel at ease. The layout of the room chosen should not be intimidating, and there should be a table or desk on which drawings can be spread out.

Selection

If only one applicant is seen, then the issue is simply whether or not the person is suitable. If there are several people interviewed for one post, then the question is which one is most suitable – bearing in mind, of course, that none may be suitable. Whatever the circumstances, it is essential to take time to make a proper decision. Unsuitable or hasty appointments can lead to problems later on and result in unnecessary expense.

The letter offering the post to the preferred candidate should state the principal terms of the offer and whether it is conditional upon anything, such as satisfactory references.

Once the candidate has accepted, the office should be informed and a work space prepared for the new arrival.

D3.3 References

Employers are not obliged to provide references, but if they do so they have a duty to those who may be influenced by those references. Even though a practice may not wish to prejudice the chances of a job for a former employee, if it knows of something which may make the person unsuitable for another practice, it has an obligation, in the case of a written reference, to give a warning. An employer will not be liable for defamation provided that what is stated is true, and that the motive in supplying the reference is a genuine exercise of responsibility to another employer.

The two kinds of reference generally sought are character references and job references. For a character reference, the referee will be expected to have known the person in question for at least five years, and comments will be expected to relate to their personal qualities and an estimation of them as decent and trustworthy members of society. Employers who ask for a general reference are usually mainly concerned to discover whether the person in question is technically competent, honest and reliable.

A reference for a technical post might include details and remarks about:

- the period worked;
- the kind of projects worked on;
- duties and level of responsibility;
- financial authority;
- competence in performance;
- competence as a team member and/or leader;
- ability to cope with clients, consultants;
- health;
- loyalty and reliability;
- reason for leaving;
- the practice's willingness to re-employ;
- a caveat if the employment was some time ago.

If there have been problems, it may be better to indicate them rather than spell them out. It is then up to the prospective employer to pursue the matter.

References should be signed by a partner (the staff partner if there is one).

The offer of any job should be subject to satisfactory references. This should be clearly stated in any job application form used, and at interview. However impressive the applicant is, it is important to take up references and evaluate them properly. It might be necessary to contact the referee and discuss the comments made.

D3.4 Induction

All staff should be informed about new appointments and their starting dates. If the practice has a newsletter, a few notes about the new employees could be included.

First impressions are important. Newcomers to the practice should be properly introduced and made to feel welcome. They should be given a copy of the office manual and an explanation of the various office procedures. Everyone should be encouraged to give their time to help new arrivals to settle in.

Where there are several new appointments, it may be useful to hold induction sessions on the practice's objectives and philosophy, past and present work, and technical and administrative procedures.

In architectural practice the business has to be managed, the projects have to be managed, and the practice's resources have to be managed. The primary resource of an architectural practice is the skill and talent of its architects, and this has to be harnessed and organised for the mutual benefit of all the members of the practice.

For the purposes of this section a simple staff structure is assumed consisting of principals, job architects, other technical staff, administrative staff, and a principal in charge of staff management.

The management of people is never a cut-and-dried operation where people and roles can be firmly identified and established. It is a complex and variable process. Some roles may be only gradually defined whereas others have to be adopted quickly, at a personal as well as organisational level. In real life, the roles and personae often intermingle in various permutations. Partners and associates are often team managers, and so are job architects, but any one of them may be a member of a team under someone else. Team members may be architects on various grades, students or technicians. Any one of them may be appointed, or may emerge, as the leader of a team or group associated with projects, technical matters, practice organisation, or in-house activities of a creative or supportive nature.

All the activities that make up architectural practice concern people, the way they work and the motives that drive them. Whatever the description and content of their job, everyone has to deal with people. To manage people it is necessary to understand the forces that drive them to function well as individuals and within a group. Above all, it is necessary to understand what will persuade them to identify with the practice's goals, the most important of which is the goal of producing good architecture.

D4.1 Managing the team or group

As soon as people come together as a group, whether spontaneously or as the result of some direction, a group identity is born. The team manager is its natural focus and representative, decision-maker, trouble-shooter and negotiator. He or she will be responsible for keeping it informed so that it can function effectively, for obtaining the resources and staff it needs, and for seeing that everyone is adequately rewarded and their careers properly developed.

In any group of people, and particularly creative people, conflicts of attitude, style and personality can arise, and handling these is a test of managerial skill. Architectural education and training place great emphasis on developing an individualistic approach towards design. Whilst this is clearly in tune with architects' creative aspirations and fundamental to their work philosophy, to some extent it conflicts with the practicalities of project work, where the architect is required to work as a member of a team as a first objective, and strongly held personal convictions have to be put aside in the general interest. As a result, tensions may build up and, unless identified in good time, can quickly develop into confrontation.

The style of a practice can sometimes lead to conflict. Some practices establish an identifiable style, a reflection perhaps of the personality of a founding partner. To architects outside the practice a unique corporate persona may be attractive – and can certainly play a useful part in staff recruitment. However, preserving a distinct 'style' means that attitudes and approaches are expected to conform with it, and new staff may find that the freedom of operation they previously took for granted is suddenly out of order.

The introduction of change into the practice can generate conflict if it is not handled with great care. A strongly-led practice, confident that it 'knows best', may not be sensitive to the hostility that can quickly build up if changes are imposed in a heavy-handed way. On the other hand, a practice that takes its managers into its confidence and leads by encouraging participation may be better able to retain the confidence and cooperation of its staff.

Conversely, practice principals sometimes have pressure put on them by staff to introduce changes in organisation or procedures, or to change the way they run the practice. There may be a very good reason for this dissatisfaction with the status quo, and it is sensible for principals to stand back and take an objective view of the way the practice is operating. A staff survey (see D4.2) can be a useful management tool in this respect.

The essence of good management is working *with* people, whether or not they are senior or junior in the posts they hold and the powers they exercise. It is a matter of taking the time and trouble to find out the patterns and approaches that will get things done. People usually respond better to decisions that affect them if they have been involved in the decision-making process that led to them.

D4.2 Staff surveys

It is essential to analyse at regular intervals the effectiveness or otherwise of the flow of information within the office. Are messages reaching the right destination? Are project staff being properly informed about technical matters? Are all staff aware of the practice's long and short term goals, its policies and philosophy? Are principals aware of any groundswells of discontent over salaries and working conditions?

One way to find the answers is to survey staff opinion. Surveys can be used to explore attitudes towards a particular issue or as occasional probes to check the well-being of practice morale; they are a useful 'neutral' mechanism and their results can be surprising as well as revealing. To encourage staff to participate effectively and honestly it is important to make sure that confidentiality is maintained and is seen to be maintained.

The example given as Fig D4.1 shows the key areas of inquiry and the underlying questions to which managers are interested in finding answers. The exercise is primarily an exploration of motivation and attitudes, and these can more easily be triggered into expression if the questions or propositions are formulated in an attitudinal way that will provoke a reaction – positive or negative. Which approach to use will be a matter for the practice to decide. Reactions can be registered on a 1–10 scale, or by marking a bar, or by ticking headings such as 'Agree/Disagree', depending of course on what is appropriate.

Fig D4.1   Example of a staff survey exercise

Areas of enquiry

1 Business strategy
Do staff perceive that there is one?

2 Organisation and structure
Is it always clear who is in charge?
Are responsibilities properly
defined? Does everyone know to
whom he or she is accountable?

3 Management style
Is the style adopted effective and
appropriate? Does it succeed in
motivating staff?

4 Staff development and training
Are staff aware of the need for
training? Are they interested?

5 Communications
Are formal lines clearly
recognised? Is there a general
exchange of information at all staff
levels?

6 Excellence of service
Are staff proud of the service they
provide, corporately and
individually? Does quality matter
to them?

7 Innovation
Do staff feel able to express new
ideas and formulate different
approaches?

		Agree ✓	*Disagree* ✗
Questionnaire A (upbeat approach)	1 It's quite clear which way this practice wants to go – on and up.	___	___
	2 We all know who's in charge and what our own responsibilities are.	___	___
	3 There's a good atmosphere here: we are allowed to get on with our work, but senior people are always around to help sort out problems.	___	___
	4 Everyone should maintain their professional competence and develop their potential, even if it means making time for it.	___	___
	5 One of the good things about this practice is that everyone talks to one another.	___	___
	6 We like to be seen as a high quality outfit. Our clients come back for more.	___	___
	7 If we pool ideas and come up with something new it usually gets a good hearing.	___	___
Questionnaire B (downbeat approach)	1 We seem to be doing all right – what's the point of worrying about the future?	___	___
	2 I sometimes wonder where the buck stops – not with me, I hope.	___	___
	3 If your face fits, it's fine. I don't believe in sticking my neck out anyway – it's not *my* practice.	___	___
	4 CPD is fine in theory, but most of us simply don't have the time.	___	___
	5 Everyone seems too busy to talk much; I get the feeling that no one want to listen anyway.	___	___
	6 We all do our best, but clients thank you one day and see you in court the next. So what's the point?	___	___
	7 I'd quite like to try out some new ideas but no one here seems interested. Better to be safe than sorry, I suppose.	___	___

D4.3 Delegation

An important attribute of a leader is the ability to delegate. Many architects find this difficult, particularly where design is concerned, which is usually a very personal matter. Delegation is often regarded as a loss of face or a sign of weakness, whereas it more truly indicates managerial competence and strength. In some situations it is essential – where for instance, the task is simply too great for one pair of hands. In others it is eminently desirable – where, for instance, staff need to be given an opportunity to demonstrate their ability and potential for leadership in situations that will test them.

Before delegating, it is important to be satisfied that:

- the task and person are compatible;
- the degree of responsibility being delegated is appropriate;
- the person has been properly briefed and understands what is expected.

Staff with delegated tasks and responsibilities should not be left to sink or swim regardless; maintaining a 'hands-off' approach does not mean abrogating duties and responsibilities that properly belong to those who are more senior. Every situation should be closely monitored, and staff should feel confident that while there is no question of interference from the top, help and support will be readily given if they get into difficulties.

It is clearly in the interests of the practice as a whole to bring on its younger or junior staff. To confine all authority and responsibility to a thin top slice of management will lead eventually to a weakened practice with its continuity at risk.

D4.4 Motivation

Motivation means 'moving' people (in the sense of persuading them) in identified directions towards identified goals. Most people will respond to motivation, but it should not be assumed that what moves one will move all. Needs and responses differ according to individual cultural and social environments and as age, health and family circumstances change.

People can be motivated by negative or positive forces. Negative forces are usually needs or demands which, if they are not met, will leave a person dissatisfied. They may concern:

- practice policy and administration;
- supervision;
- working conditions;
- salary and benefits;
- working relationships;
- status;
- job security.

Positive forces are needs which, if they are well handled, can be used to motivate people to realise their potential. They may be associated with:

- achievement;
- recognition;
- the nature of the work;
- responsibility;
- advancement;
- personal development.

It can be argued that staff will be broadly content if their pay and conditions are satisfactory, but this does not necessarily mean that they have been motivated to give of their best. To achieve that, it is important to offer a worthwhile task, the possibility of growth with the job, recognition, and the opportunity to contribute constructively to the aims of the practice as a whole.

D4.5 Stress

Motivation can be described as bringing a controlled amount of pressure to bear upon people to enable them to maximise their potential for their own benefit and that of the practice. Where such pressure is too great or is applied thoughtlessly, the result can be harmful stress.

Although most architects enjoy being 'stretched' and having to cope with the problems and challenges that arise in professional practice, some may suffer stress as they strive to match their own and the practice's expectations, and to achieve the goals set them. This may mean that they have to try to be something which is contrary to their natures. A practice that sets out to motivate people to achieve more, always runs the risk of putting them under stress as a result. In extreme cases this can lead to physiological or psychological failures which are tragic in personal terms and can be costly to the practice.

Staff partners need to be alert to the signs of stress in all levels of staff, and should not forget to look out for such signs in themselves. Obvious danger signals are:

- excessive working hours;
- a drink problem;
- heavy smoking;
- unexplained absences;
- frequent errors;
- deteriorating work relationships;
- problems left unresolved;
- departures from normal behaviour.

Stress sufferers are often considered by the more robust to be inadequate in some way, but they are more often the victims of situations generated by others.

Some individuals take on too much work, or tasks which are beyond their ability, and are afraid or too proud to admit it; they may accept programmes and deadlines which they know are too tight. Others worry that they have too little to do and may be accused of being idle or of coasting along. They fear that they will be in the front line if redundancy threatens.

A job that is inadequately specified may cause stress because of the uncertainty of the situation. The incumbent does not know exactly what is expected and may be faced with having to make decisions which risk criticism as being beyond his or her remit on the one hand, or as not going far enough on the other. Stress may have been built into a job by, for example, a demand for high quality within too tight a programme. It may be impossible to meet both objectives.

Partners may cause stress by failing to support or trust their job architects and by not allowing them sufficient authority to carry out their responsibilities. They may pay lip service to 'participation', yet at the same time demand that staff 'get the work out regardless'.

A team that has been thoughtlessly constructed may have a potential for internal conflict that is far beyond the management capability of the job architect. It may be impossible to reconcile differences and motivate the team to pull together.

A practice which prefers to tell its job architects what to do rather than consult them can cause stress to staff who are not inclined to answer back. On the other hand, a practice which is so loosely organised that its managers have no framework in which to operate will make staff feel insecure.

Unhappiness about career prospects can also cause stress; some members of staff may be afraid of change or of being overtaken by the younger or abler. Others, on reaching a career ceiling, may feel that they have failed to fulfil earlier ambitions and promise.

Not everyone is stressed in the same way: some event or factor may be a source of stress at one moment in a person's life but not at another. When a person is stressed but just coping, one small addition can be the last straw. It is essential to be aware of the dangers of stress, know what signs to look for, and be prepared to respond appropriately. Regular medical checks for staff and managers alike are a sensible precaution.

Conflicts of responsibility

Generally speaking, architects are people of moral and ethical integrity; they will usually only work for a practice whose methods and philosophies they respect. However, there may be occasions when they will feel unable to work on a particular project. Where this kind of conflict occurs, the practice will want to know the reasons for it. If they are sound, and the person concerned is a respected member of the organisation, then a quiet reassignment to another project may be the best solution.

Conflicts of responsibility may also occur for other reasons, often arising from commitments outside the office. The practice should maintain an open-minded policy towards private work or individuals who are studying to obtain higher professional qualifications. Such activities may be time-consuming, and any serious conflicts should be averted if possible before problems arise.

Some staff believe that their only chance of promotion is by demonstrating a level of commitment well beyond the call of duty. It is true that there are times when an exceptional project demands nothing less than an all-out effort by all concerned. However, a practice that expects a blind allegiance at all times and total commitment regardless of private and family responsibilities is inhumane as well as unrealistic. Attitudes such as these may achieve short term results, but they are likely to be self-defeating in the long term.

Self-induced pressures are also a problem. Some staff are so proud of their dedication to their work that they do not allow themselves sufficient time to relax and recharge the batteries. Inevitably they end up mentally stale and physically exhausted, and may become a burden to their families and a liability to the practice. It is important to watch out for the workaholic, and to make sure that all staff take their full holiday entitlement.

Counselling

People who have a problem need to talk, and often need help in identifying the cause of the problem and the possible courses of action open to them. However, there may not be anyone suitable or available, the problem may be difficult to explain, or it may be about something that arises from some conflict of personality. Family problems can be so acute that they affect a person's performance at work and yet are too personal to discuss with friends and colleagues. Problems at work are often difficult to talk about with colleagues or senior staff because they themselves may be part of the problem.

Staff with problems need to know to whom they can turn for help. Larger practices may have a staff partner or personnel officer with a counselling role, but this is rarely the case with smaller practices. People will tend to look for someone at their own level in the practice who is likely to be sympathetic. Team managers may find themselves taking on the role of counsellor simply because they are the first to notice if someone shows signs of not being able to cope.

However, it is more a matter of luck whether a practice has someone prepared to help others in this way, and designating someone as the practice's 'counsellor' might be considered. Whatever his or her title, staff would have the reassurance that there was someone in the practice with the time and will to listen to their problems.

A practice with an authoritarian approach may see counselling as a soft option which allows staff to avoid reality. However, people who seek counselling are essentially asking for help; telling them off or prescribing solutions is a waste of time. It is better to allow them to explore and explain their problems and feelings while the counsellor steers them in the direction most likely to lead to some acceptable solution.

Managing the commission

Part **E**

Management is the process by which a particular group of people are brought together in order to achieve organisational goals. Plan, organise, direct and control are key words in that process. In a project-orientated group, the skills needed are a mix of technical knowledge and experience, together with the ability to understand and cope with complex situations – an essential attribute for senior managers. Strategic as well as operational foresight is required.

E1.1 Principles

The management principles relevant to managing a commission differ from those that are applicable to practice management, although there are some common features. The practice is assumed to be permanent, although regular reviews and adjustments will be needed, whereas a commission is of relatively short duration. Once it has been properly set up and procedures agreed, the goal is to complete to time, within cost, and to predetermined standards. Practice management can be seen as a cyclical process, in contrast with a linear track for managing the commission; the analogy is not perfect, of course, because lessons learnt on one job can be implemented on the next by way of a loop of feedback and renewal.

The management cycle

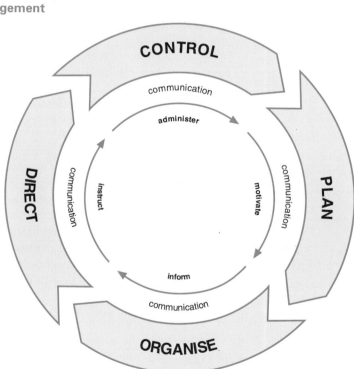

E.1.2 Application

Design, technology and production processes are often complex, and involve many people with various skills and abilities in all but the simplest projects. For a commission to be successful it is necessary to motivate people, organise, coordinate and control their work, and identify and put in place appropriate procedures for monitoring and assessment. Much also depends on having defined and adequate lines of communication throughout.

The management structure adopted must be appropriate for the particular commission; there is no standard type or format for management. It will depend on the nature of the job, its time span, and the mix of people and resources involved. A simple structure with clear lines of authority and responsibility is usually more effective than one with a complex hierarchy and uncertain web of command.

A building project, for example, generally requires management of the client's objectives through a network of short life organisations (the design and construction teams) supported by the permanent structure of the firm or practice which runs the business overall and manages its resources.

Each project brings together a range of specialist skills that need to be managed sensibly and economically through a controlled series of stages. Because the process of building design is evolutionary, its management must be sensitive to changing conditions and able to respond flexibly. A building project rarely runs its course without unexpected changes in requirements, pace or budget, or without conflicts of interests and priorities that need resolving.

Commissions for architects today can be varied and diverse. They might include services relating to:

- preparing reports on existing buildings;
- studies and reports, eg feasibility reports or computer presentations illustrating development potential;
- acting as independent design consultant, or subconsultant to a lead consultant of contractor;
- acting for developers of schemes that may depend on successful funding or grant applications;
- providing advice on energy conservation and upgrading of buildings;
- advising on the implications of compliance with current construction legislation;
- a traditional full service where the architect is designer and administrator under the building contract.

Whatever the commission, the management issues that arise, and the matters on which management decisions are needed should be identified, together with an operational framework that will enable decisions to be implemented by designated people at the programmed time.

Clients nowadays generally expect more than just a competent service from their professional advisers. They expect measurable quality, regardless of the fee they have agreed to pay. That quality should be demonstrated not only in the end product – whether this might be a building or a report – but also in the management process that brings it about. Effective management and sound administration are the essential cornerstones of a properly handled commission.

E2.1 The team

Although the Latham Report was entitled 'Constructing the Team', the actual composition of the team and its operating procedures was largely a matter of inference. However, the Review on which the report was based clearly identified certain practices which impaired efficiency, and stressed the importance of the client's role as an active participant in the team. Other points strongly made include the need to define and establish design responsibilities, the respective roles of consultants and specialist designers and installers, and the respective responsibilities of contractors and subcontractors.

The simplest operation will involve a small team consisting of client, designer and constructor, where direct communication is possible and basic procedures will be sufficient. However, relatively few projects today are as uncomplicated as that, and project strategies are essential, together with an operational framework and a clear definition of roles and responsibilities. The larger and more demanding the construction process and the more complex the team relationships in both the design and construction phases, the greater is the need for sound management.

E2.2 The client

The client has a central role and can make a significant contribution to the success of the project, particularly in the design stages. Where the project is complex, the client might decide to seek specialist advice concerning his role. For example, the client might provide his own management team or designated representative to manage the scheme on his behalf or to work directly with others appointed. Such a representative should be vested with adequate power to ensure the smooth collaboration necessary for the design team to progress effectively, but in addition he may have a permanent company role.

A corporate client might have an in-house team – for example an authority with its own architects' department – which might handle the work entirely, or in collaboration with outside consultants. Such a team might handle all building procurement for the corporate client and be responsible for advising on suitable methods and the appointment of consultants, and for issuing orders to contractors engaged to provide a maintenance or small repairs service.

Other arrangements might include the following:

- The client may appoint a consultant to identify and develop an initial brief and later recommend the setting up of an appropriate organisation for the project procurement and management.
- The client may make first contact with a consultant from any suitable discipline, who may in effect become a lead consultant and thereafter take up a management role. Either way, the client may appoint an architect to undertake the traditional role of providing advice on the project and on the appointment of other members of the design team.
- The client may appoint a designated agent or representative from outside the organisation, particularly in the case of a sectional building or a design–build project. Such a person will probably have only a limited management role, however important his or her administrative duties.
- The client may appoint an independent project manager, who could be a member of the client's staff, a contractor, or an independent consultant. The scope of the manager's role and authority will vary according to the project.

Where a project manager has already been appointed, the architect should carefully establish his or her own terms of appointment with the client, and relationship with the project manager. The latter may have prepared the client's invitation for architects to tender, or have recommended an appointment.

The matters to be agreed might include a comprehensive statement of the project requirements, the *modus operandi*, a brief for the architect's programme of work, the resources to be provided, and the check and control procedures to be used by the project manager. Alternatively, the project manager may give the architect a general briefing orally, and this should be confirmed subsequently in writing.

It is important to establish at the outset the respective roles of the architect, the other consultants and the project manager, and how they interrelate. For example:

- What is the extent of the project manager's authority and to whom is he accountable? How does this affect the roles of the architect and other consultants?
- How are decisions to be made and by whom?
- How will differences of opinion be resolved (such as the project manager not accepting the professional advice offered by the architect or consultants)?
- What functional relationship, if any, will exist between the architect and the client?

The more clients distance themselves from the design team, the greater the risk that vital aspects of their requirements may be lost, together with the opportunity for effective design. This could become a source of friction and frustration between the project manager and the design team. Architects acting as lead designers would do well to insist on the right of direct access to clients during the design stage; creativity is the architect's main strength and unique professional attribute.

If the project manager's experience is outside the construction industry, the architect should carefully consider what impact the proposed management structure and constraints will have upon his or her own activities and resources.

E2.3 Consultants

The architect's role and responsibilities should be clearly established at the time of appointment. If acting as the lead consultant, the architect should check whether a quantity surveyor has been appointed and, if not, whether the client has a name in mind. It is desirable that the appointment of a QS is made early.

The role of the QS might typically be as follows:

- to assist in advising the client on financial and budgetary matters;
- to collaborate with the design team to ensure that there is a proper balance between the client's requirements and considerations of quality and cost;
- to prepare bills of quantities and assist in preparing tender documents;
- to examine and report upon tenders;
- to monitor costs during construction and undertake valuation and measurement;
- to ascertain legitimate claims from contractors and prepare final accounts.

The architect, if appointed as lead consultant, might also expect to advise on the need for additional consultants. There are obvious benefits for the architect in working with people who are known, but the ultimate test must be whether a consultant has the ability to provide the quality of expertise required.

The *Architect's Job Book* describes in some detail the range of services offered by civil, structural, mechanical and electrical engineers and their duties. On larger or complex projects it is increasingly common to find important 'second tier' consultants on matters such as landscape, geotechnics, health and safety, insurance, security, site lighting, handover and commissioning.

The architect, if appointed as lead consultant, is likely to provide:

- assistance in developing the brief;
- advice on special studies and surveys for design development;
- collaboration with the design team to develop design and cost control;
- advice on developing drawings, specifications and other tender documents;
- commenting on installation drawings;
- inspecting work on site with regard to quality, cost and time;
- attending commissioning and acceptance testing and completion of relevant work;
- assisting in valuations and the settlement of accounts.

Architects who have been involved with the process of selection and appointment may know or have previously met the prospective consultants. Whether or not this is the case, it is important to establish a sound and friendly working relationship from day one. Extra effort will be needed if appointments have been made 'cold'.

E2.4 Site staff

The need for site staff should be discussed with the client at the outset and where possible details should be set out in the architect–client agreement.

It should be understood that architects do not have a supervisory role on site. Their role is normally restricted to inspection of progress and quality, and site visits are made as provided for in the agreement and depending on the stage of the works.

The presence of a site architect or a clerk of works could be said to indicate recognition of the need for continuous inspection. The architect should always ensure that such personnel receive a clear brief on their duties and responsibilities and the procedures to be followed. This is so whether the clerk of works is an employee of the architect or a member of the client's permanent staff, or is appointed by the contractor, or is appointed in the traditional way by the client to be inspector for one particular project. On large or complex projects there may be more than one clerk of the works, and this makes it even more important to define roles, duties and lines of communication.

The *Architect's Job Book* and the *Clerk of Works Manual* give useful guidance on these matters.

E2.5 Contractor's role

In some procurement methods, such as management contracting, the contractor will obviously have an important management role both pre-construction and during the operations on site. In other procurement methods, for example one of the 'turn-key' or design–build variants, the total management role will reside largely within the contractor's own organisation. In recent years some clients have been attracted by such non-traditional procurement methods for a variety of reasons, but they require particular types of management and forms of contract.

In the traditional procurement method which still accounts for a substantial proportion of work in the United Kingdom, competitive tendering for contracts is widely used by both private and public clients. The *Architect's Job Book* illustrates the stage by stage approach to the traditional design process and how the contractor's involvement can be advanced into it. In considering the basic sequence of the *Plan of Work* the contractor is seen primarily in his role of builder without design responsibility for the work. Even if he joins in with design team discussions, for example on a negotiated contract, it will be in an advisory capacity only.

The contractor's role in a traditional procurement method contract will be specifically as set out in the building contract between him and the client – who is now termed the 'employer'. Unless the contract contains anything which expressly places a design responsibility with the contractor, his role will be to carry out and complete the work designed by others for whom the employer assumes responsibility in the first instance. Responsibility for supervision and management of the operations on site is solely the contractor's. He is also responsible for the coordination and supervision of all subcontract work, materials and supplies.

The role of the contractor's site management team may be particularly important in projects which are very large, very complex, or constructed under difficult conditions. In some contracts it is an obligation for the contractor to name key personnel and not to change them without first informing the architect. Indeed when selecting management contractors it is usual to expect the contractor to bring key site or management staff to the interview and for their employment to be a condition of selection.

The matter of quality assurance on site is now being addressed in the industry, and some large contractors have appointed their own quality management staff. Codes of practice such as BS 8000: Workmanship on Building Sites are an important contribution to achieving standards, but the standards specified in the contract might be higher than those described in the BS.

On any project, site supervisory staff provide valuable support, but will not usually figure large in the overall context of management. However the contractor should establish at the start of site operations the role and duties of his site staff; their presence can be important, especially in relation to quality control. It is also important for architects to establish with the contractor at the outset agreed procedures and lines of communication.

E2.6 Subcontractors and specialists

Specialist subcontractors have an increasingly important part to play in projects. In some, a major part of the contract sum is accounted for by design and installation work carried out by specialist firms.

In terms of management, the responsibility for bringing about the timely appointment of specialist subcontractors and suppliers rests largely with the architect. The provision of necessary information, including contractual and programming matters, is something for which the architect will be responsible initially, although when the subcontract is placed this duty falls on the main contractor. The integration of subcontractors' work and the supervision of their operations is one of the more difficult areas of the main contractor's management function.

Sometimes with a simple scheme these specialists need not be introduced until after the basic design has been formulated. Very often, particularly where the specialist firm has a nominated status, the involvement in design matters will be in two stages. The first will be to provide information and advice necessary for the architect to complete the scheme design. The second will be when the subcontract is confirmed and detailed information such as installation information and shop drawings are needed.

It is common for specialist subcontractors to carry out design work, but architects should recognise that they carry the responsibility for any design work they have done prior to the specialist's appointment. The client's written approval to any subletting of design should always be obtained.

Where contractors or subcontractors carry out design work, architects should coordinate this with their own work; they will remain responsible for its integration into the general design. It is essential for architects to draw the attention of the client to the benefits of obtaining a written warranty to cover the design work carried out by specialist firms, for the contractor will generally have no design responsibility under the building contract.

E3.1 Planning the work

One of the most crucial aspects of design team working is the planning and coordination of contributions from all the members of the team – and this should include the client. Every project passes through identifiable stages, to facilitate direction and control, and this process can be set out as a plan of work.

There are established methods and procedures on which to base a suitable structure for managing building projects. The RIBA *Plan of Work*, used with a conventional form of contract and competitive tendering procedures, provides a firm operational base for traditional methods of procurement, and may be adapted for other methods.

The RIBA *Plan of Work* was originally published in the first edition of the *Handbook of Architectural Practice and Management* in 1964 as an operational model for design team work. The Tavistock Institute reports *Communications in the Building Industry* (1965), and *Interdependence and Uncertainty* (1966), stressed the need for long term research into the organisation of communication techniques in the building industry. Since then much work has been done in this field, and there is an extensive family of related techniques. *Plan of Work* itself has become widely accepted throughout the building industry, and professional institutions have developed compatible services and fee structures in line with it.

The *Plan of Work* as originally devised offered a procedure for design team working suitable for traditional procurement methods, and certain assumptions were made:

- that it was applicable to a building costing about £300,000 at 1964 prices (about £2 million at today's values) with a full team of consultants;
- that the architect was responsible for leading the design team;
- that the architect would be appointed as early as possible;
- that the full services for the type of project assumed related to stages (set out sequentially in the Outline Plan of Work, Fig E3.1).

Whether or not *Plan of Work* is used as a model, a quality management plan or system is advisable for every building project. This is in effect a statement of what has to be done and the requirements to be satisfied: the key staff involved, respective responsibilities, the project programme, procedures to be followed, and arrangements for review, assessment and audit. It is a system which should encourage consistency of approach, and provide the opportunity for regular monitoring.

Plan of Work can be used as an adaptable framework, subject to the following considerations:

- because it represents a model method of working, it will need tailoring to suit the needs, size and complexity of particular projects;
- it represents a logical sequence of actions to ensure that sound and timely decisions can be made;
- success depends on everyone carrying out the required actions at the right times;
- most of the detailed actions described are matters of sound professional practice, but they need the support of good administrative procedures (covered in the *Architect's Job Book*);
- where designers other than the architect and engineers noted are required, they must be appointed in time to join the team at Stages C or D at the latest to make an effective and timely contribution to the development of the design.

Fig E3.1   Outline *Plan of Work*

Stage	Purpose of work and decisions to be reached	Tasks to be done	People directly involved	Commonly used terminology
A Inception	To prepare general outline of requirements and plan future action.	Set up client organisation for briefing. Consider requirements, appoint architect.	All client interests, architect.	**Briefing**
B Feasibility	To provide the client with an appraisal and recommendation in order that he may determine the form in which the project is to proceed, ensuring that it is feasible functionally, technically and financially.	Carry out studies of user requirements, site conditions, planning, design, and cost, etc., as necessary to reach decisions.	Clients' representatives, architects, engineers and QS according to nature of project.	

Stage C begins when the architect's brief has been determined in sufficient detail.

C Outline Proposals	To determine general approach to layout, design and construction in order to obtain authoritative approval of the client on the outline proposals and accompanying report.	Develop the brief further. Carry out studies on user requirements, technical problems, planning, design and costs, as necessary to reach decisions.	All client interests, architects engineers, QS and specialists as required.	**Sketch plans**
D Scheme Design	To complete the brief and decide on particular proposals, including planning arrangement appearance, constructional method, outline specification, and cost, and to obtain all approvals.	Final development of the brief, full design of the project by architect, preliminary design by engineers, preparation of cost plan and full explanatory report. Submission of proposals for all approvals.	All client interests, architects, engineers, QS and specialists and all statutory and other approving authorities.	

Brief should not be modified after this point.

E Detail Design	To obtain final decision on every matter related to design, specification, construction and cost.	Full design of every part and component of the building by collaboration of all concerned. Complete cost checking of designs.	Architects, QS, engineers and specialists contractor (if appointed).	**Working drawings**

Any further change in location, size, shape, or cost after this time will result in abortive work.

F Production Information	To prepare production information and make final detailed decisions to carry out work.	Preparation of final production information i.e. drawings, schedules and specifications.	Architects, engineers and specialists, contractor (if appointed).	
G Bills of Quantities	To prepare and complete all information and arrangements for obtaining tender.	Preparation of Bills of Quantities and tender documents.	Architects, QS, contractor (if appointed).	
H Tender Action	Action as recommended in relevant NJCC *Code of Procedure for Selective Tendering.*	Action as recommended in relevant NJCC *Code of Procedure for Selective Tendering.*	Architects, QS, engineers, contractor, client.	
J Project Planning	To enable the contractor to programme the work in accordance with contract conditions; brief site inspectorate; and make arrangements to commence work on site.	Action in accordance with RIBA Plan of Work.	Contractor, subcontractors.	**Site operations**
K Operations on Site	To follow plans through to practical completion of the building.	Action in accordance with RIBA Plan of Work.	Architects, engineers, contractors, subcontractors, QS, client.	
L Completion	To hand over the building to the client for occupation, remedy any defects, settle the final account, and complete all work in accordance with the contract.	Action in accordance with RIBA Plan of Work.	Architects, engineers, contractors, QS, client.	
M Feedback	To analyse the management, construction and performance of the project.	Analysis of job records. Inspections of completed building. Studies of building in use.	Architects, engineers, QS, contractor, client.	**Feedback**

Even with a traditional method of procurement, departures from the Plan will often be necessary, some planned and some unforeseen. Obviously the more unplanned departures required, the greater the risk of abortive work and loss of overall control.

For an architect who is not appointed at the outset, Outline Plan of Work will help in the first task of identifying any omissions to be rectified. It will also serve as an operational structure for the client, who must provide necessary information at the appropriate times, make decisions and keep to them, and understand the consequences of not doing so.

From the time of appointment, the architect has two distinct functions:

- as manager – to ensure that the project as a whole is effectively planned, coordinated, directed and controlled;
- as designer – to contribute the creative skills particular to architects, and by harnessing the technical expertise available through the team.

E3.2 Adapting *Plan of Work*

Although *Plan of Work* was devised to reflect the sequence of stages found in traditional procurement, it can be adapted to suit other methods of procurement. The same stages will be present in some form or other, but they may not be so neatly compartmented nor in the same sequence as shown in the original *Plan of Work*. The design team consultants may not always be present in their traditional roles, and the division between design and construction may not be so clear-cut.

Whatever procurement method is used, projects move through five phases, and in this Handbook these are described as Pre-design, Design, Preparing to Build, Construction, Completion and Post-construction. Their application to the three principal methods of procurement is shown in Fig E3.2.

Traditional

In the traditional method, a project progresses from inception to feedback, ie from Work Stage A to Stage M. Progress is linear, requiring the completion of one stage before proceeding to the next. *Plan of Work* ascribes to the architect both a design and a management function, together with a role as leader of the design team. In the Figure the inception and feasibility stages (A, B) constitute the Pre-design phase. The Design phase extends from concept or outline design through its detailed development (C, D and E). Preparing to Build starts with production information and ends with tender action (F, G and H). The Construction phase (J, K and L) moves from project planning to completion. The Completion and Post-construction phase (L and M) includes the vital activities of commissioning, instructing maintenance staff, preparation of service manuals and health and safety file, as well as the increasingly important need for de-briefing. Specialist servicing arrangements are normally required under separate service contracts. There is then the analysis of feedback for incorporation into the early stages of subsequent projects.

Fig E3.2 *Plan of Work*: sequence of stages for traditional procurement

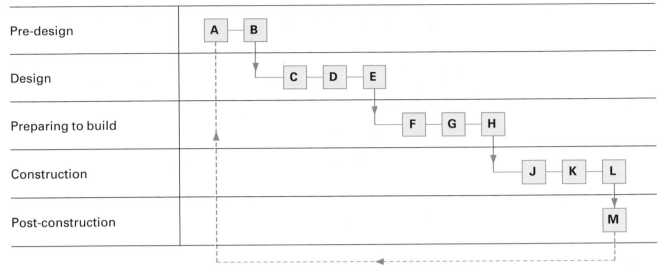

Plan of Work: possible sequence of stages for design–build procurement

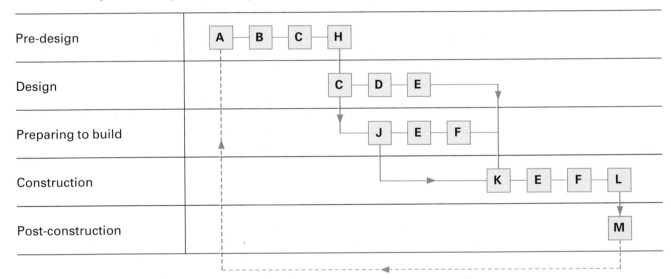

Plan of Work: possible sequence of stages for management contracting procurement

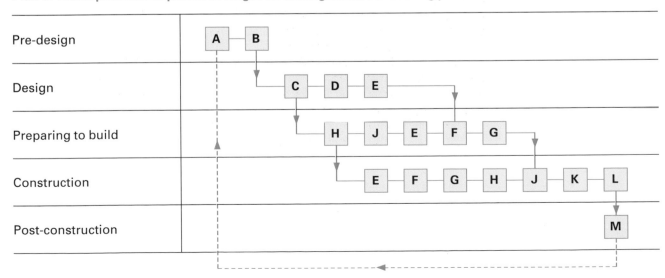

Design–build

With design–build procurement, the adapted *Plan of Work* shows that the Pre-design phase could include some concept design by the client's consultants as part of the employer's requirements on which the contractor will base his proposals. Tender action could also take place in this first phase as the major part of the design work is to be entrusted to the contractor. Tenders could be on a two-stage basis, in which case there might be some design development by the contractors selected for the second phase. However, this has not been shown in the Figure, to keep it as simple as possible.

In the Design phase, it is unlikely that all design work will be undertaken before construction begins. It commonly proceeds in parallel with site operations, and Stage E activities could continue into the next two phases. Similarly the preparation of production information (Stage F) required by the contractor could take place at the Preparing to Build phase and also well into the Construction phase. The amount of activity in the Post-construction phase will largely be determined by what was included in the employer's requirements. Whilst there are always lessons to be learned from any degree of involvement in a project, in this method of procurement the results of any analysis and feedback will of course mainly benefit the contractor.

Because of the absence of an architect in the traditional role of designer and contract administrator, and because consultants have a limited professional contribution, the *Plan of Work* will need adaptation. There are many and varied types of design–build operations, so that different versions of the Plan would need to be specially devised to meet particular circumstances. *Plan of Work*, suitably adapted, might still be a worthwhile management tool for the employer, and as the contractor will normally include design activities as part of the construction programme, it may have a limited application here.

Management contracting

Management contracting usually involves the appointment of a professional team, and the appointment of a management contractor at an early enough stage to cooperate over the development of the project design. The architect has a design and management function relating to the project, but the design may be only at outline stage (C) when the management contractor is appointed (J) on the basis of project information available at tender stage. In this way the Design phase and the Preparing to Build phase differ from the model *Plan of Work*.

Design development may be appropriate through these phases, with that in the Construction phase related mainly to the packages for the works contracts. Because of this, *Plan of Work* will be valuable in a suitably adapted form for use with management contracts. Depending on the number of works contractors, the management function is likely to be complex, and all construction operations are the responsibility of the management contractor. However, because of the probability of parallel design working throughout the construction stages, a plan of work for professional team working is an essential management tool.

In adapting the *Plan of Work* it will probably be helpful to arrange the work stages into an appropriate sequence. The persons or organisations involved and their roles will then head the columns. Key operations can be tabulated as they are in the original model, so that critical interactions and timings can be clearly established.

E3.3 In-house teams

For a large project the architect might need to set up an in-house project team, and if consultants from other professions are appointed, they also may need to set up project teams within their respective organisations. These consultants will have responsibilities and allegiances to their own offices and professions as well as to the design team. To bind them together and allow their work to be properly controlled and coordinated, a common sense of purpose must be generated and key targets agreed and understood. Each team must be carefully structured, with levels of responsibility and authority clearly defined. An adequate and efficient substructure of administrative and technical procedures should be established which can quickly be activated when a commission is accepted.

For a team to operate effectively, its members need to trust one another's professional expertise and judgement and be prepared to subordinate personal ambitions to the greater good of the common objective. This is usually easier when the parties are known to each other, particularly if they have collaborated successfully in the past. Otherwise, trust must be built up by conscious effort. People from different disciplines often see a situation in a different way, and there is always the possibility of conflicts of personality arising in any group of people who have to work closely together. Team members should be carefully selected to ensure as much compatibility as possible at the start, and to minimise the risk of the collective effort being eroded by the actions or inadequacies of individuals.

Good leadership is essential. Team members must accept and respect their leader, who in turn must be capable of earning that respect. Whatever profession he or she comes from, the team leader must be appropriate for the job and have the necessary organisational and technical skills.

For successful working relationships, clearly defined lines of communication must be understood and observed to avoid uncertainty and to enable effective control to be maintained. Effective communication can do much to lift morale and strengthen team spirit.

As well as the architect, the client and each consultant or practice represented on the design team may have its own in-house team for the project. In the case of architects, it is likely that a partner or director will take charge of the project; he or she is often simultaneously responsible for several projects. This of course assumes that strategic decisions have already been taken about the staff and other resources needed to service the project in the overall context of the total complement of practice resources available. It will then be the responsibility of the partner in charge to plan allocated resources according to the needs and constraints of the project in question, deciding what is needed, when, and who is available and most suitable to staff the project.

In the case of a small office or a project which, although small, needs some particular expertise, the partner in charge might be able to cope single-handed. More often he or she will work with a job architect who will be responsible for day to day matters and head the project team, with in-house logistical support. The job architect may on occasions have to understudy the partner, so it is important that he or she is kept fully briefed. Depending on circumstances, the job architect may attend design team meetings.

Similarly the partner in charge must be kept fully informed of the progress of the project by the job architect; it might be just one of several for which the partner has responsibility, so that his or her direct involvement is necessarily limited.

Fig E3.3   Lines of communication: design team and in-house teams

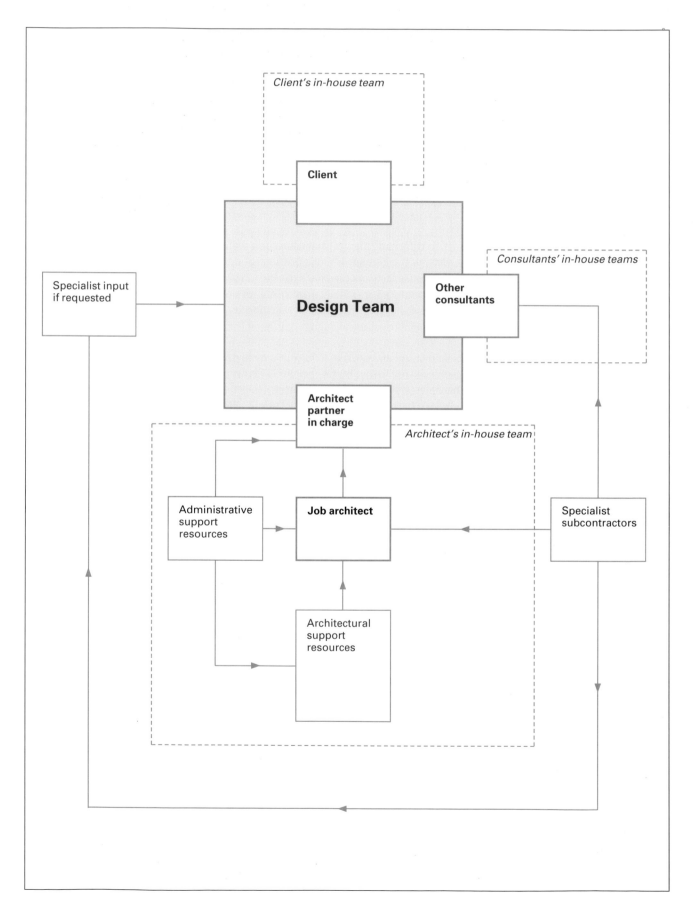

Close and effective liaison between partner, job architect and team is important in maintaining morale and enthusiasm. However hard-pressed, the partner in charge should always try to be accessible when needed, to have a regular pattern of formal and informal meetings with job architects and teams, and to act promptly and fairly to resolve any difficulties that arise.

Choosing the right team is obviously of critical importance. The partner in charge will be responsible for this, and the first step is to assess what abilities are needed: design talent, technical expertise, presentation skills, personal qualities etc. The next step is to fit the faces to the abilities and attributes identified, making sure that the level of staff effort relates to budgetary constraints as well as other factors, human and economic, specific to the project. The result will ideally be a balanced and compatible group of people who are likely to work in harmony. The internal hierarchy of the group needs to be clearly understood, lines of communication defined, and appropriate technical procedures prescribed.

At Stage A (Inception) the architect manages the terms of his or her appointment. The client clarifies the initial statement of requirements. There is preliminary discussion about possible courses of action and the formation of the project organisation.

At Stage B (Feasibility) the design team meets to appraise the implications of the physical, technical, legal and financial aspects of the client's requirements. The client will need firm advice about the feasibility of the project before being able to instruct the team to proceed to the design phase.

Points to watch out for at this Phase include the following:

E4.1.1 Appointment

Many claims against architects arise because the commission was not properly defined and recorded – in some cases not recorded at all. Until a proper basis for the commission has been agreed and recorded in writing, no work should be started. It is wise to spell this out to the client.

Clients sometimes present architects with their own terms for engagement. If possible, these should be resisted as they often impose greater burdens upon the architect while not providing many of the protections built into the conditions set out in the standard RIBA appointing documents. If they have to be accepted, it is essential to understand the different liabilities and costs they entail and the effect they will have on the value of the fee the architect receives, and to check with insurers that cover will not be at risk.

Some clients with in-house professional departments offer to provide part of the service themselves, or provide services to the appointed architect. In the latter case, the architect may become responsible for the appropriateness of the service provided, and will be responsible for its implementation. The division of responsibility must be clearly defined and recorded. It is possible to become liable inadvertently for the work of others, particularly in design–build contracts.

Architects who undertake a partial or reduced service should be extremely careful not to let it become extended beyond the defined conditions and responsibilities without first reviewing them and considering whether they are still appropriate. A typical instance might be when an architect is paid off on completion of drawings because client and contractor agree that further involvement of the architect is unnecessary. Or it might be that an architect involved in design for a design–build contractor, despite completing the agreed number of drawings, is then called to site to advise or to interpret details.

Partial or reduced services are full of pitfalls. Great care should be taken when setting up the appointment to define as precisely as possible the services covered by the appointment and the limits of responsibility accepted. Where Work Stages are omitted because of a partial service, architects can be exposed to additional risks when attempting to carry out the remainder. For example, an architect might be commissioned to take a project only up to production information stage, and thereafter have no involvement in how that information is used (or misused) when the building is constructed. Alternatively, an architect not engaged to inspect operations on site might nevertheless be asked to certify that the contractor had carried out work in accordance with the drawings. When taking over somebody else's work, it is essential to establish the limits of the service at appointment stage and allow sufficient time and money for checking and familiarisation.

E4.1.2 Fees

Risks arise in fee bidding, setting the targeted profit margin for projects, and collecting payments due from clients. Risks can be reduced by acquiring a good understanding of job costing, making sure that arrangements for paying invoices are clearly set down in the terms of the commission, and by instituting and operating strict administrative procedures for the issuing of invoices and for their prompt payment.

When invited to quote a fee, architects should recognise that it is impossible to state a realistic fee if the extent of the service required is not yet defined. Where the service can be fully described it may be reasonable to quote a lump sum figure, but where the service cannot be fully described it would clearly be unwise to agree to a fee basis which did not allow proper reimbursement for the professional work involved.

Many claims against architects surface as counterclaims in actions for recovery of fees. Therefore a first line of defence is to avoid the need to sue clients for fees by carefully defining the appointment and the arrangements for paying fees. On all but the smallest of jobs it is advisable to arrange for payment at regular intervals rather than upon completion of work stages. A hostile client who owed a large sum in fees might well capitalise on the situation if it suited him. It is worth remembering that if credit is extended there is always a risk of default, so that the extent of credit should always be limited to what the practice could afford to write off in the worst case.

The rendering of monthly accounts is becoming standard practice, and with new clients it is in order to request an initial payment in advance. Once arrangements have been agreed, it is important to keep to them and make sure that accounts are rendered at the specified intervals and honoured by the due date. If a client is tempted to 'try it on', he should be given fair warning and if he does not pay, then the architect should stop work. At the very worst such action will merely have precipitated a problem that was going to arise anyway, and the practice will not have wasted more time and effort than was unavoidable.

E4.1.3 Consultants

Many claims arise partly or wholly from actions or omissions by other consultants. The risks attaching to the use of consultants can be managed and thereby minimised. Consultants should preferably be appointed directly by the client, who will hold them responsible for the service they provide. Where the client insists on a single appointment for all professional services, architects should establish a proper structure of control and only accept their own nominees.

Whether a single or team appointment is to be made, architects can manage the risks by ensuring that correct procedures are followed, viz:

- by selecting their own team, and using consultants whom they know and trust;
- by setting up formal agreements that properly lay down the nature, allocation and standard of duties, the level of service required, and the right to terminate;
- by obtaining evidence of consultants' current insurance cover and getting it checked by the architect's insurers for adequacy.

It is important to keep insurers informed. Architects are often required to state on their insurance proposals that they always require clients to appoint the consultants and have a duty under most policies to advise of any 'consortium' arrangements. These are often excluded by insurers.

When consultants are employed direct by the architect, their fees become part of the turnover figure on which the architect's professional indemnity premium is based. Although this may be heavily discounted, there is a residual insurance charge which may be as much as 0.5% of the fees, and this should be allowed for in the architect's own fee agreement.

The employment of consultants, even under standard conditions, does not relieve architects of their own liability for advice that is patently incorrect. An architect should always check advice from consultants 'with the skill and care of the average architect'. If anything appears to be amiss, the architect should say so and ask the appropriate questions. Blindly accepting the advice of consultants is bad practice and a needless risk, and so is doing the consultants' job for them. It is in order to question, criticise and suggest, but it is never in order to tell a consultant how to do something.

It is also thought that the architect has a duty to warn the client of serious shortcomings in the performance of consultants appointed direct.

E4.1.4 The brief

The brief should be as comprehensive as possible, clearly expressed and accurate. It may be a formal document, used as a point of reference throughout the project, and as a yardstick by which the completed building is measured. No assumptions should be made. It is a professional duty to question the client's proposals and information and to identify ambiguities or omissions, establish a firm basis for progress, and reduce the risk of misunderstandings later. Brief-taking should not be hurried; any temptation to rush in with preconceived ideas and solutions should be firmly resisted.

All the information elicited at briefing meetings should be carefully recorded and dated – in particular, all instructions and decisions from the client. The other consultants involved at this early stage must be kept informed of changes and additions.

E4.1.5 Programming

The first programme for the project arising from the initial brief will probably be broadly based and provisional, indicating only key dates and an approximation of the *Plan of Work* stages relevant. It will be developed and refined throughout the subsequent design stages. It is important to see how the timescales of the various project activities fit into the overall programme, so that staff and other resources can be properly allocated and scheduled within the constraints of the practice's general workload.

The programme should contain the essential information about tasks, time, and coordination. Hand-prepared charts must be amended promptly and kept up to date with changes and developments; superseded versions should be dated and retained for record purposes. Where programmes are maintained on computer software, the old version should be printed out and filed.

Programmes should be as simple as possible. Bar charts are easy to devise and allow a large amount of interrelated information to be understood at a glance.

Computer flow charts or critical path analysis diagrams have their place on large or complex projects where options have to be constantly evaluated and where patterns of tasks and events have to be integrated.

The programme is usually built up by working back from the key dates set by the client's brief, or may be determined by particular procedures that have to be followed. It is important to build in enough time to allow stage reports to the client to be compiled, submitted, discussed and approved, bearing in mind that a corporate client may have to consult various departments or committees before giving fresh instructions to proceed.

E4.1.6 Financial appraisal

The client may feel entitled to specific financial guidance from the architect. As well as building costs, he may well want to discuss the commercial potential of sites or properties, sources of funding, and tax allowances. It is reasonable for clients to assume that an architect has a useful general knowledge of such matters, but it should be made clear that it would be foolish as well as dangerous for architects to pretend that they were expert in this field. Clients should be told that for an independent professional view on specific financial matters, it is in their best interests to consult their own advisers.

All budget and other cost estimates should be given to the client in a written form. They should always define precisely the bases, rates and indices adopted; without these, financial forecasts may be misleading. It may be necessary to explain the figures at a meeting with the client.

The client should be informed promptly if anything happens to bring about a significant change in the figures given. Clients are often reluctant to take on board any revisions upwards to the original estimates, so estimates should be realistic and supported by as much information as possible. The baseline factors adopted for financial appraisals are typically these:

- a specific base date for costing, for instance the projected date for starting on site;
- an allowance for inflation, which can be in line with one of the recognised inflation indices;
- the estimated contract period;
- any other relevant constraint or trend affecting the cost of construction, on a local or national basis, which can be realistically quantified.

E4.1.7 Investigations

An appraisal of the site or an existing building is often needed during the Pre-design phase. The client might not yet be the owner, although he might have valuable information to hand. However, drawings of existing buildings and site survey drawings prepared some time ago by firms unknown should always be treated with caution and carefully checked for accuracy.

Surveys and investigations should be undertaken early in the design phase because this is when the architect needs full information about the site or building. The client should be persuaded that the cost of surveys undertaken by specialist firms is a sound investment. The architect should arrange for the specialist firm to be properly briefed and asked to submit quotations for the work. These should be presented to the client accompanied by a recommendation for acceptance from the architect. The timing of surveys can be crucial to the progress of the early stages of design.

The more that can be discovered about the nature of ground conditions at this stage the better. Any site investigation work needed should be commissioned directly by the client and undertaken by specialists working to a brief compiled by the structural consultant. Borehole drilling might be needed to reveal ground conditions, water table levels and any obstructions, natural or artificial.

Information available from local authority departments such as town planning, engineers, surveyors, and highways can be checked on early. The availability of services should be checked with the relevant statutory bodies or other providers.

Although clients are responsible for providing information about known legal constraints affecting the site, they rarely volunteer it, and specific requests will have to be made. Matters such as rights of support, way and light can have a considerable influence on feasibility and can constrain design.

E4.2 Design phase

At Stage C (Outline Proposals) the client is presented with proposals which show the design team's general approach to planning, design, construction and services. A procedure for cost planning and control needs to be agreed and operated from now on, although at this stage the client can be given only an approximate estimate of costs.

At Stage D (Scheme Design) the design is developed from the approved outline proposals and the cost estimate is revised. This work will involve the full design team and coordination of specialist input. This is also when the various authorities and other bodies will need to be consulted and planning and other permissions applied for. The brief cannot be modified after this without serious implications.

At Stage E (Detail Design) the approved scheme design is developed further as necessary prior to the preparation of production information. This stage again requires a coordinated and properly managed team approach.

The sequence of stages and their work content will depend upon the requirements of the project in question, the method of procurement, the timescale, and the availability of information. It is essential to determine at this point what stages will be used and what work is to be carried out in them.

Points to watch at this Phase include the following:

E4.2.1 Design management

Design means recognising the constraints of the law, the agreed budget, and the requirements of the brief as it is developed. However, it is also a creative process that involves both analysis and synthesis reflected in four main stages of activity:

1 Understanding –
of the brief, the site conditions, requirements imposed by law, cost constraints, the standards of quality to be attained, relevance to similar problems elsewhere, feedback from previous projects. This is where analysis, knowledge and experience come together to form the basis for developing the design solution.

2 General study –
to bring order and balance into the accumulation of data and opinions, exploring the relationship of design elements, identifying the nature of problems, creating ideas and concepts, and testing them.

3 Development –
working up those solutions that seem most promising, refining planning and design more precisely, working out the implications on the general design of structure, services and other specialist contributions, coordinating and integrating them, reviewing and checking the result against the brief.

4 Communication –
presenting solutions in an appropriate form. This might be by visual display, written report, oral presentation, or a combination of all or some. The presentation may be for purposes of discussion with colleagues in the office, as information for the benefit of the design team, or aimed directly at the client organisation.

In the course of the design process, group decisions often have to be taken. Where views are positive and convictions strongly held, these are often difficult to achieve without the design becoming compromised and diluted. Design thinking must be coherent, clearly formulated and lucidly expressed; regular review sessions should be held at which there can be a step by step appraisal of the way the design is evolving and proper evaluation of the various options.

E4.2.2 Design communication

To make an effective contribution, the client may need to engage in a considerable amount of consultation within his own organisation and set up his own in-house procedures. Reactions or approvals will take time, and the architect leading the design team should take this into account. Lines of communication between the client and the architect or other professional acting as lead consultant must be clearly defined and appropriate. Many clients have difficulty in reading drawings, and to help them fully understand what is being proposed, three-dimensional computer generated images are useful. Models, mock-ups and other ways of physically demonstrating spaces or heights could also be considered.

Design team meetings are the central forum for progressing design development, and each member of the team must be prepared to account for his or her performance. Minutes should record all agreements and decisions taken and can usefully include an 'Actions' column to remind people about agreed actions and commitments. Minutes should always be issued promptly, and sent out with a covering letter drawing attention to those items on which action should be taken by the recipient. The architect should issue any further detailed instructions, and any necessary supporting drawings, schedules etc promptly after the meeting to ensure that any information required from other members of the team is produced and made available promptly.

At the first design team meeting the architect should put forward the directive for the stage and proposals for design development, clearly set out by work stages within the overall programme. The directive should reflect the client's brief as then understood, and will include requirements for cost, time and quality, and the procurement method to be adopted. The proposals will include:

- the design concept and strategy for its development, with any innovative aspects highlighted;
- the overall programme and *Plan of Work* stages to be adopted;
- the planned contribution of each member at each design stage;
- agreed procedures for coordinating, monitoring and controlling operations through design team meetings, for which there should be a standard operational agenda so that the full spectrum of work can be kept in view.

E4.2.3 Design factors

Clients are increasingly being made aware of environmental considerations, and the RIBA has recommended the following actions when designing:

- specify insulation standards above those required by current Regulations where appropriate;
- specify low energy, high efficiency plant fittings and appliances;
- employ up to date controls which will ensure that buildings respond appropriately to internal and external conditions;
- consider adopting passive solar design and study the site micro-climate to take advantage of solar orientation and natural air currents for ventilation;
- test the effects of building height and form on the site micro-climate, including wind turbulence;
- specify timbers only from sustainable forests;
- design the building to permit natural or simple mechanical ventilation and thus minimise the need for full air-conditioning and associated refrigeration plant;
- where refrigeration plant is necessary, try to ensure that consultants specify compliance with the Chartered Institute of Building Services Engineers (CIBSE) policy on the use of CFCs;
- where possible, avoid the use of halon fire control systems, as fire tests usually involve full-scale release of the gas.

The Health and Safety at Work etc Act 1974 lays duties on employers to ensure that their employees are not exposed to risks to their health and safety. Further obligations arise from the six Regulations which became law in 1992, and in particular the Workplace (Health, Safety and Welfare) Regulations 1992 has direct application to the design and operation of premises. Architects should draw the attention of clients to any implications, and take these into account when designing or remodelling existing premises.

The Construction (Design and Management) Regulations 1994 lay duties on designers to avoid foreseeable risks and to combat risks at source when designing, which requires risk assessment procedures to be adopted. Designers must also include necessary health and safety information in documents. The Approved Code of Practice reminds designers that when making design decisions they must take into account costs, fitness for purpose, appearance, practical buildability and environmental impact. In practice, this might mean considering such matters as the weight and handling of materials or components, noise and fumes which might arise from any process, and access for persons carrying out work. Other aspects include stability and temporary support of work during construction, site access and working, life expectancy of installations, provision for persons involved in regular maintenance and cleaning.

Architects should always design within the limits of their knowledge and experience. If something more is needed, further expert advice should be sought.

Otherwise, architects should keep to the brief and watch the budget, and if these are incompatible, the client should be advised in writing as soon as possible. Many claims arise from attempts to meet the client's cost limits regardless of the consequences, or by agreeing amendments to the basic brief without considering the cost implications.

While the vast majority of claims against architects arises in respect of ordinary traditional buildings, innovative design presents special risks. The first essential is to inform the client, explain the risks, and ask for written approval to proceed. In a recent case (which was settled after many weeks in court, but before judgment), it became clear that although the architect had exercised extreme care in developing an innovative design, he would lose the case because he had failed to advise the client of the inherent risk – in spite of the fact that the client had specifically asked for an 'outstanding' building. An innovatory approach can apply to new design concepts, and to the use of new materials or components. In all cases there must be full and careful research, and records kept.

Where new materials and components are concerned, manufacturers' information must be treated with extreme caution: it tends to be limited to physical characteristics tested and assessed under laboratory conditions. Individual materials and components might appear to be satisfactory in isolation, but when joined together under particular circumstances the assembly can fail. Accelerated testing of mock-ups can be a more reliable test, but it is often costly. It is unwise to accept at face value a statement that a material or component has been used successfully in other buildings. Checks should be made on the type of building involved, the context in which the material or component was used, and the length of time the building has been in use.

E4.2.4 Design development

During the development of the design, many decisions have to be made which may involve some compromise. Any departures from the brief must be agreed with the client. Other decisions, while not necessarily in conflict with the brief, will be taken for purely design reasons. At some later stage a query may arise as to why a decision was made. Therefore it is safe practice always to record the reasons for decisions made during the design process to demonstrate that decisions have been made with careful thought and good reason.

Any authorised changes to the brief should be collected and kept in one file (or set of files) and set down in writing. A copy should be sent to the client, and a copy kept on file. A comprehensive briefing file is the best defence against allegations that the brief has not been fulfilled. Development of the brief may reveal requirements which have a significant effect on the client's stated budget. Where there are cost implications, the client should be informed. The project quality plan should include proper procedures for recording design changes.

Cost checks should be carried out frequently during the design process to avoid exceeding the budget. If designs are far advanced before the cost implications are known, any re-designing may have to be done in a compressed timescale, resulting in errors and increasing the potential for claims.

E4.2.5 Design authorship

The overall design of a project is essentially the province of the architect. The importance of this is reflected in law because works of architecture are regarded as artistic works in which copyright subsists. However, this personal identification with the created work carries a parallel degree of design liability.

Copyright in the design, drawings and documents including software remains the property of the firm or practice which produced them, unless otherwise agreed. This should be clearly stated in the conditions of appointment.

Ownership of the documents prepared for a project at the client's expense passes to the client, except for those drawings produced by the architect for his own purposes when preparing and developing the design. These remain the property of the architect. What use the client is allowed to make of the drawings will largely depend on the conditions of appointment and on copyright law. The client is usually entitled to carry out the project in question on payment of the requisite fees.

Architects have a right to withhold actual drawings and the beneficial use of them until fees are paid. Even in the rare cases where copyright is assigned to the client, this will generally be in respect of the overall design concept and is not likely to preclude architects from using their standard details on other projects.

The restriction on the use of the design for one occasion only and for the purpose intended could be particularly important in the context of design–build projects, where the architect is working for the contractor.

The conditions of appointment should set out the position in respect of design copyright, design by consultants, and design by specialist subcontractors and suppliers. The extent to which design is to be carried out by others should always be agreed with the client.

E4.3 Preparing to Build phase

At Stage F (Production Information) the detailed requirements from other consultants and specialist firms need to be incorporated into the production drawings, schedules and other descriptive material which can now be prepared.

At Stage G (Bills of Quantities) the quantity surveyor will need to receive the amount of drawn information necessary under the measurement code, and specification information for incorporation into the bills. Decisions on the form of contract to be used and specific information which might affect tenders and programme will require consultations with the client.

At Stage H (Tender Action) the main contract tenders will be invited and obtained. Time will be needed for these to be thoroughly examined, and appropriate advice given to the client.

Points to watch at this Phase include the following:

E4.3.1 Transition

In preparing to build, the architect is chiefly concerned with translating detailed design proposals into information from which the contractor can construct the project. This includes the procedures and preparations necessary before the main contract work starts on site. In practice, there is seldom a clear distinction between Stage E detail drawings and Stage F working drawings.

In traditional procurement, it is essential to give the contractor sufficient information at tender stage and to allow him adequate time to mobilise resources. However, in restoration or refurbishment work, where a lump sum may be impracticable, this cannot always be done.

In design–build or management contracts the approach is different. In design–build, construction work might well commence with a minimum of information available at the outset, although contractors usually have a clear idea about what can be included within the price already agreed. Even where a management contractor participates throughout the design stages, there will inevitably be many design decisions to be taken as the works packages are developed and integrated during the construction period, and experience tends to suggest that a certain amount of re-design is often needed to accommodate later packages.

E4.3.2 Drawn information

Production information drawings should convey precise instructions simply and clearly to enable operatives to construct the work. Whether produced manually or by computer, production drawings are entirely impersonal in character. They should carry the minimum of information required and should be produced to an agreed and uniform system for arrangement, annotation, dimensioning, line thickness, symbols, coding and reference.

Production information needs to be properly structured and coordinated. Information will come from many sources, with drawings produced by various members of the design team. Whatever method is used (eg copy negatives, overlay draughting, computer draughting) there must be effective communication within the design team. In this context the adoption of Coordinated Project Information (CPI) conventions will be beneficial for the majority of projects. When adopting CPI, the code of procedure for production drawings should be followed.

It is important to allow sufficient time for preparing production information and to challenge the client's timescale if it is too tight to allow production information to be properly prepared. If changes made by the client will set back the programme for production, the architect should insist upon being given more time. The same applies if consultants appointed by the client do not comply with the architect's programme. Changes made late in the course of preparing production information may have a knock-on effect on the detailed design. Architects should insist on time to make thorough checks on the implications, particularly any relating to Building and Fire Regulations.

The issue and receipt of drawings also needs to be carefully recorded. Not every member of the design team will need every drawing, but it is essential that important information is passed to all who might be affected, and that this also is recorded. It is wise to cover the issue of all information with a slip which ensures that the recipient knows why a particular item of information is being sent, particularly in the case of revisions.

Drawings produced by the architect should if possible be checked by another person as part of the quality management system. Drawings produced by other members of the design team are the responsibility of the originators, although the architect should be satisfied that their proposals can be properly integrated into the overall concept and that there is no conflict.

A high proportion of the work in many buildings is designed by specialist subcontractors, and this design work should always be the subject of a formal agreement. It is essential to check that the specialist enters into an employer/subcontractor agreement which clearly covers such matters as the issue of information, design responsibility, and performance to programme.

Drawings originating with specialist subcontractors or suppliers which come with a request for the architect's approval should be treated with caution, particularly if (as is probable in this phase) no contractor has yet been selected. It should be made clear that any approval given to such drawings is purely in respect of their integration into the overall design; the contractor, when appointed, will be responsible for checking that dimensions are correct and construction is practicable. It should be made clear that checking will not relieve the specialists of their responsibility for design and documentation.

Drawings are potentially the most costly vehicle for formal communication, so it is important to make sure that they are really necessary and that information is not repeated needlessly. Many of the problems that arise on site are caused by inadequate, contradictory or late information. It is the architect's duty to provide adequate, clear and unambiguous information when the contractor needs it.

E4.3.3 Written information

Written production information will include items described and/or measured, irrespective of the form that a particular document might take. Complementary documents may contain diagrams, where these are likely to prove clearer than descriptions. Documents will usually be specifications, schedules of work, or bills of quantities.

A specification is a description of the work, workmanship and materials to be provided by the builder in constructing the works. It should be clear, unambiguous and complete; many claims arise from inadequate specifications. The best person to prepare a specification is the designer; the best time to prepare it is while the drawings are being prepared; and the best form of specification is one that uses a standard format and terminology. What not to do is delegate it to somebody else when (nearly) all the drawings have been prepared.

Specifications should be produced in accordance with the Common Arrangement of work sections advocated by CPI. The use of standard wording for clauses is advisable, and those most commonly available are:

- National Building Specification (in standard, intermediate and minor works versions) as hard copy or computer disk, fully compatible with Common Arrangement;
- National Engineering Specification (sponsored by the Chartered Institute of Building Services Engineers (CIBSE) and structured in accordance with Common Arrangement).

The specification may be the only written document; it may be general, simply to allow a global price, or sufficiently detailed to be a priced document which may be used as the basis for the valuation of subsequent variations. It can simply be a compilation of descriptive clauses or, if appropriate, a hybrid document which also includes some items in bill and schedule format. Even if a detailed bill of quantities is to be the contract document, specification clauses might be indispensable.

In building contracts with quantities, a specification may be incorporated into the bills of quantities and thus be given the status of a contract document. This can be done by treating it as a separate bill (eg 'Bill 2 Specification') or by dividing it up as specification preambles (replacing the formerly used trade preambles) to the various sections of measured work. The adoption of CPI conventions and SMM7 makes this a worthwhile possibility.

A schedule of work is a list of items of work to be done, usually set out on a room-by-room basis. It can be a detailed priced document which can be used instead of a bill of quantities. A schedule is usually most suitable for work to existing buildings, particularly for housing refurbishment work, where it can obviate the need for heavily annotated drawings.

The bill of quantities, produced in accordance with a Standard Method of Measurement, provides the fullest detailed information for tendering purposes. Traditionally it has three parts: preliminaries, preambles, and the measured work. The first two sections are largely the responsibility of the architect, although they are usually prepared by the quantity surveyor and presented for approval. They need to be checked carefully for content and consistency with other documents.

Bills produced to the Standard Method of Measurement, Seventh Edition (SMM7) in accordance with the CPI Common Arrangement of work sections start with a Preliminaries/General Conditions section. This will contain items not specific to work sections and items (eg plant, supervision, temporary works) which have a fixed and time-related cost. There is a requirement for certain drawn information to be provided to tenderers, and architects should note that in addition to Location and Component drawings which must accompany the bills (listed in Appendices 1 and 2 of the SMM7 Measurement Code), dimensioned diagrams are to be given in the bills.

Two issues which the architect should be careful about when preparing production information for a project to be billed using SMM7, are the use of 'an approximate quantity', and whether provisional sums are to relate to 'defined' or 'undefined' work.

Whatever type of bill is recommended by the quantity surveyor, cooperation between architect and QS will be necessary throughout the period in which bills are prepared, and query sheets should be dealt with fully and promptly. At final draft stage, the architect should carefully check the bill, particularly the preliminaries section and specification section. This of course is also where information relating to health and safety is most likely to be found – and which will assist a successful tenderer in preparing his health and safety plan.

E4.3.4 Tender action

Great care must be taken in selecting contractors for a project. The architect should only select those who appear to be competent and trustworthy, and whose references are impeccable. It should be remembered that a contractor is not likely to supply the name of an architect for whom he has done a bad job, and it may be necessary to speak to other architects for whom the contractor has worked.

Lists of approved contractors and subcontractors will show the project types and contract price ranges for which the firms are thought to be suitable. It is important to take up references for any firms recommended by the client about which little is known and to make sure that all firms invited to tender competitively are compatible in capability, size and reputation.

On large projects, or where design–build or management procurement is to be adopted, the client will probably wish to interview firms before the tender process is initiated. In the case of management procurement it may be advisable to interview not only potential management contractors but also those works contractors whose packages are key elements in the overall programme.

In traditional procurement it might be sufficient to rely on the use of standard enquiry forms and tendering questionnaires, but pre-tender meetings or interviews are often held as part of the selection process. They might be appropriate:

- where the contract is unusually complex (eg in design, phasing, because of working restrictions) or of high value;
- if the contractors are not personally known to the architect or client, or where the firm is known nationally but their local organisation is not;
- where it is essential to identify and meet the personnel likely to be involved (eg designers in a design–build contract, or key staff in a management contract);
- if the contractor needs to be appointed during the design development.

Pre-tender meetings can be expensive and time-consuming, and should be kept to a minimum. Contractors should be given adequate information about the project beforehand (eg details of the works, approximate anticipated value, access, form of contract, key dates, specialist works, tender arrangements), and meetings should be based on a strictly limited agenda. Information for prospective tenderers might be circulated with a questionnaire 14 days before the interviews. It might include questions about directors' qualifications, the firm's annual turnover for the preceding three years, details of completed projects of a similar size, information about management and site personnel.

Certain types of projects, notably public sector construction contracts above a specified value, have to be advertised, via the *Official Journal*, throughout the European Union. This allows interested contractors from member states an opportunity to be placed on selective competitive tender lists.

The National Joint Consultative Committee (NJCC) did much to ensure that tendering is competitive and fair. It published tendering codes which, although not mandatory, were drafted in the interests of all concerned, and recognised as good practice in the Latham Report.

Once a choice has been made about which contractors to list or approach, the tender action required will include making preliminary enquiries about the firms to be invited, assembling the tender information, inviting the tenders, evaluating them, advising the client and notifying tenderers of the results.

When preliminary enquires are made, prospective tenderers should receive information about the site location, a general description of the works, approximate cost range, key dates, identity of consultants, what form of contract is to be used and which optional clauses are to apply. All tenderers should expect to receive the same information. It should be as full as possible so that tenders can be reliable and realistic.

E4.3.5 Post tender period

It is seldom wise (or possible) to make an immediate and unqualified decision about appointing the contractor after tenders have been opened. The architect should submit a report with recommendations for acceptance to the client. It might include part or all of the quantity surveyor's report.

Before recommending that a tender should be accepted, the architect should be clear about what working with the firm in question might mean. The greatest danger area is where the contractor is recommended (or insisted upon) by the client, particularly if price is a major consideration. Contractors whose tender price is unexpectedly low need closer watching, and may increase the architect's risks. In these circumstances the architect would be wise to warn the client that additional fees may have to be charged for an exceptional degree of inspection. However, simply charging additional fees will not overcome the risks run where the contractor is clearly not capable of carrying out the work properly.

Priced bills or some other itemised priced document should be called for and checked by the QS for errors. The report from the QS should cover not only the arithmetical check but pertinent comments about the pricing generally and any special observations about the contractor's approach.

If an error in pricing is found, the tenderer in question should be informed. The NJCC codes set out alternative courses of action to follow in that event. Should it be necessary to correct or amend the documents used for tender purposes, it is important to ensure that appropriate pricing adjustments are made, and that the subsequent contract documents are consistent with the accepted tender. Unless changes have been deliberately introduced after tenders have been invited, the tender documents and the contract documents should be identical. Any changes agreed in the interim should be embodied in the contract documents.

It would be wise to require the contractor to submit a programme and a health and safety plan, albeit a provisional one, when tendering. It is also sensible to allow the contractor adequate time to plan the project properly and organise resources.

It can be part of the architect's duties to advise the client on the most appropriate form of contract. Standard forms of building contract should be used whenever possible. The JCT range of forms covers most methods of building procurement; the contracts are accepted by the industry and a body of case law exists. It is undesirable for standard forms to be used when heavily amended, but if the client insists on this he should be warned of the risks entailed, and expert advice on the amendments should be obtained – at the client's expense.

However, items in the contract appendix are *not* standard. They must be discussed with the client, the implications explained, and the client's instructions taken. This advice applies not only to the items needed to complete the Appendix, but other items connected with site conditions, possession, insurances, neighbours etc.

E4.3.5 Appointing the contractor

These days main contractors are primarily managers, and their ability to plan operations, direct and coordinate subcontractors, monitor quality and progress, and generally keep the whole project on target is a key consideration. Their financial standing (as far as it can be reliably established), record of contracts completed, and management resources should also be taken into account.

The client might assume that because contractors have been recommended for inclusion on a tender list, the architect is prepared to guarantee their subsequent performance. The architect should state unequivocally that this is not the case: the best assurance that can be given is a truthful confirmation that the firm in question has done well on previous jobs. Nevertheless, great care should be taken to establish the suitability of firms before they are included on tender lists.

The contractor and selected subcontractors are usually, but not always, appointed after competitive tendering. Negotiated tenders, particularly two-stage where the first-stage tender is selective on some notional basis, can retain a competitive element. So-called 'open tendering', where any firm (regardless of suitability) is able to tender, is generally not recommended.

If the scheme is altered between the inviting of tenders and the appointment of the contractor, the architect must ensure that there is sufficient time to amend all the drawings and documentation before the contractor is given possession of the site. Scrambling to keep up with demands for information invariably leads to errors and delays, and subsequent claims.

Similarly, if the contractor offers to speed up the programme and complete earlier than expected, the architect must be sure, before recommending acceptance, that it will be possible to meet the contractor's requirements for information.

Clients are increasingly demanding performance bonds from main contractors and principal subcontractors. These are legal documents, and should be standard, or otherwise only be drafted by lawyers. The terms of any bond required should always be stated in tender documents. The bond should always be obtained *before* the contract is signed – it may be impossible to obtain later.

E4.4 Construction phase

At Stage J (Project Planning) the contract documents should be prepared. They should take account of any adjustments made prior to acceptance of the tenders. This is when the site inspectorate will need briefing, and the contractor should receive full information. The initial (or 'pre-contract') meeting will be convened. Adequate time should be allowed for the contractor to set up the site and plan operations.

At Stage K (Operations on Site) the construction of the project takes place, from possession of the site through to completion. Because arrangements for completion are sometimes given insufficient attention, for the purposes of this book only, this important part of Stage K has been identified for fuller coverage under the next phase. In the *Plan of Work* however, completion is clearly the culmination of Stage K. This stage also covers contract administration matters such as the issue of information, instructions, statements in writing or certificates as required in accordance with the relevant procedural rules.

The management role of the architect during construction will depend on the method of procurement adopted, the extent of the commission for professional services, and the wording of the particular form of contract used. The architect could be responsible for the total management of a project where there is a series of separate trades contracts to be coordinated. With a design–build contract the architect is likely to be no more than a consultant to one of the parties, with no management or executive function during construction. In traditional contract situations, the architect's role is to administer the terms of the contract even-handedly between the parties with the authority imparted by the contract in question.

E4.4.1 Starting up the contract

The contractor must have reasonable time to mobilise resources and plan operations on site, and the architect should therefore deal promptly with these three issues:

* the assembly of information that the contractor will need before construction starts;
* the appointment (or confirmation of appointments already made) of the site inspectorate, and their briefing;
* arrangements for convening the initial project or pre-contract meeting.

The contractor will need certain information as soon as the contract arrangements are settled. This will comprise whatever is stipulated in the contract conditions – normally one certified copy of the contract documents and at least two copies of all drawings, schedules (including those from consultants) and unpriced copies of bills and/or specification. Instructions and documents relating to named or nominated subcontractors and suppliers should also be made available.

Information supplied to the contractor by consultants should always be issued through the architect. Information from named or nominated specialist firms is usually multi-phased and supplied direct to the architect in the first instance to enable completion of the design before the contractor is appointed. Later, installation or 'shop' drawings may follow so that the contractor can properly accommodate the work or fittings. Timing will be important, and delays could seriously affect the progress of the works. It might therefore be prudent to include clauses in specifications for specialist work which refer to the preparation, issue and timing of such information. It might also be wise to require production of specialist drawings within a specified time from the acceptance of subcontractors' tenders.

Information from specialist firms is often accompanied by a request for the architect's approval, and it is important that adequate time for this is allowed in the contractor's master programme. Once the contractor has been appointed, all information or drawings from the specialist firm should go direct to him. The contractor should first check the information for dimensional accuracy and buildability before passing it to the architect, who should check that it is suitable for integration into the overall design. The architect should then return it via the contractor with a clear statement that any approval given in respect of suitability for integration does not relieve the subcontractor or supplier of responsibility for specialist design and documentation.

It is often good sense to supply the contractor with some presentation material showing the finished building for display in the site office. Identification of the goal to be achieved encourages staff and enhances their sense of purpose.

If a clerk (or clerks) of works is needed, appointments should be made or confirmed before work starts on site. The architect is usually responsible for their direction, for ensuring that they are properly briefed about the procedures to be followed and supplied with report forms, etc. It is important that clerks of works are clear about the limits of their designated authority.

At the initial project or pre-contract meeting, usually the first time all those involved in the project are assembled together, it is crucial to establish proper working arrangements and agree procedures to be followed throughout the contract. The design team members likely to be involved with inspection, the site inspectorate, and the contractor's management and site supervisory team should be present. It is also desirable for a representative of the client to attend.

E4.4.2 Site communications

General lines of communication must be established and rigorously observed throughout the construction phase. Consultants may be tempted to discuss technical matters direct with subcontractors, but it should be made clear that the only valid instructions are those issued formally by the architect to the main contractor. Ignoring this rule is likely to lead to confusion and unauthorised expenditure; worse, it will allow one party to play off another in the event of a dispute.

The employer similarly must understand that communication with the contractor must be through the architect. For their part, architects must make sure that instructions are given only to authorised representatives from the contractor's organisation, and not to site operatives. Some contracts (eg the JCT Management Contract) require the contractor to name individuals, and it is sensible in all projects to require the person in charge to be identified. Difficulties can arise in the case of small projects, where the contractor's agent may be covering several small jobs simultaneously, but it is still necessary to establish unequivocally the normal channels of communication.

It is important that administration of the contract follows the procedures as set out in the particular form of contract, and that this is done in the manner required and to the timescale stated. Doing so meticulously may take time, and problems can arise if a backlog builds up. It is not unknown for a contractor to saturate the architect with paperwork and then take advantage of the situation; this is a matter to be sorted out firmly at head office level. Requests, claims, or notifications from the contractor can usually be aired at the architect's site meetings where the rest of the design team is present and a thorough check of the situation can be made. Any decisions should be formally confirmed in writing.

Contractors often fax requests for information from site, and ask for the reply to be faxed back. Although this is a valid medium of communication and can save time, it is important to remember that faxes should always be followed up by the original document. Fax transmission is often used to impart a spurious note of urgency to a normal situation or as a simple matter of the contractor's convenience. Architects should not be pressurised into responding hastily simply because a fax has come in.

E4.4.3 Site meetings and visits

Architects' site meetings are generally helpful in regularly monitoring progress and integrating activities. However, meetings are time-consuming and expensive and they should always have a purpose. Site meetings will be convened and chaired by the architect (if contract administrator); they are the central point at which the management functions of both architect and contractor meet. All those invited to attend should command an appropriate level of responsibility, have an interest in aspects of the current stage of construction, and should have the authority to make decisions as necessary.

Minutes are best taken by the architect and distributed as soon as possible after each meeting. They should be both a true record of the business conducted and a checklist for action. They should be sent out with a covering letter drawing attention to those items on which action should be taken by the recipient.

All visits to site should be made during normal working hours and with the consent of the contractor, who has been given possession and who is responsible for site security and safety. Inspection can be periodic, or take the form of spot checks, or be 'predictive'. Predictive inspection is specifically included for in some building contracts and is concerned with situations where work is to be covered up. Where this arises, the contractor will be required to give the architect adequate notice that certain works are ready for inspection and will remain so for a stated period.

How much inspection is necessary and when it is best carried out will depend on what was provided for in the appointing document, the architect's professional judgment, and will relate to the intervals appropriate to the stage of construction.

Others with an interest to inspect might include consultants and the clerk (or clerks) of works. They should be properly briefed and understand the nature of their respective roles and limits of authority. They are there to inspect and report back to the architect, not to advise or instruct the contractor or any subcontractor.

All visits and inspections should be recorded by the site inspectorate and will form a valuable job record. They will also feature in the regular reports submitted by the clerk of works. The architect's own reports should also be systematically completed and filed so that an independent dossier of facts, comments and photographs is compiled. Photographs taken regularly at predetermined positions may help to show the way the work is being carried out, and should be dated to provide evidence of progress.

Site visits should be made with a clear purpose in mind. It is helpful to use a standard checklist to avoid things getting overlooked. Checks on workmanship will take note of standards, accuracy, correct sequence and regular progress, as well as the need for proper protection. Checks on goods and materials might require reference to the specification, approved samples, and vouchers. Architects will also want to be satisfied that the work is being carried out in a proper and workmanlike manner.

Contractors might be required to provide a method statement at tender stage about how they intend to operate quality control. The architect can then check whether their intentions are proving effective, although quality control remains the responsibility of the contractor regardless of what audits of diligence the architect carries out. Where contract documents refer to specific Codes of Practice or British Standards, it is prudent to look these up before making a site visit, or require that copies are made available on site for reference.

E4.4.4 Programmes and progress

Contractors on all but the smallest projects prepare schedules and programmes to help in the ordering and allocation of resources. A programme showing the sequence of operations, the duration of each activity, and the critical points of information supply for the contract period is an essential management tool. It might take the form of a simple bar chart or precedence diagram, or a computer-based network, according to the complexity of the project. It should enable the architect, the rest of the design team, clerk of works, and the employer to understand the contractor's intentions.

The wording of some contracts refers to the provision of the programme prepared by the contractor for the architect's information as a contractual obligation. For most projects, the bills or specification should require the preparation and submission of a programme and might stipulate the form it should take. Many architects require a programme, albeit interim, to be submitted at the time of tendering.

Architects should take care not to approve a contractor's programme in such a way that it could become a document that binds the architect to supply information or instructions to unrealistic dates. Programmes show by the use of symbols critical dates for the supply of key information by the architect, and these should be carefully noted, as they could constitute a specific application even though submitted in the early days of the project.

Nevertheless the programme is an indispensable document against which the contractor's actual performance can be monitored. The programme should extend to the duration of the contract period and it is important that the dates shown on the programme and in the contract documents are the same. The programme is likely to be the first point of reference in the event of notices of delay, assessments of reasonable diligence or use of best endeavours.

One of the more difficult areas is relating subcontract programmes to the overall programme for the works. Integration of subcontract work is generally the contractor's responsibility, but difficulties can arise where the architect names or nominates firms who are found to be unable to perform to the requirements of the master programme. The architect can do a great deal to assist the proper setting up of such subcontracts by carefully checking requirements at an early stage.

E4.4.5 Architect's instructions

Under a traditional contract the architect has the crucial duty of issuing instructions and certificates. Contract forms rarely prescribe any particular format or pattern for these documents, but as their content must accord precisely with what the wording of a contract requires, it makes good sense to use standard published forms where these are available.

Matters on which instructions should or may be given are stated in the form of contract, and it is prudent to check that an instruction is empowered before issuing it. Even where the issue of instructions is discretionary, there may be occasions when it becomes a necessity, and failure to issue could mean that the employer is put in breach of contract. It is helpful to establish with the contractor at the outset what is to be regarded as a valid instruction; for example, it might be made clear that site or other minutes are not to be construed as instructions.

Oral instructions should be generally avoided. Even if they are necessary in some emergency, they should be recorded in the architect's site notebook, and confirmed formally on return to the office. The particular contract may spell out the options for confirmation, but it is best that confirmation should come from the architect.

If variations or changes of a material kind are proposed or ordered, the employer must be made aware of the associated cost implications. Pre-pricing of variations was a recommendation in the Latham Report, and some contracts provided for this. Whilst a figure may be entered against an architect's instruction, this cannot usually take account of the knock-on effects (eg in direct loss due to disturbance, or of any extension to the contract period).

If there are modifications or variations to the project, some drawings may need revision. Later information should be clearly identified and dated, and a record made in the drawing register. All obsolete documents should be kept in the architect's office in case they need to be referred to subsequently, but it is wise to insist that consultants and others destroy their copies of anything superseded so that there is no confusion about which version is current. A careful watch should be kept for inconsistencies between earlier and later issued drawings, or between those for which the architect is responsible and those for which others are responsible. If any discrepancies are discovered, the contractor should immediately be given an instruction to clarify the situation.

The action to be followed should be as provided for in the particular contract, and any financial adjustments made accordingly.

E4.4.6 Certificates

With traditional contracts other than for minor works, valuations will normally be prepared by the QS at the periods prescribed in the contract, leaving the architect responsible for issuing the associated monetary certificates.

The QS measures the work as it is seen to have been done, regardless of whether or not it is in compliance with the contract – the architect is responsible for checking for compliance. Architects who follow the QS's valuations regardless may find that they have included for work which has not been properly executed. A monetary certificate should never be issued without proper care and attention; it is important to remember that under most contracts its issue binds the employer to pay the amount certified.

Interim certificates are not conclusive, but they are issued as a general indication that work has been properly executed and that payment is now due. Careful inspection should always be made before issuing any such certificate. The power for issuing instructions for dealing with work that does not conform to the standards of the contract will be set out in the particular contract. The contract may provide for the employer to accept nonconforming work, subject to an abatement. Opening up may be needed to establish conformity or otherwise, and details of defective work should always be recorded (in words and photographs). Such failures should be dealt with promptly and firmly in accordance with the provisions of the contract.

The contractor has a contractual and legal responsibility to maintain a safe site (and the architect should check that he does so), but the architect also has responsibilities as designer. The bills or specification will include a pre-tender health and safety plan from which the contractor must prepare his own plan before starting site work. They might also require the contractor to submit method statements, and the architect should check that these are being properly implemented before certifying that work is being 'properly executed'.

The contract will doubtless also refer to other formal statements or certificates (eg at practical completion) to be issued by the architect. Precisely when such statements or certificates are issued depends on the circumstances and, above everything else, on the opinion of the architect. In some instances this is a matter for the architect's professional judgment; in others (such as partial possession) it is largely a matter of confirming fact. In all matters of judgement the architects should try to be objective, fair and reasonable.

E4.5 Completion and post-construction phase

At Stage L (Completion) the completed project is handed over and the fact formally recognised. The employer will have been advised in good time beforehand about the implications of practical completion, eg insurance responsibilities, liability for defects, the adjustments at final account, and the significance of the final certificate.

At Stage M (Feedback) there is an opportunity to review aspects of the design and construction performance. Unless the client has a continuing building programme, this activity is likely to be mainly for the benefit of the design team.

The arrangements for practical completion, which might include commissioning and testing as required by the contract before handing over the project, are still part of Stage K. However, their importance, often overlooked, is given emphasis here by identifying them as part of the post-construction phase.

Completion and handover should be a properly programmed and well-managed sequence of operations to ensure that the completed project functions satisfactorily as a whole. With some complex and heavily serviced buildings, commissioning may have to be done in stages and will involve various consultants. For all projects, regardless of size or complexity, it is essential to allow for the cost of 'proving' installations, and the time for this must be reflected in the contractor's programme.

Although actual construction work may cease at the completion stage, the contractor will have a continuing obligation to rectify defects. There will also be obligations to supply the employer with the health and safety file, including operating instructions, a maintenance manual, and recorded drawings. All buildings need programmed maintenance, and the employer needs adequate information to carry it out.

E4.5.1 Practical completion

At completion date the contractor is obliged to have the whole of the work ready. It is his, and no one else's, responsibility to notify readiness for handing over the completed project. This is the time for the architect to make a crucial examination of work done in particular by the finishing trades, and it is usually helpful for the architect or clerk of works to compile a snagging list. This is purely an *aide-mémoire* and should not be divulged to the contractor (who will be producing his own) in case he is tempted to regard it as a set of requirements which, if met, will imply the architect's satisfaction. Unsatisfactory or unfinished matters should continue to be raised at the architect's site meetings, and a record kept in the minutes.

The contractor should state when, in his view, completion will be achieved. However, the point at which the works are judged to have reached practical completion is for the architect to decide, and is arbitrable. It may not be contractually defined, but it is clear from the case law that only *de minimis* matters should be tolerated when certifying practical completion. The architect has a difficult judgement to make, often in the face of pressure from the employer or the contractor to accept completion.

E4.5.2 Commissioning and testing

Commissioning is the process whereby static completion is brought to the state of full working order for proving. Testing is a matter of checking an installation and evaluating the measured performance against the specified requirements.

Even the simplest services installation needs systematically checking and testing. When installations are sophisticated and costly, consultants and subcontractors bear a heavy responsibility not only for the initial design but also for ensuring that plant is properly installed and that it works as it should.

Commissioning might include water systems, medical gas or air systems, heating and ventilation or air-conditioning systems. It might also be needed for emergency generators, oil-fired or steam boilers, and automatic control devices and systems. Many large client bodies expect particular codes to be observed and stated procedures to be followed. A common difficulty is the precise definition of responsibilities. Whilst architects might have a duty to see that appropriate measures are provided for and satisfactory arrangements made, responsibility for the carrying out of the commissioning and testing clearly lies with others.

The tender documents should have stated clearly what method of commissioning and testing is required, and reference made to appropriate CIBSE, IEE or BSI Codes. The master programme should have allowed adequate time for testing, and it should be scheduled to fit in with current work by other trades. It may be helpful, even on small jobs, to ask for at least a bar chart showing the day-to-day activities that might constitute the itemised handover checks for mechanical and electrical services work.

With large or very sophisticated installations, the process of progressive performance testing and balancing can involve specialist firms and be lengthy. Completion of such work might not be attainable until the building has been in full and regular use for a given period.

If commissioning tests involve running the plant for long periods, the contract should include for the replacement of certain parts (eg filters) thereafter. It is important that the employer is presented with a completely new and fully operational installation at handover. If it is likely that full commissioning tests will not be completed until the building is in use (ie after practical completion of the works), account should be taken of this at tender stage, and appropriate clauses incorporated into the building contract should make provision for it.

E4.5.3 Handover

Practical completion should be marked by a formal handing over of the project to the employer by the contractor, who thereafter relinquishes possession of the site which he has assumed for the purpose of carrying out the works.

A problem often arises when specialist installations (eg lifts, electrical or heating) have been completed before practical completion of the building, and have subsequently been used by the contractor. Phased handover is possible, with the necessary relevant provisions, or the contractor should be required to take steps to present the employer with the equivalent of a newly completed project (involving checking by specialists and replacement of worn or used parts or components).

At handover, outstanding items of work should have been carried out and patent defects rectified, and the site should be clear of all rubbish. The contractor's plant and equipment should have been removed from site. Except for special cases where final balancing cannot be completed until the building is fully operational, commissioning and testing should be carried out before handover.

The employer may be in a hurry to occupy the building – sometimes before practical completion. Even where partial possession is provided for under the building contract, the employer should be warned about the implications. Although the contractor will in most respects cease to be responsible for the occupied part, he might still require reasonable access to complete or rectify work and may allege that he is being forced to operate in an uneconomic manner, and be generally uncooperative. The presence of other people on part of the site can be disruptive and lead to claims and a blurring of responsibilities, as well as creating a security risk. Partial possession is best avoided unless it has been fully thought through and is carefully administered.

Contractors and subcontractors are usually anxious to finish a project and leave the site as soon as possible to undertake new contracts. As a result, key personnel are often transferred elsewhere too soon before final completion, and the result is poor finishing. Site management and supervisory staff have an important part to play towards the end of a project, and every effort should be made to keep the team together until the project is complete. It is important to continue to hold regular architect's site meetings until practical completion. The architect's involvement in site monitoring is likely to be greater towards the end of the job.

The employer may wish to put in hand arrangements for fitting out and furnishing. If these are not part of the contract they are best left until after handover. The contractor might agree to store items delivered in advance, in which event insurers should be informed and cover extended if need be.

The employer should be reminded that whatever arrangements were made under the contract for insurance of the works during construction, this cover will cease to be effective when practical completion is reached. The reminder is best given in writing, and in good time for the employer to take out whatever insurance cover he wishes.

E4.5.4 Post completion procedures

After practical completion, various administrative procedures and actions need to be carried out.

The final inspection which the architect will make at the close of the defects liability period is the last chance which the architect has under the contract to identify those defects for which the contractor has a responsibility. The contractor will nevertheless continue to have a liability for workmanship and materials throughout the limitation period. The employer and/or the occupier should accompany the architect during the inspection and any defects should be scheduled. This schedule of defects should be prepared by the architect and issued as an instruction to the contractor.

When the scheduled defects have been rectified (assuming that the employer has not decided to take an appropriate reduction of the contract sum instead), this must be formally certified. Certification means that the contractor's work has been completed and, for the architect, it entails a further inspection.

Adjustments to the contract sum should now be computed and agreed. Outstanding amounts due to nominated subcontractors and suppliers should be discharged. The final account is settled.

The way is now clear for the issue of the final certificate. The status of this certificate with regard to conclusiveness will depend on the wording of the particular form of contract. The architect is obliged to issue it, but not until he or she is completely satisfied that the contractor has met all his contractual obligations. The issue of the final certificate is the last act of the architect as empowered under the contract. Any matters or claims arising subsequently will be for the parties to resolve; any dispute can be ultimately referred to arbitration or adjudication, or made the subject of litigation.

The CDM Regulations 1994 require the contractor to obtain and prepare information for the Health and Safety File. This must be in a very advanced state before the architect can certify practical completion. It will usually contain guidance on maintenance, as well as record information and operating instructions.

Plan of Work Stage L refers to the architect providing record drawings. These should accurately show the main lines of drainage and services as executed, and in particular work that has now been covered up. This is unlikely to involve specially prepared drawings, but rather marked up prints prepared with the assistance of the clerk of works or the contractor. Drawings of services installations should be supplied by the consultants.

Architects acting for contractors under the JCT With Contractor's Design form (CD 81) should note a more stringent requirement. Here the employer will expect to receive 'as built' drawings as a contractual right before the defects liability period starts. It is always wise to check with the contractor what drawings are to be provided under the particular contract.

E4.5.5 Defects after completion

If complaints of defects arise after completion, architects must notify their insurers, as these are events likely to lead to a claim. These complaints should always be treated seriously. A charge should be made for investigating them, because if an architect undertakes investigation without charge, it might be interpreted as an acceptance of fault. If the fault lies elsewhere, the architect should make every effort to support the client in pursuing those at fault. The architect's evidence both from records and memory will be invaluable.

If the client has already called in experts to report on the problem, the architect should try to obtain a copy of any report they may have made and ask for facilities to make an inspection. However good the architect's relations have been with a client, the possibility of being sued cannot be ruled out. Clients are usually guided by their lawyers, who may recommend legal action.

It has been held by the courts that architects have a continuing duty to warn interested parties if they become aware of an error or defect in a building, even after completion. Because of the way architects work, the same error or defect or unsatisfactory detail or component may be used on a number of jobs. This could be described as a Catch-22 situation. If the architect fails to warn owners of completed projects, it may precipitate a claim; if the architect fails to warn them, it will have breached the architect's duty to warn. On balance, it is probably preferable to warn as quickly as possible, because in that way the damage may be minimised and the owner will be able to mitigate his loss. Insurers should be kept informed throughout.

Managing risks

Part **F**

The quality of most professional relationships depends upon the degree of willingness on both sides to exchange information freely. The client will want to know what skills the architect has, what resources the practice can offer, and what work it has completed or has in progress. Such questions should be answered truthfully and fully.

F1.1 Client identity

The architect will need to discover the true facts about a client's requirements, expectations and sources of finance, and whether there are any constraints on time and budget critical to the project's success. Architects should not feel diffident about making discreet checks on the financial status of new clients before accepting a commission, and, if circumstances suggest it, even asking for money up front. They need to be confident that clients are creditworthy, particularly where large sums of money might be at risk.

An important first step is to clarify the identity and status of the client in relation to the project. For example, if the client is a company it is vital to know whether it is the parent company, a holding company, or just a subsidiary – a subsidiary may be more vulnerable to insolvency. With corporate clients it is essential to have a single point of contact, one named person who can be held accountable and have authority to act. The client organisation needs to be studied – how it is structured and how it functions.

The client might be an unincorporated body. It could be a church or club or some other association. If the client is a committee or board, it is important that there is one named person authorised to make decisions, convey instructions, and sign cheques.

The client might simply be an individual looking to build an extension to his own house for his own occupation. However, if 'the client' seems to be a couple, it is essential to establish which one will give instructions, sign the agreement and cheques etc – or will they both insist on doing this, and could there be potential for friction and delay.

It is also important to find out where the client is 'coming from' in relation to the project. Clients build for different reasons and purposes, and their degree of interest in the project will vary accordingly. A client might see development as a speculative initiative or investment, and be interested primarily in the financial return; matters of building design and construction may largely pass him by. On some projects there might be a commissioning client, and a user client who could be the eventual purchaser of the completed work – or even an occupier under a pre-let agreement. The client may have backing from a funding organisation which will seek to secure safeguards by way of collateral agreements. It is wise to establish in the early days of the architect–client relationship just what and whose interests have to be taken into account.

F1.2 Client perceptions

Normally clients have personal aspirations about their projects as well as a shopping list of the functional and operational requirements to be satisfied, and architects should make a point of discovering what these are and identifying with them. With most building projects a compromise has to be made between cost, speed of completion and quality, so that it is essential to understand the client's real objectives and priorities.

In this respect there are lessons to be learned from some of the conclusions reached in the RIBA *Strategic Study of the Profession* concerning architects and clients, which were that:

- practices were too often introverted;
- practices were 'more concerned with rationalising their own processes than explaining the power of design';
- clients were disappointed by 'the gap between the aspirations they had been encouraged to harbour and the realities of poor delivery';
- architects should 'replace perceived arrogance and disappointment with mutual respect';
- architects should devote as much energy to managing relations with clients as they devote to designing buildings.

Clients who have built before should have a relatively clear idea of their needs, and what the chosen procurement method will entail. A client who has not built before is likely to lean heavily on the guidance of advisers and consultants. It is worth remembering that in several legal cases it has been held that a professional's duty of care relates to the known experience or inexperience of the client. A client new to building may not realise that he or she will have to be accessible for the duration of the project, make decisions quickly when necessary and abide by them, and respond to requests for information promptly. The implications of disregarding critical points in the agreed programme will need spelling out.

F1.3 Client guidance

It is important to explain to clients at the outset that every building project involves some degree of risk, and that it is rarely possible for their aspirations about time, cost and quality to be realised without some compromise being necessary.

To help identify and explain the services architects can provide, and to remove areas of potential misunderstanding, the RIBA publishes a series of client guides ('yellow books') on engaging an architect. Topics covered to date are these:

- the Brooks Method of Architect Selection;
- Architect's Services for Small Works;
- Health and Safety – the CDM Regulations 1994;
- Architects' Fees;
- Party Wall Procedures under the Party Wall etc Act 1996.

The guides offer concise and constructive advice and are addressed directly to the client. Sending an appropriate guide under a covering letter early in the relationship is a convenient and helpful way of informing clients about important aspects of their project.

The range of advice expected from architects today can be wide and varied, depending on the type of client and the nature and scope of the services to be provided. The architect may be appointed to act in various capacities, with varying measures of accountability and liability.

F2.1 Professional advice

When giving professional advice, as for example when reporting on the potential of a development proposal, or when preparing design drawings, the architect will be expected to exercise a duty of care – ie to use reasonable skill and care. This is a duty in tort, but will probably also be a contractual obligation. Some essential points to bear in mind follow.

- Architects should not attempt to advise on matters beyond their expertise. This is not just contravention of the Code of Professional Conduct, it could amount to misrepresentation.
- Architects should not attempt to advise or make recommendations on matters which are beyond their control (eg that a particular result will be achieved, or that a particular contractor will 'do a first class job').
- Architects should not volunteer advice gratuitously, or offer advice that goes beyond contractual obligations or what is required under legislation, without first assessing the risk.
- The professional duty to exercise reasonable skill and care is based on an objective standard, but the degree of skill and care which can be expected in particular circumstances can vary.
- Advice should always be based on the best information obtainable at the time. Any caveats or conditions meant to be taken into account should be clearly stated and explained if necessary.
- The extent to which the architect may be expected to give advice should be set down in the terms of the professional appointment, which should be clear and unambiguous. In cases where such matters are not covered expressly and assumptions made, the courts have been known to decide that terms were implied, particularly where the parties had contracted previously.
- The RIBA Code of Professional Conduct requires members, when acting between parties or when giving professional advice, to exercise independent judgement impartially to the best of their ability and understanding. Furthermore, members are required to seek appropriate advice when faced with a situation which is outside their experience or knowledge.
- The ARB Code of Professional Conduct and Practice requires registered persons to exercise due skill and care and diligence, and to carry out professional work without undue delay and, as appropriate, within any agreed time limit.

F2.2 Professional duty

There may be situations where the architect has accepted more than the normal duty of care. Liability in tort could coexist with a duty of result – for example where a 'fitness for purpose' warranty is given. In such situations merely exercising skill and care may prove insufficient if the intended purpose is not achieved.

Although the architect's duty will normally relate to the client in tort and in contract, a tortious duty may also arise with third parties who have no contractual relationship. For example, a contractor might be able to sue an architect in tort where there has been advice culminating in intended interference in the running of the building contract, as a result of which the contractor has suffered loss. There will also be a tortious and contractual duty to third parties, eg funders, lessees etc, where collateral warranties have been given.

From the earliest stage of negotiation, everything agreed with the client should be set down in writing and filed. When the work is in progress, all instructions, approvals and decisions should be meticulously recorded. It is important not to assume everlasting goodwill, even where the client is well known to the practice, or the personal friend of a principal. Records can be produced as evidence in years to come, whereas good will can vanish in a moment.

Claims still commonly arise against architects because the original commission was not properly defined and recorded – in some cases, not recorded at all. The RIBA Code of Professional Conduct requires members 'to have defined beyond reasonable doubt and recorded the terms of the engagement', whilst the new ARB Standard requires architects not to undertake professional work 'unless the parties have agreed in writing' the terms of their agreement and in particular scope, responsibilities and fees.

F3.1 The appointment

The client's agreement in writing to all the conditions of appointment must be obtained. Any departures from standard conditions should be clearly stated in the document used. Architects should never proceed with any work until they are sure that a proper basis for the commission has been established with the client and recorded in writing, and that they have the necessary authority to proceed.

Clients should always be given an explanation of the need and purpose of each work stage; if they do not wish to pay for a full service, they then have the choice of making other arrangements. However, providing a 'partial' service can have dangers if the scope of the service is not clearly defined, and architects would be wise to state clearly what this does *not* cover, in order to avoid any misunderstanding. Where the client's own organisation provides part of the service, or an architect is asked to take over work started previously by others, both the scope and the limits of responsibility should be set out in writing.

It is always advisable to use a standard form of appointment. At the time of writing, the RIBA publishes appointing documents which relate (very approximately) to major commissions under JCT 80, less complex projects under the Intermediate Form IFC 84, and commissions of up £100,000, possibly under the Minor Works Agreement. All the appointing documents have a similar and logical structure which consists of a Memorandum of Agreement (or a model Letter of Appointment), and Schedules which set out the services to be provided, the fees to be charged and how these are calculated, and details of any other appointments necessary for the project. Each document also includes the conditions of appointment applying to the project. The RIBA publishes accompanying guidance on the use and completion of its forms of appointment.

F3.2 Other consultants

Many claims arise partly or wholly from an action, or a failure to act, by other consultants. Consultants should preferably be appointed directly by the client, who will hold them responsible for the service they provide. Where the client insists on a single appointment for all professional services, architects should establish a proper structure of control and only accept their own nominees.

Architects should insist on their right to check the terms of appointment and services of consultants and, if necessary, ask for them to be changed. If the client disagrees, the architect should put a disclaimer of responsibility in writing. The terms under which consultants are appointed should state their responsibility for complying with the architect's requirements regarding time and programme.

Clients are increasingly reluctant to make individual and separate appointments, and often insist that the architect appoints and accepts responsibility for the whole professional team. An architect who refuses to do so may risk losing the job, but that is a matter of commercial judgement.

Every architect who undertakes a commission exposes him or herself to some degree of risk, because this is the nature of business. It is always necessary to balance an assessment of the risks entailed against a judgement about the potential for profit. Risks can be reduced by acquiring a good understanding of job costing, making sure that arrangements for paying fees are clearly set down in the terms of the commission, and by instituting and operating strict administrative procedures for the issuing of invoices and for their prompt payment.

F3.3 Rejecting the impossible

Commissions that are clearly impossible should not be accepted. Prospective clients frequently lay down a brief, with a budget and a timescale, as a precondition of appointment. These may be incompatible and one or other of them even unattainable. As a result there may be a claim – or the architect will not be paid. A commission should never be accepted under one set of terms and operated under another. Changes to the conditions of a contract require the agreement of both parties in writing.

Similarly, it is essential to avoid over-committing practice resources. As well as sound commonsense, it is a requirement of the RIBA Code of Professional Conduct that architects undertake to establish that their competence and resources are adequate before accepting a commission. Over-commitment can lead to an inadequate service, a dissatisfied client, and eventual claims.

The tendency has increased in recent years for clients to offer commissions to architects on their own purpose-made terms. These often seek to transfer all risks to consultants, and sometimes include requirements which are uninsurable. Architects should study the terms and conditions carefully and consult their legal advisers and insurers before accepting appointment.

Another situation to watch out for is the 'creeping commission' – one that gradually becomes something far in excess of what was originally agreed, often without any recognition that adjustments need to be made to the appointment to reflect the true situation, and the architect's fee increased accordingly.

F3.4 Collateral warranties

Architects are often put under pressure to give collateral warranties to third parties; these may be institutional funding organisations, or prospective purchasers or tenants. It is uncertain what effect warranties may have in respect of future claims on the profession, but they certainly increase risk and should be avoided if possible. Insurers must always be informed about any warranties proposed and asked whether they are prepared to cover the additional risk. Not all insurance policies cover claims arising from contracts with third parties. At the time of writing only the RIBA scheme insurers have stated that they will cover, without further reference to them, claims arising from the use, unamended, of the Form of Warranty in favour of funder issued jointly by the RIBA and the British Property Federation (BPF). It should be borne in mind that cover for these additional risks might well affect the practice's professional indemnity insurance premiums in future years as well as the current year.

Collateral warranties to persons providing finance for a project usually require the architect to act for the third party if that party becomes the owner of the project before completion. It is crucial for architects to retain their rights of termination. Often the third party will only come into ownership through the failure of the original client and there may well be a legacy of ill will affecting all the professional advisers. Continuing to work for the third party under strained circumstances can lead to trouble.

Forms of collateral warranty can sometimes introduce obligations greater than those set out in the original contract. The wording of 'duty of care agreements' and any attempts to obtain 'fitness for purpose' undertakings should be treated with great caution and be checked by a lawyer. Architects who sign documents incautiously may find themselves in breach of their insurance policy conditions, and without professional indemnity insurance cover as a result.

In the past, competitive fee bidding, sometimes conducted under conditions which were not always fair and reasonable, resulted in architects undertaking work with a fee inadequate for the proper standard of service required. As a result, corners were cut in an effort to meet client demands, and risks taken which should have been assessed as unacceptable. The RIBA *Strategic Study of the Profession* noted that 'the desperation of practices to win work dictates that they will enter a fee competition at cost – or below'. Too low a fee, too tight a programme, too vague a brief are the ingredients of potential disaster.

F4.1 Risk potential

Risk potential is great if work which has a known bad record for claims is undertaken. Insurers have identified the following as areas of high risk:

- taking over someone else's work (or vice versa) on a partial service basis;
- structural related surveys;
- post-completion certification for building societies or other funders;
- one-off houses built by non-NHBC registered builders;
- working for some housing associations;
- design and build contracts, particularly those which do not limit design liability;
- approving drawings by specialists and subcontractors;
- acting as a subconsultant without a proper appointing document.

Responsibility for design, in the absence of anything expressly to the contrary, rests wholly with the architect and cannot be assigned or sublet to others. The duty of the architect is a wide one, and may be interpreted to include a duty to warn in the case of innovative design or untried systems and materials. It applies equally to gratuitous advice, and has been held to extend to investigating alternative solutions and advising on relative costs.

Unfamiliar construction methods and new products have considerable risk potential. There is often a failure to investigate fully the durability of materials, components or systems relative to a required life cycle, the risks of differential movements or chemical reactions in particular circumstances or combinations. Typically, too much credence is given to manufacturers' claims, which are often based on tests under laboratory rather than real-life conditions.

To summarise, risks can be avoided or substantially reduced by:

- being sure that resources are adequate and available before making any commitment;
- making sure that the service offered is properly described and confirmed, and that the client's expectations are realistic;
- making sure that the fee or other remuneration is fixed before work starts and, unless agreed otherwise, work is never carried out 'at risk';
- making sure that the legal obligations are attainable and that the assessed risks are acceptable;
- making sure everything is systematically documented and recorded. In a dispute, the person with the best and most accurate records has a head start;
- checking and if need be questioning the brief at the outset;
- keeping the client fully informed about cost check procedures and the implications of any changes;
- only subletting specialist areas of design to consultants or subcontractors with the client's authority and acceptance that such persons are solely liable for their design work;
- putting manufacturers' claims and test figures for new material or methods into the particular context, and never 'borrowing' attractive design ideas without fully investigating their suitability for the application intended.

Exposure to risks can be reduced generally by adopting sound practice management and establishing standard procedures for both projects and office business. A quality management system, regularly audited for effectiveness, will reduce a practice's overall risk potential and should be seriously considered by all practising units.

F4.2 Liability

Liability concerns matters for which the architect can be held accountable or responsible at law. Most claims against architects are for alleged breaches of contract, or for negligence in tort. The duty of care expected of a professional is usually that of exercising due skill, care and diligence. However, this can be modified and become more arduous or reduce in certain circumstances. It will depend largely on what the architect has undertaken to perform.

Liability arises in the context of common law obligations, and those duties which are founded in statute. For architects, it can be limited in the following ways:

- by adopting an appropriate form of practice;
- by incorporating appropriate terms in the appointing document and obtaining the client's agreement;
- by the intervention of statute (ie claims becoming statute-barred with the passage of time).

Some architects choose to practise in the form of a limited liability company, but this does not mean that the company and/or its directors and other employees are entirely protected from claims in negligence. (See B1.5, where the advantages and disadvantages of incorporation, and the attaching liabilities, are reviewed.)

It is possible to limit liability by only entering into tightly drafted contracts which clearly set out the extent of the services to be provided. These should restrict liability to that of the standard of reasonable skill and care normally to be expected of the professional. A simple contract is to be preferred, in that it has a shorter liability period than a deed.

Liability can be expressly excluded in some areas, or can at least be limited through the provisions of the contract. For example, current RIBA appointing documents provide in the Memorandum of Agreement for the architect's liability to be limited in time and amount. A clause allows for the insertion of any time that the parties might agree, and this should effectively override the limitation period arising from statute. There is also a 'net contribution' clause, which is an attempt to limit the architect's joint liability to his or her fair share. Another clause allows the insertion of an overall ceiling limit to liability, as a matter of normal commercial practice.

As discussed above, architects should avoid unnecessarily widening the net of contractual liability by entering into third party warranties or collateral agreements. Where these are inevitable, care should be taken to ensure that a liability greater than that under the main contract does not result.

Liability will also be limited by the intervention of statute, in that the law offers a defence to any actions brought after the period of liability. The periods are set out in the Limitation Act 1980, as amended by subsequent legislation (see Fig F4.1). Actions founded in tort (S2) are to be brought within six years of the date on which 'the cause of action accrued'. Actions founded in contract (S5) simple or (S8) specialty are to be brought within six years or twelve years respectively from the time of the breach. The limitation starting point is critical. In the case of tort

Fig F4.1   Limitation periods for different classes of action

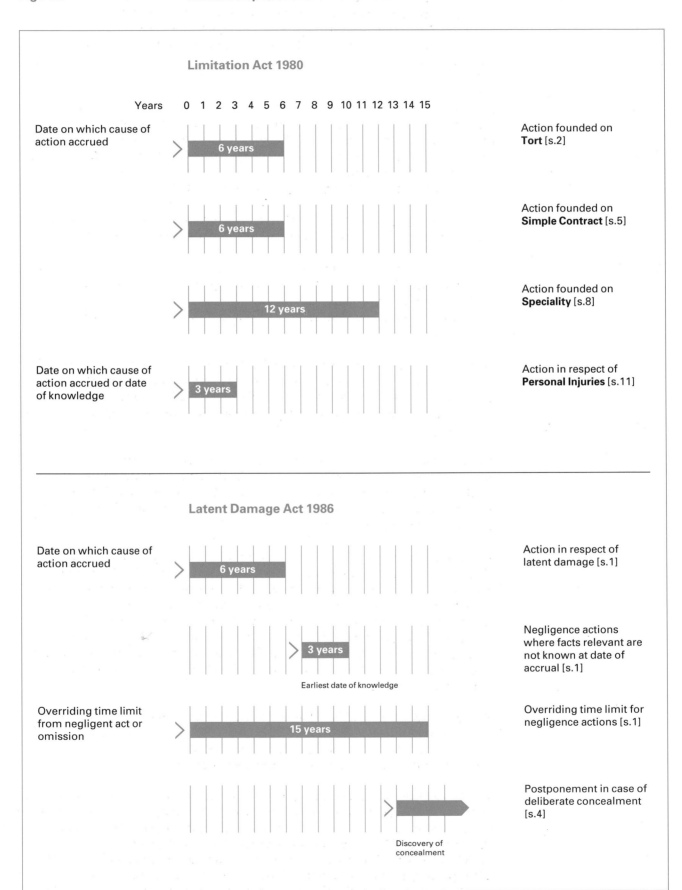

Limitation Act 1980

	Years	0 1 2 3 4 5 6 7 8 9 10 11 12 13 14 15	

Date on which cause of action accrued — **6 years** — Action founded on **Tort** [s.2]

— **6 years** — Action founded on **Simple Contract** [s.5]

— **12 years** — Action founded on **Speciality** [s.8]

Date on which cause of action accrued or date of knowledge — **3 years** — Action in respect of **Personal Injuries** [s.11]

Latent Damage Act 1986

Date on which cause of action accrued — **6 years** — Action in respect of latent damage [s.1]

— **3 years** (Earliest date of knowledge) — Negligence actions where facts relevant are not known at date of accrual [s.1]

Overriding time limit from negligent act or omission — **15 years** — Overriding time limit for negligence actions [s.1]

— (Discovery of concealment) — Postponement in case of deliberate concealment [s.4]

actions for personal injury it is three years from 'discoverability'. In the case of tort actions arising out of building latent defects it is six years from the date that the damage occurred.

The Latent Damage Act 1986 imposes further limitation periods for tort actions (see Fig F4.1). There is a three-year discoverability period, but this depends on the 'starting date', 'the knowledge required', and a 'right to bring such action'. All this is defined under S1 of the Act, which introduces a new S14A into the 1980 Act. In addition there is an overriding time limit of 15 years from the date of the negligent act which caused the damage.

None of these limitations applies where there is 'fraud, concealment or mistake'. With so many limitation periods, the major problem is uncertainty, because each period might have a different starting date.

Under the Civil Liability (Contribution) Act 1978 the courts can order a contribution to damages awarded from parties who are held to be responsible in some measure for the injury caused. This order can be made up to two years following the award of damages, and this further increases the period of liability.

F4.3 Indemnity

Responsible architects in the UK have traditionally protected themselves and their clients by arranging adequate professional indemnity insurance cover. Sometimes clients stipulate the required level of cover before agreeing to appoint the architect. Insurance is not a cover for incompetence on the part of the architect: it is a responsible precaution against unfortunate and often unforeseeable circumstances.

Under the RIBA Code of Conduct, members undertake to inform clients whether or not professional indemnity insurance is held. However, under the Architects Registration Board's Standard 7, all architects undertaking professional work must now have adequate professional indemnity insurance cover. The term 'professional work' is very broad, and the Standard applies to all architects including those undertaking work on a spare time basis. The question of what is adequate is not defined, but obviously will relate to reasonable requirements on the part of the client and to the size and nature of the work.

F4.4 Professional indemnity insurance

A PII policy is an annually renewable contract with a premium payable each year, giving protection against claims arising during that year. In return, the insurers indemnify the insured against certain stated losses up to stated limits which they are 'legally obliged to pay'. Insurance contracts depend upon a basis of good faith where there is total honesty in completing proposal forms and absolute disclosure in all matters.

Cover can be either for 'each and every claim' or on an 'aggregate' basis. The former is recommended as most generally suitable, and will comply with the general requirements of public sector clients. At the time of writing, the amount of cover should be not less than £250,000 for reasonable security. Even small jobs can give rise to claims which, with legal costs, can run into six figures.

Special insurance arrangements may be needed for multi-discipline practices, or where architectural practices operate with other firms in a group practice or joint venture. Architects bidding for joint venture projects should be able to meet a requirement that each member of a consortium should be jointly and severally responsible for performance under an agreement. The risk must be acceptable to professional indemnity insurers.

When planning to buy or when reviewing professional indemnity insurance it is important to consider the following aspects. The level of indemnity required is unlikely to be less than £100,000, but many clients will not accept less than £250,000, and some big clients require £5 million plus. The guide used by insurers for a suitable level of cover is between two and three times annual gross fee income, including VAT, in the previous financial year.

Policies also need to cover the risk of more than one claim arising in the same year. To offset this risk, the policy can be written on an 'each and every claim' basis. There are no standard policy wordings, and to assume that all policies are much the same is dangerous. It is essential to be clear about the protection offered. Policies that exclude cover using retro restriction clauses or endorsements should be rejected.

To obtain terms or a quotation for a policy, architects should ask the RIBA Insurance Agency or a broker to provide a proposal form. This should be completed and returned immediately, or if there is existing cover about one month before it is due to expire. Completing the proposal form accurately is vitally important; if it is not completed precisely, honestly and fully it could lead to a policy being void at the critical time. Non-disclosure is a very serious matter.

The level of premiums is influenced by many factors, such as any record of previous claims, the type of client, the nature of the project (eg degree of technical innovation, physical risk factors etc). Some client groups are seen as higher risks than others. The average premium paid by architects is about 5% of gross fee income, but this can vary widely. Architects engaged to do feasibility and design work only, ie free from all forms of attendance and inspection, will tend to be treated more favourably.

Clients should be made aware of the benefits of appointing an architect who is considered by insurers to be a good insurance risk. They should also appreciate that some demands for collateral warranties could place the insured practice in breach of normal insurance terms with the result that the warranted work is no longer covered, and the warranty is therefore worthless. Settlement of any claim arising will depend entirely upon the personal resources of the person or firm who signed it.

Policies should include a 'non-subrogation' clause to protect employees from being sued by insurers to recover any losses for which they were held responsible whilst employed. Architects who are self-employed or in short term contracts are not automatically or even usually covered under this clause. It is necessary to get written agreement or an endorsement from insurers to extend cover. Most PII policies state that the insured is obliged to notify insurers of any claims, and of circumstances which might lead to a claim. This is a duty which exists throughout the life of the policy and is a condition which must not be ignored.

Fig F4.2   Some typical notifiable situations

- Where the architect's client, or a third party, alleges that damage, financial loss, or personal injury has occurred.

- Where an architect discovers his office has made a mistake, even though no one else is aware of it.

- Where another member of the team (another consultant of the contractor, say) alleges that the architect has made a mistake.

- Where a problem arises with design work undertaken by another consultant but which the architect coordinated.

- Where the contractor claims delay due to late receipt of information (not due to changes instructed by the client).

- Where the client contacts the architect some time after completion regarding a latent defect.

- Where a dispute arises between other parties connected with the project.

- Where the client jokes about suing the architect for a particular reason.

- Where the client refuses to pay the architect's fees.

- Where someone is injured in an accident on site.

When planning for retirement, architects should recognise that liability continues beyond the date of retirement – at worst, it can continue beyond death and into the deceased architect's estate. The premiums paid in retirement may not qualify for tax relief, so architects should consider appropriate tax-efficient action while still working to mitigate this future liability and should obtain sound professional advice on the matter.

The RIBA Insurance Agency provides a PII scheme tailored to the needs of architects and has recently introduced a 'compact' insurance policy to suit small practices. The schemes have a number of special benefits:

- the protection of a policy negotiated by architects for architects;
- dealings with experienced PII specialists who understand the problems that architects face;
- regular information about reducing exposure to claims;
- assurance that the policy will not be suddenly voided because some item or event has not been notified, provided that there was no dishonest intention in the omission;
- any claim arising will be handled by an expert in the field;
- large premiums can be paid in instalments;
- in the event of a dispute, the RIBA can intercede on a member's behalf;
- the scheme is backed by reputable insurers who are all members of the British Insurance Association, which ensures the continuity of the scheme and the protection of its members.

Information about the schemes can be obtained from the RIBA members insurance line, or direct from RIBA Insurance Agency.

Architects should be careful not to lead clients to assume that they will automatically include work which is additional to whatever services have been scheduled (eg surveys of site or buildings) under the terms of their appointment. If architects deliberately choose to undertake such services without any additional fee, then that is a matter for their commercial judgement. However, it should be recognised that such actions can bring considerable risk if they are not properly resourced. It is always advisable to make appointing documents very clear as to what is, and what is not included with the services agreed.

F5.1 Other consultancy services

RIBA appointing documents typically include a range of services which could be provided by the architect in addition to services specific to building projects. Of these 'other services', some are advisory in character whilst others are directly related to sites or buildings investigation. Many of the latter can be accommodated under the appropriate standard appointing document, whilst many of the listed consultancy services require a separate agreement outwith the normal RIBA appointing documents.

Professional services for which architects could well be appointed include:

- to act as expert witness;
- to act as arbitrator under the Arbitration Act 1996;
- to act as adjudicator under Part II of the Housing Grants, Construction and Regeneration Act 1996;
- to act as expert (ie not as arbitrator) in dispute resolution;
- to act as Planning Supervisor under the CDM Regulations 1994;
- to act as party wall surveyor under the Party Wall etc Act 1996;
- to act as project manager.

Some of these appointments can be made under an RIBA standard form of appointment; others will need an agreement specially drafted by a lawyer, since a simple exchange of letters is rarely adequate.

However, some services often undertaken by architects can have pitfalls, and should be regarded with a degree of caution. They are extensive, and examples of some are described in the following sections.

F5.2 House surveys

Structural surveys for the house purchaser are a major area of risk for most small practices. Unless this kind of work is to be a regular and major source of income, architects are best advised to avoid it. Any architect who does undertake house surveys should establish some sound procedures to be followed in all cases.

A house purchaser commissions a survey for one reason only: he wants a realistic indication of his likely future commitment. However enthusiastic he may be about the property at the time he commissions the survey, if faced with an unexpected cost some time in the future, his first reaction will be to try to recoup his costs from the surveyor. And if he is insured against, say, subsidence, then his insurers will bring an action in his name to recover their loss. In recent years, judicial findings on what constitutes professional negligence in surveys have been extremely punitive. Architects should remember the following points.

- They should never carry out a survey for a friend for a reduced fee, or for no fee at all. Responsibility is not limited by the size of the fee.
- Any warning required by their indemnity insurers should be included in all reports. An architect who fails to do so is likely to carry the whole burden of any claim.

- The report should include a statement about the physical and climatic conditions under which the survey was carried out and the vantage points from which inaccessible parts of the property were viewed, eg roof slopes. It should be made clear what was not inspected, or where it was not possible to inspect.
- They should have available a full complement of instruments and tools with them on site so that the condition of the property can be properly established.
- There must be access to all the principal parts of the property, particularly roof spaces and drains. It may be necessary to ask for the attendance of a builder to provide access and opening up; if so, this should be arranged in advance.
- It is best to work to a tried and tested checklist. Many good ones are published, and can be adapted to suit particular circumstances.
- Architects should not allow their judgement to be clouded by explanations from the owner or his agent about obvious defects.
- If any doubt remains about about any aspect, the architect's report should include a recommendation that there should be further inspections by specialists (see also C5.1).

Architects should remember, particularly when surveying unoccupied properties alone, to avoid hazardous situations where it might be difficult to get out again. They should make sure that the office knows where they have gone and what time they expect to return. Recommended health and safety guidelines should be followed (see D2.3).

F5.3 Building society inspections

Building society and similar inspections of existing properties are usually carried out for a considerably smaller fee than full house surveys. The reports are usually recorded on a standard form provided by the society. The drafting quality of these pro formas and the degree of responsibility that they place upon the surveyor can vary widely. Some are made available to the purchaser, and some are not. Even in the latter case, the courts have decided that the purchaser can rely on them.

Architects should not hesitate to delete words or paragraphs that are inappropriate to the inspection they have carried out, or to add caveats. The point from which visual observations are made should be stated, eg 'The condition of the roof, when viewed from the ground only, was . . .'.

As well as inspections and reports on existing buildings, architects are sometimes approached to carry out inspections in connection with mortgage advances on new property. Building societies or banks often stipulate that money will be advanced in instalments upon completion of certain stages, subject to inspection by an architect or surveyor who is required to submit an inspection report and ultimately sign a certificate. Provided the architect is approached before work starts on site, inspection may be reasonably undertaken, but the client must alert the architect that a stage is ready for inspection before any covering up of work takes place. Where the architect is approached late during construction, it might prove impossible to complete stage reports and certification.

It is important for architects involved in such work to understand the difficulties and recognise the dangers. Inspection can only be on the basis of periodic visits to check generally the quality and progress of the work to the extent that this is possible by visual inspection. Any statements which might amount to absolute warranties (and these frequently appear in standard certificates produced by building societies) are unacceptable. They go far beyond the legal duty to use reasonable skill and care and should be resisted.

F5.4	Surveys of commercial buildings

These surveys are usually carried out either before purchase or when entering into a lease. They present less of a risk to architects because of the nature of the client and because an adequate fee can usually be charged to allow the job to be properly resourced. On all major buildings it is usual to employ specialists to report on services. The same general rules apply as with house surveys, but some additional caution is required.

- With newly constructed property, architects should establish the rights of the purchaser in relation to the latent defects provisions of the building contract. If the rights are not to be assigned, they may be unenforceable.
- With leased property, architects should always insist on having a copy of the lease so that the full responsibilities of the lessee can be established, if necessary by taking legal advice. Repairing leases can be onerous.

Even where only part of a building is being leased, it is still essential to inspect the whole building, paying particular attention to the roof and main services, as the tenant will almost certainly bear a proportion of any costs of repair and maintenance.

F5.5	Quinquennial church inspections

The 1955 *Inspection of Churches Measure* requires that every parish church in the Church of England is the subject of an inspection and report by a 'suitably qualified' architect, at least every five years. This is work usually undertaken by a sole practitioner, or by a named architect. It is specialised work, and it is important to make sure that a policy of professional indemnity insurance covers the person actually doing the work. In some cases this work will be the firm's work, but in others it will be a personal appointment and the named architect is acting in an individual capacity. This should be checked with insurers.

A Guide to Church Inspection and Repair is published by the Council for the Care of Churches, and gives sound and helpful advice. Refer also to the RIBA Journal *Practice* supplement for August 1987 on liability and insurance aspects in relation to church inspections.

F5.6	Additional services with risk aspects

Architects are sometime asked to certify compliance with Building Regulations or some other standard of satisfactory completion, to meet the requirements of a finance organisation. This is often the case where the owner has self-built, or has engaged with an unregistered building group to erect his private house. An architect who has not been engaged to visit the works in progress would be unwise to undertake this service.

Inspections of work in progress

Architects are sometimes engaged to inspect works in progress which are not of their own design, perhaps for a client who has entered into some kind of design and build or package deal contract. They should always establish in advance what rights they have under the building contract in question. If these are limited (and they will often be nonexistent) it is important to advise the client of the limits of the architect's powers before accepting the commission. Architects should never attempt in any way to amend the design or any constructional details during visits; they should simply inform the client of any problem and let him sort it out with the contractor.

Grant-aided work

Architects involved with grant-aided housing improvement work should be thoroughly conversant with all the rules and conditions and not risk disqualifying the client by breaching them. It is also essential to avoid risking any suggestion of collusion with a client by obtaining grant aid to which the client may not strictly be entitled – some clients tend to take a 'relaxed' view of the rules. The real risk to the architect who becomes involved in such dubious practices is that if at some later date the client makes sole claim against the architect, the latter will not be in a position to defend the claim for fear of exposure of any malpractice.

Handling clients' money

Architects sometime handle money belonging to clients. This may be a matter of disbursement such as the clerk of works' salary, or fees connected with statutory approvals. They may be asked to administer separate trades contracts, making payments to the various firms with the client's money. It is important to make certain that these monies are always paid from a 'client's account', and record that the payments are being made for and on behalf of the client. Architects should never pay out any of their own money, or they may find, for example, that they have taken on the responsibilities and liabilities of the builder – and they will not be covered by their professional indemnity insurance. Architects are required to conform with the Members' Rules for Clients' Accounts under the RIBA Code of Professional Conduct.

Many other or additional services require special expertise, which all architects may not have. Clients still tend to assume that architects are omniscient because of their traditional image as the people who know about everything to do with buildings. In reality, the growing complexity of the building process and the legislation surrounding it means that few firms now encompass all the skills and expertise that may be required by clients. It is essential to establish that competence and resources are adequate to provide a service which meets the RIBA Standard of Professional Performance before accepting any commission.

Index